RISING STAR

RISING STAR

The Meaning of Nikki Haley,
Trump's Unlikely Ambassador

JASON A. KIRK

The University of Arkansas Press
Fayetteville ★ 2021

ISBN: 978-1-68226-182-8
eISBN: 978-1-61075-756-0

25   24   23   22   21   5   4   3   2   1

Manufactured in the United States of America

Designed by Liz Lester

♾ The paper used in this publication meets the minimum requirements of the American National Standard for Permanence of Paper for Printed Library Materials Z39.48-1984.

Library of Congress Cataloging-in-Publication Data

Names: Kirk, Jason A., author.
Title: Rising star: the meaning of Nikki Haley, Trump's unlikely ambassador / Jason A. Kirk.
Other titles: Nikki Haley, Trump's unlikely ambassador
Description: Fayetteville: The University of Arkansas Press, 2021. | Includes bibliographical references and index. | Summary: "In Rising Star, political scientist Jason A. Kirk analyzes Nikki Haley's ascendance in the Republican Party, from her governorship of South Carolina to her elevated profile as Donald Trump's representative to the United Nations"—Provided by publisher.
Identifiers: LCCN 2021022929 (print) | LCCN 2021022930 (ebook) | ISBN 9781682261828 (paperback) | ISBN 9781610757560 (ebook)
Subjects: LCSH: Haley, Nikki, 1972– | United States—Foreign relations—2017– | United States—Politics and government—2017– | United States. Mission to the United Nations—Officials and employees—Biography. | Ambassadors—United States—Biography. | Women ambassadors—United States—Biography. | Governors—South Carolina—Biography. | South Carolina—Politics and government—1951– | East Indian Americans—South Carolina—Biography. | BISAC: POLITICAL SCIENCE / Women in Politics | BIOGRAPHY & AUTOBIOGRAPHY / Cultural, Ethnic & Regional / Asian & Asian American
Classification: LCC E901.1.H35 K57 2021 (print) | LCC E901.1.H35 (ebook) | DDC 327.730092 [B]—dc23
LC record available at https://lccn.loc.gov/2021022929
LC ebook record available at https://lccn.loc.gov/2021022930

For Arun and Uma

Contents

Preface

When you really want to read a book, sometimes you have write it. I began thinking about this book, in a somewhat different form, in April 2012, at the annual meeting of the International Studies Association in San Diego. I was there to present a draft paper, following up on a 2008 article I had written on the US-India Political Action Committee (USINPAC),[1] and to tack on a family vacation. My wife and I, North Carolinians, had never explored California, and we thought our kids, at nine and six, might be just old enough to appreciate the experience.

After my early morning panel at the conference Hilton, I went up to our room. Deepa and the kids were waiting on me to drive to Torrey Pines State Beach so we could feel how cold the Pacific is in April. I found the three of them watching *Good Morning America* on ABC. We were about to shut off the TV when a new segment came on profiling Governor Nikki Haley, of our state's southern sibling. She had just published a memoir. ("Wait, wasn't she *just* elected, like two years ago?" I remember thinking.) Seen from the opposite coast, the Carolina landscape felt familiar. We kept watching.

More precisely, I shifted between watching Governor Haley on TV and watching Deepa, Arun, and Uma as they watched Governor Haley on TV. Much of the five-minute segment, filmed at the South Carolina State House in Columbia and in the governor's birthplace of Bamberg, was devoted to her family background and home life, framed not so much as a curiosity but as a grounded, relatable story—unique in some ways, universal in many. It was all carefully curated and packaged with network production values, but it worked. Haley's policy positions were only lightly touched on in the profile, and seemed (or were made to seem) almost beside the point. Here was a Republican politician who pressed the Family and Faith buttons in new ways—specific, but somehow more inclusive—and who broke the mold of the stereotypical southern governor, even while presenting herself as thoroughly southern. And she was Indian American.

I thought back to a book I'd picked up in Virginia a few years earlier, when we first moved back south after living in a northeastern city for six years. As historian James Cobb elegantly argues in *Away Down South: A History of Southern Identity*, southern-ness has been a form of "otherness" in the United States—and can remain so, despite the South's increasing centrality in national politics and culture and in the global economy.[2] For the news media, the main question about Nikki Haley seemed to be, "How in the world did *this* woman get elected governor of *that* state?" The answer to this dually exoticizing question seemed fairly straightforward: Haley had won as a conservative Republican, and South Carolina voters were neither all unreconstructed racists nor all budding multiculturalists.

But one detail from the *Good Morning America* interview, in particular, struck a chord with me, and with my wife. It has been mentioned in many other media profiles, becoming part of the Nikki Haley lore. The governor was asked about a childhood experience in Bamberg.

When she was five, she and her sister had entered the Wee Miss Bamberg pageant, only to have organizers tell them that in the event's tradition of crowning dual Black and white[3] winners, they fit neither category, and would have to be disqualified. In the talent show, Haley was allowed to sing Woody Guthrie's "This Land Is Your Land." She got a beach ball as a consolation prize.

The story reminded my wife of a tradition at her high school in eastern North Carolina, still in place in the early 1990s, of crowning separate Black and white couples for the annual Homecoming Court. We both thought of the parallel, and I thought of that indelible line from Faulkner, "The past is never dead. It's not even past."[4] For many Americans growing up in the decades after the civil rights movement, that history—and the racism that spawned it—might have seemed to belong to another time. But "What *was* that like?" had the wrong verb tense.

What would this country be like, I sometimes wondered, when someday, somebody born in the 1970s—born "after history," as it were—inhabited the governor's mansion or the White House? In my mind's eye, that person hadn't looked like Nikki Haley. Now she did.

★ ★ ★

Nikki Haley has been widely hailed as an emerging force in American politics, her star power burnished over a whirlwind decade in which she rose from the State House to the world stage. The initial fascination about the three-term state legislator's gubernatorial candidacy, nomination, and election in 2010 owed much to her state's complicated history and efforts at self-reinvention in a globalizing world. Then, shortly after Governor Haley's reelection in 2014, the state confronted a series of extraordinary challenges and tragedies. The year 2015 would be a turning point for Haley's political trajectory, and for the Palmetto State, as South Carolina reckoned with race and history as dramatically as any state in recent memory.

In North Charleston that April, a white police officer shot a Black man in the back following a routine traffic stop, killing him in broad daylight as an eyewitness captured it on video. In Charleston that June, a white supremacist murdered nine Black Americans in church, during weeknight Bible study. There were renewed calls to take down the Confederate flag, long a source of controversy, from the State House grounds in Columbia. In due course, Governor Haley would join the chorus and would preside over the flag's removal, following soul-searching debates and votes in the legislature. In October, a deluge of rainwater from a "thousand-year storm," Hurricane Joaquin, fell on the state, causing devastating flooding and property damage.

South Carolinians showed remarkable resilience, civility, and grace in the face of these tragedies. Governor Nikki Haley was a prominent figure throughout: a woman of color leading a state that remained divided economically, politically, and racially—but that also seemed to offer glimmers of hope for a better, more united America.

And then, seemingly against long odds, the following year saw Donald Trump's takeover of the Republican Party and, remarkably, the president-elect's announcement in November 2016 that Haley was his pick to represent the United States of America at the United Nations. A daughter of Indian immigrants would be the face of Trump's America First policy to the world. The period since 2010, when Nikki Haley first drew wide notice beyond South Carolina, has seen massive changes in American politics and international relations.

This book's emphasis is on Nikki Haley's two-year UN ambassadorship, more than her six-year governorship in South Carolina (an asymmetry reflecting its author's scholarly concentration in international relations). The emphasis also reflects two key premises: that Nikki Haley may return to national politics and to the world stage, and that important clues as to how she might position herself and how she might lead can be found in her body of work since 2015—and especially in the Trump administration—more so than in her early governorship. Moreover, foreign policy encompasses many areas and issues; the focus here is mainly on the "high politics" of US national security and relations with politico-military allies and rivals, and to some extent on human rights diplomacy, and less on humanitarian diplomacy and aid. (So, for example, the book does not follow Ambassador Haley's diplomacy in sub-Saharan Africa, even though the region seems to have had a significant impact on her).

President Trump, as so many pundits have said, has been as much a symptom as the cause of deep strains and fissures in American political institutions and American society. The Donald may have decamped to Florida in January 2021, but Americans and global observers will debate the meaning of his spectacle presidency for a long time. And there will be no turning back the clock in political time.[5] Given the support Trump retains among Republican voters, if Nikki Haley seeks the presidency in his turbulent wake, she will have to embrace her legacy as a Trump cabinet member while at the same time appealing to a good many Americans that just as persistently disapprove of (or loathe) the president she served.

It is a narrow needle to thread, but Nikki Haley just might be the person to do it. Strategically, she can lay claim to the rare, perhaps singular legacy of a Trump administration official who departed on their own terms, and with her prior reputation more or less intact. A loyalist, but a knowing one; an instinctive politician in her own right, with a distinctive persona and power.

In early 2014, a New York real estate developer and fading reality-TV star dashed off a fax to a telegenic South Carolina governor who had just won reelection by a fifteen-point margin. "Nikki—You're a winner!" the memo read, followed by Trump's jagged signature.[6] In Ambassador Nikki Haley's unlikely arrangement with President Donald Trump, who was the bigger winner?

★ ★ ★

An author should not be a part of the story, but one's background and limitations may at times be relevant and thus merit acknowledgment. I teach undergraduate courses in international relations and comparative politics at Elon University, in central ("Piedmont") North Carolina. My course on international organizations covers the main UN institutions—the 193-member-state General Assembly and the fifteen-member Security Council—along with the International Monetary Fund, the World Bank, and the World Trade Organization. I also teach and study India's politics and international relations.

I majored in journalism as an undergraduate. In graduate school for political science, my first-year seminar in American Political Development taught me to seek understanding of the American experience in comparative and historical-institutional contexts. The professor, Marie Gottschalk, had been a journalist and editor and had taught in China. She helped me learn how to switch, mentally and lexically, between journalistic and academic writing. I trace a line from that course, over twenty years ago, to this book. In some corners of academia, writing "journalistically" is an offense. Professor Gottschalk gave me permission to think otherwise.

I hope that in presuming to write this book, and traversing some academic boundaries, I am not presuming too much. There is no shortage, in American politics and American political science, of white men with Something to Say. The best work on women in politics is generally by women scholars. The best writing about the political lives of South Asian Americans is by South Asian Americans.

I am close to Nikki Haley's age, having grown up in the age of Reagan.[7] I am a southerner, raised in an evangelical Christianity that leaves an indelible mark even after "losing my religion," as the Georgia band's song said. (I am also, like this book's subject, an acolyte of the rock canon.) I am grateful every day that an Indian American family and its east Carolina community accepted me as one of its own; they have enriched my life immeasurably. But if I white-mansplain Nikki Haley's "meaning," then none of this really matters—so I simply offer these personal details that the interested reader might recognize my biases, which hopefully do not distract or detract from this book's treatment of its significant subject.

Ultimately, this book is most interested in reflecting how various observers have seen Nikki Haley; it considers a range of perspectives, without advancing any one of them as definitive. A journalism class taught me "show, don't tell"; this book endeavors to follow that advice. "So, what's the argument?," some academic colleagues will want to know. This book is a work of narrative contemporary history,[8] distilled from the reporting of many fine journalists and infused with interpretations reflecting various perspectives that (with only a few exceptions) all share one attribute: they take Nikki Haley seriously, and they conclude that she is a significant figure in American politics. But there is no single claim here as to Nikki Haley's significance, in the sense of just what she signifies. The subtitle invokes "the meaning of Nikki Haley," but the book assumes that Haley will mean different things to different observers and readers: indeed, the book's approach depends on it.

If the book has a central conviction, it is simply that we may learn something—some things—about American political possibilities and limits from Nikki Haley's decade in American politics. We the People do contain multitudes. But leaders, and by extension the electorate, must confront more particular choices as they seek to remake possibilities and transcend boundaries.

This book draws almost entirely on published sources. A great deal has been asked, said, and written about Nikki Haley over the past decade. The reportage and commentaries assembled here—ephemeral fragments of the digital ether—may take on new meanings when gathered together under one cover as part of a larger narrative, with distinct chapters seen from multiple perspectives. While the account here inevitably lacks some of the granular detail of some of the source material (and the interested reader should follow each chapter's endnotes to original sources), its broader frame hopefully allows for a different, more nuanced picture to emerge.

Nikki Haley has also written two memoirs, which the interested reader should consult alongside this book. In these books, Haley has had much to say about how she sees herself, how her background has shaped her political outlook, and why she has taken certain personal and political decisions. The account here seeks to represent Haley's self-presentation faithfully, albeit briefly; for obvious reasons, she should be read directly for her own unique perspective. Ultimately, this book is more interested in what others have asked and observed.

Who is the real Nikki Haley?, some readers may seek to discover (like the audience member who put this question to me, in a talk I gave at the university where I teach). Nikki Haley is, of course, a politician. The through line of her public career has been to present a consistently distinctive persona and voice, across multiple domains of policy and politics, from state government in South Carolina to multilateral diplomacy at the United Nations. The observation need not carry the implication of artifice. As modern American politicians do, Haley has made her personal background a big part of her political appeal; if she has done this more than most, let the reader weigh the balance of personal agency and external expectations confronting Haley as she writes, figuratively and literally, her "American story."

While writing this book, I visited South Carolina several times over several years, both as dedicated travel for this project and for my son's frequent soccer tournaments in the state. I am grateful to several South

Carolinian professional political analysts and scholars—who spoke freely and generously with me, and in the mutual understanding that their insights were not for personal attribution—for helping me to understand some of the internal cultural and political nuances of their fascinating state, which can be oversimplified or exoticized in many accounts. If I err similarly here at times, the fault lies in limitations of the student and not in their lessons.

There were four pilgrimages I had to make: to the State House in Columbia (two years, it turned out, before that divisive Confederate flag was removed); to Mt. Horeb United Methodist Church in Lexington, where Governor Haley's family attended during her tenure; to the Gurdwara Guru Nanaksar gurdwara of the Sikh Religious Society of South Carolina in Chapin, where the governor's father and mother could be found on a warm October Sunday in 2013; and to Emanuel African Methodist Episcopal Church in Charleston. Politics, religion, and their intersections should be taken seriously (politicians and their public performances of faith, perhaps less so). These are all hallowed places, in their own ways and in this story, so it seemed important to visit them and honor those who had come before and effectively made this book. I visited the others alone, but I stood with my teenage son at Mother Emanuel; he didn't need to be reminded what happened there.

☆ ☆ ☆

The week after Nikki Haley ended her UN ambassadorship, I was in another hotel for another conference. The fourth annual Raisina Dialogue on global politics and economics, in New Delhi, was an interesting vantage point from which to consider America's international relations in January 2019.

I stepped out of my hotel room and into the corridor to find, after a half-night of jetlag sleep, a newspaper flat on the freshly swept floor—on it, two familiar faces and the headline, "Nikki Haley, Ivanka Trump in Race for World Bank Chief." Surreally, India's *Hindustan Times* reported that Haley might be in the running for presidency of the World Bank, after a surprise announcement by its president Jim Yong Kim that he was leaving two years into a second five-year term.

My previous book was about the World Bank in India. Now it was time to wrap up this book about Nikki Haley. That the two subjects would intersect felt like some weird alternate universe. I double-checked the reporting to make sure. From London, the *Financial Times* reported the same. The scenario seemed so unlikely—but then again, Donald Trump was president of the United States.

After three days, the *New York Times* reported that White House officials said Nikki Haley would *not* be a candidate for the World Bank presidency. The official denial only reinforced the strangeness of the story. (Ivanka Trump, it was now reported, would help lead the nomination of the next World Bank president, but the president's daughter would not be a candidate herself.) Eventually David Malpass, a former US Treasury official and frequent World Bank critic, would be Trump's pick. Even so, it was a sign of Nikki Haley's standing (and of the "anything goes" nature of Trump's presidency) that her name was, in fact, floated to lead the World Bank—and that this was front-page news on the other side of the world.

It is widely expected that America and the world will see more of Nikki Haley in the future. This book is an effort to understand what has been seen so far.

Acknowledgments

This book has had two institutional patrons and many supporters. First, I would like to thank the Eagleton Institute of Politics at Rutgers University for a 2013 research grant through its Center on the American Governor. This was, at one time, going to be another book, called something like *South by South Asian American: Bobby Jindal, Nikki Haley, and the Remarkable Rise of Two Governors*. I began to move away from that notion in early 2015 when Jindal, in his faltering presidential campaign, said of his family, "We are not Indian Americans." But as comparisons often do, this one helped me to clarify certain unique contours of Haley's governorship and its reception, even before her UN appointment in late 2017 ultimately made this a different book. For their consistent support and flexibility as the project evolved, I would like to thank especially Kathy Kleeman and Ruth Mandel, both also with the Institute's Center for American Women and Politics, along with David Redlawsk and Kristoffer Shields. I also learned from fellow attendees at the CAG grant recipients' conference at Rutgers in December 2013, and I am grateful that this group of Americanists was politely accepting of me as an interloper from "IR" (international relations).

Second, I would like to thank my institution, Elon University, for Faculty Research and Development support. Through the Political Science and Policy Studies Department, I also received support from the Turnage Family Faculty Innovation and Creativity Fund for the Study of Political Communication, overseen by my senior colleague Laura Roselle. Elon's Office of Sponsored Programs also helped administer the Rutgers grant noted above, and I thank its director Bonnie Bruno and the entire staff there for this support.

I am fortunate to work with smart and supportive colleagues. For our conversations over the years that helped shape my thinking for this book, I would like to thank especially my Elon Department of Political Science and Policy Studies colleagues Damion Blake, Jessica Carew, Carrie Eaves, Sean Giovanello, Jason Husser, Baris Kesgin, Laura Roselle (again), Joel Shelton, Sharon Spray, Safia Swimelar, and Kaye Usry, along with our wonderful program assistant and colleague Melissa McBane and former colleague Dion Farganis (now "Far Dion"). Likewise, I would like to thank several friends in the Department of Religious Studies: Amy Allocco, Brian Pennington, and L. D. Russell. Beyond Elon, I am grateful to Vikash Yadav in the Political Science Department at Hobart and William Smith Colleges in Geneva, New York, for hosting me for a talk about this project early on, and for his encouragement and friendship throughout.

I won't begin to name former students here, but they know who they are: I am especially grateful to the ten Elon students who took my India and South Asia course in Spring 2019, which included travel to Delhi and Punjab. About half of them were at my end of the dinner table one warm evening in Amritsar and were kind enough to listen, through the din of an electrical fan blasting our table, as I talked about this project and about how the mother of America's UN ambassador had been born "right here in the shadow of the Golden Temple" (as Haley had told an Indian audience in 2018).

At the University of Arkansas Press, I would like to thank editor-in-chief David Scott Cunningham for taking an interest in this project, and for supporting its evolution through Nikki Haley's transition from South Carolina governor to UN ambassador. D. S. has been very understanding of delays arising from my personal and other professional obligations, always responding with good (sometimes wickedly funny) humor. Every author should be so lucky as to have someone like him to work with. Two anonymous readers were patient enough to wade through an earlier version of the manuscript and offered invaluable suggestions for making revisions. Janet Foxman and Jenny Vos have been supportive managing and project editors, respectively, and Matthew Somoroff's line-by-line parsing of the manuscript yielded so many language and organizational improvements, I wish I could send him everything I ever write. (I take responsibility for any remaining errors in the text.) The cover design by the marketing team is better than anything I had imagined; thanks to Melissa King, Liz Lester, Charlie Shields, and everyone else involved in those aspects of book production and promotion that may seem like alchemy to the author, but that require their special talents and insights.

Although some of my previous research has relied significantly on interviews, I decided early on that this project would be based on sources already in the public record, and would not attempt to "break" news about its subject's background or political career. Even so, several professional observers of South Carolina politics were generous in their willingness to speak with me in off-the-record visits during Governor Haley's first term. I would also like to thank the former senior staff person in the governor's office who was willing to speak with me, also off-the-record—and as it happened, just days before Haley's UN resignation announcement. These conversations provided helpful confirmations and clarifications. In particular, I appreciated the former Haley staffer's candor in saying that it was sometimes hard to remember details from life in the governor's office before the events of 2015, which was a detail I found interesting in itself.

My deepest source of inspiration is my family. As noted in the preface, it was a moment with my wife, Deepa, and our children, Arun and Uma, watching Nikki Haley on TV in a San Diego hotel room, that first sparked my interest in writing about the governor. They were good sports then to let a family trip be organized around my conference travel. They have done far more since then to tolerate my frequent distractedness. My previous book was for Deepa, and so is this one, but it is specially dedicated to our children, Arun and Uma, who are writing their own American stories.

I would also like to thank my parents-in-law, Drs. Tripuraneni Laxmi Perumallu and Tripuraneni Anjanadevi Perumallu, and sister-in-law Rekha Perumallu and her husband, Patrick Mucklow. Their love and support nourish me, and they are the best family I could hope for.

We lost three of the men in my family while I was working on the initial draft of this book; then, while I was revising and editing, we lost Nana and two more men who were dear to me. My grandfather William Smith Kirk, whom I called Papa, loved photography and flying. He was a Presbyterian of deep faith: reticent, but with the generosity and foresight to write certain things down, so we could better understand how he understood things. He and my grandmother Lois Smith Kirk (Nana) have been solid rocks in my life, teaching me about our family's roots in North Carolina and Pennsylvania while growing gracefully in their acceptance of new interfaith traditions in the family.

My uncle John Thomas Spicknall remains indelibly tied to this book. I learned of Tom's diagnosis from an email I read in that same hotel room in San Diego. I was able to see him one more time, at home in Dalton. His ALS progressed quickly, but we talked for many hours over two days, and he could lift his arms: he made the signal for "Touchdown!" when I told him my idea for this book. *Got some things to talk about, here beside the rising tide.*[1] The Dude Abides. My aunt Peg and cousins John and Susan are strong in character and in faith, and their examples inspired me when we suddenly lost my father, William Smith Kirk Jr., on January 10, 2017.

The man my children called Daddy K had a big heart; it simply gave out. He loved the Carolinas, especially the coast. I'm glad he moved closer to it for the last year of his journey. He died the night of President Obama's farewell address. We would have enjoyed arguing about politics in the Trump era. Maybe.

Then, across 2020: Lois Smith Kirk, my grandfather Charles Martin Severance, and T. L. Perumallu. None from COVID-19, but all in its unmoored time. Tom was fond of quoting Kurt Vonnegut's Billy Pilgrim on being "unstuck in time,"[2] or some such metaphysical possibility. Where does the time go?

Sometimes, the departures leave me at a loss for words, but the spirits are in the music so *I'll see you in my dreams.*[3]

Don't you ever ask them why, if they told you, you would cry
So just look at them and sigh, and know they love you.[4]

RISING STAR

1 ☆ This Land Is Your Land

THE BUZZ BEGAN THE MOMENT SHE EMERGED AS AS CANDIDATE for governor in South Carolina's 2010 election. Amid the Tea Party revolt taking aim at Barack Obama's historic presidency and congressional incumbents alike (including Republicans), Nikki Haley cut an intriguing profile. She seemed "in" the Tea Party movement, but not quite of it.[1] She made pointed criticisms of the party establishments, but always in measured tones, in a light southern accent, and did not traffic in the rage and resentment permeating some corners of the movement. Haley, then a state lawmaker, was an Indian American woman poised to be the Republican nominee for statewide election in South Carolina, in the national psyche a bastion of racial division and dirty politics. In the lingo of the times: *Wait, what?*

Haley made the cover of *Newsweek* (still a cultural barometer, if not quite what it used to be) for the July 12, 2010, issue. The magazine ran a striking portrait of the candidate in a red jacket, against a red background, under its red title banner. Haley stared into the camera, arms folded, her pose confident. Against the crimson monochrome, a small detail stood out from her lapel: the US flag mirrored by the South Carolina state flag, white palmetto tree and crescent moon on an indigo field. To the left of Haley's picture, bold black letters heralded her "The Face of the New South"; on the right, white type invoked "Diversity in the GOP."

Haley was in 2010 a five-year incumbent in the South Carolina House of Representatives, representing its Eighty-Seventh District, for Lexington County, west and south of Columbia. In June she had captured 49 percent of the four-way GOP primary vote in the governor's race, forcing a runoff with Gresham Barrett, a white man and the US representative for the state's Third Congressional District in the western Upstate, bordering Georgia and North Carolina. The month before, an endorsement by former Alaska governor Sarah Palin—two years after her own star-making turn as John McCain's running mate in the 2008 US presidential election—had instantly elevated Haley's national name recognition. She won the runoff, 65–35 percent. In November she went on to defeat Democrat Vincent Sheheen, another white man, 51–47 percent, in the general election.

Haley's historic governorship raised great expectations, often far beyond her state. Some critics seemed to relish that she might fail the tests they set for her and so confirm what they already knew about South Carolina and its possibilities. To some, whatever Haley might symbolize as a self-identified "brown"[2] woman elected to her state's highest office, that state's abiding symbol stood right there on the grounds of the State House, where Haley had served in the legislature and where the governor's office had its home.

For nearly forty years, the iconic battle flag of the Confederate States of America had flown over the capitol dome in Columbia, just below the US and South Carolina flags. It was raised in 1961 to commemorate the centennial of the Battle of Fort Sumter, which had begun the American Civil War. A legislative resolution in 1962 affirmed its display. The flag's symbolism soon became inseparable from white defiance in the face of the civil rights movement and federally enforced desegregation. As years passed, its presence had remained a subject of tension and controversy. Governor David Beasley, a white Republican, had reversed his earlier defense of the flag to call for its removal in 1996, only to lose his 1998 reelection bid.[3]

By the turn of the millennium, South Carolina was the only state of the former Confederacy still dedicating an official display to the battle flag (though its image was also featured within the state flags of Georgia and Mississippi). The National Association for the Advancement of Colored People (NAACP) demanded its "removal and relocation . . . to a place of historical rather than sovereign content" and called for a statewide commercial boycott, beginning on January 1, 2000, and continuing "until such time that the Confederate Battle Flag is no longer displayed in positions of sovereignty in the state of South Carolina." In an uneasy compromise voted on by the legislature, it was removed from the capitol dome and relocated to a new flagpole on the grounds of the State House, next to an existing thirty-foot monument to fallen Confederate soldiers; a new African American History Monument was installed elsewhere on the grounds in 2001.

Ten years later, South Carolina's first nonwhite and first woman governor would be called on by the national president of the NAACP, which had never accepted the compromise, to settle the symbolic score once and for all. The organization maintained that the flag's relocation did not remove it from a position of sovereignty in South Carolina; if anything, it only made it more visible to passersby: a fluttering, living symbol to all, and especially to Black South Carolinians and visitors, of slavery and segregation.

In July 2011, at the organization's annual convention in Los Angeles, NAACP president Benjamin Jealous put forward a challenge to Governor Nikki Haley:

> Perhaps one of the most perplexing examples of the contradictions of this moment in history is that Nikki Haley, South Carolina's first governor of color, continues to fly the Confederate flag in front of her state's capitol. Given the similarities between our struggles to end slavery and segregation, and her ancestors' struggle to end British colonialism and oppression in India, my question to Governor Haley is one that Dr. King often asked himself: *What would Gandhi do?*[4]

Jealous's question for the governor was widely reported. Haley's press secretary Rob Godfrey responded:

> More than a decade ago, under the leadership of a Democratic governor, South Carolinians Republican and Democrat, black and white, came to a compromise position on the Confederate flag. Many people were uncomfortable with that compromise, but it addressed a sensitive subject in a way that South Carolina as a whole could accept. We don't expect people from outside of the state to understand that dynamic, but revisiting that issue is not a part of the governor's agenda.[5]

In fact, Haley did not have the legal authority (or political power) to take down the flag. But the Jealous entreaty was really about historical and political symbolism. What kind of "governor of color" would Nikki Haley be?

The answer to Jealous's question, "What would Gandhi do?"—if taken literally as well as seriously—really was not so self-evident. In his own time, Mohandas Karamchand Gandhi, the Mahatma (Great Soul), had to accept an agonizing political compromise, in the bloody 1947

Partition that separated Pakistan from India (amid Hindu-Muslim tensions and competing visions for national identity and institutions). The worst violence was in Punjab, which also had a large Sikh population that happened to include the future South Carolina governor's mother and father, who emigrated roughly fifteen years after Partition.

Still, Jealous rightfully and righteously invoked a history of solidarity between Indian freedom fighters and Black Americans, well into the American civil rights movement. Martin Luther King Jr. often invoked Gandhi's teachings.[6] Despite Haley's press statement demurral at the time, the question posed by Jealous—eventually and in the course of events—would become *the* question of her governorship. Taking down the Confederate flag was not part of her agenda. But it would be.

It wasn't that Haley was indifferent to historical significance or racial symbolism. She just preferred to focus on other things. Haley led with a small-government, pro-business message she said she came by naturally, as a daughter of immigrants who started keeping the books for the family business when she was thirteen. As governor, she directed state employees across cabinet agencies to answer their phones cheerily, "It's a great day in South Carolina. How can I help you?" She talked about government accountability and transparency (particularly for votes in the legislature), about taking on the "good old boys' network" that for too long had abetted self-dealing lawmaking, including within her own party. Those were the kinds of changes she said South Carolinians deserved, and should expect from their government: forward-looking, easy for everyone (apart from those "good old boys") to get behind. She had to set priorities, as governors must do; the flag would be a distraction at best, and possibly a divisive derailment.

Still, Haley showed her own knack for symbolism and an ability to read the political moment even as the historic presidency of Barack Obama sought to expand the federal government's role in many areas: auto-industry bailouts, consumer protection, environmental regulation, health care. In 2012, Haley was handed an opportunity to appoint a US senator to fill a seat vacated by the early retirement of Jim DeMint, who was leaving Congress to head the Heritage Foundation, a conservative think tank in Washington, DC. Governor Haley appointed Tim Scott, a conservative Republican and Black businessman from Charleston who had been elected to the South Carolina House of Representatives in 2009 (briefly making Haley and Scott legislative colleagues) and to the US House of Representative for South Carolina's First District in 2011.

At Haley's appointment, Scott was the first-ever African American to represent South Carolina in the US Senate. The governor insisted Scott had earned the seat for "who he was," and not through tokenism.[7] (Scott retained the seat in a special election in 2014 and was elected to a full term in 2016.)

Haley also won reelection in 2014, a rematch with Sheheen, by 56 to 41 percent. The more than comfortable victory marked something of a comeback. In 2012 she had narrowly trailed the Democrat in statewide polls, as she brushed off ethics investigations into her campaign's finances and her relationships with companies doing business with the state.[8] Even as her approval had temporarily slipped at home, her national profile continued to rise.

She was frequently mentioned as a potential running mate for Mitt Romney, the Republican presidential nominee to challenge Obama in 2012. Haley liked the former Massachusetts governor when she met him individually, as she did with all the leading GOP candidates—men seeking her endorsement. Ahead of South Carolina's GOP presidential primary election, she endorsed Romney. (Newt Gingrich won the state by double digits.) She later waved off speculation she would join the Romney ticket, saying, "You know, I've got the best job being governor of South Carolina. . . . Even if offered, I would decline."[9] Haley seemed to understand the power of acknowledging she might have the opportunity—and the ability to say no.

When the eventual Mitt Romney–Paul Ryan ticket failed to defeat Obama, a post-election "autopsy" within the GOP—acronymically christened the *Growth and Opportunity Project* and led by Republican National Committee chair Reince Priebus—encapsulated an emerging conventional wisdom that the party faced a bleak future if it didn't shed its "stuffy old men" image problem to present more racially diverse candidates to a changing American electorate. Priebus, who happened to turn forty-one the week of the report's publication, told the media, "Our message was weak."[10] (A few weeks earlier, Louisiana's governor Bobby Jindal, also forty-one, had said his Republican Party had to "stop being the stupid party.") Along with other forty-something luminaries like Marco Rubio, the junior US senator from Florida, it looked like a foregone conclusion that Nikki Haley would figure prominently in this emerging Republican Party for the twenty-first century.

But in 2015, the crucible of events would define Haley's governorship more than anything from her previous agenda, thrusting her into a national spotlight more glaring than any portended by her historic election, first term, and reelection. That same year, the Republican primaries were about to be upended by Donald Trump, in a presidential campaign that went right to the rage, resentment, and racialized political appeals that the GOP wisdom had sworn off—and that Nikki Haley as much as anyone had steered away from. The eventual collision would make Haley, more than ever, one of the most intriguing political leaders in the United States, as the country veered from Barack Obama's historic presidency into something like its antithesis under Donald Trump's divisive insurgency.

If the earlier GOP had a sometime history of coded "dog whistle" appeals to white voters (over affirmative action, welfare, and other issues eliciting racial resentments), Trump traded it for a bullhorn.[11] The celebrity businessman from New York gave voice to explicit racial and ethnic stereotypes, and to "the forgotten men and women of this country" who would help him "Make America Great Again." Trump's MAGA mantra hearkened back to a pre–civil rights movement America, a time before the 1960s immigration reforms when Nimrata Nikki Randhawa had not even been born—and likely would not have been born in America, let alone in South Carolina.

Haley's rise—from SC lawmaker in 2004 to governor in 2010 and UN ambassador in 2017—has been remarkable. She was the first Indian American to hold each office. In her first term in the South Carolina House of Representatives, she was elected chair of the freshman caucus. In 2005, after just a year, she was named a majority whip by the House Republican Caucus—the only freshman lawmaker given this responsibility of lining up votes and helping shape the GOP legislative agenda. "I'm honored to be recognized again by my peers and I know this new position helps me serve my constituents," Haley said. "This position will help me drive legislation that will benefit Lexington County and the entire state." Haley's whip appointment was even a brief news item in another state capital, half a world away: Chandigarh (which India's Punjab state shares jointly with neighboring Haryana).[12]

Haley herself has had much to say from her perspective on events, and about her journey from state politics to the global stage. The first of her two memoirs, *Can't Is Not an Option: My American Story*, was published in 2012, not two years into her governorship.[13] A second, *With All Due Respect: Defending America with Grit and Grace*, was published in November 2019,[14] following Haley's departure from the UN post in the Trump administration that January (and after this book was mostly completed).

There are political science literatures on women as candidates, legislators, and executive leaders—all three roles that Haley has inhabited effectively. In her study of women in leadership positions in state legislatures, for example, Cindy Simon Rosenthal found that women tend to differ from male colleagues in observable ways, and often "approach politics with an understanding and skills that have been shaped by family, community, volunteerism, and education."[15] (She also found that women spend more time on constituent concerns and on building coalitions within and across party lines.)

Women as individuals may or may not reflect general or perceived gender traits, of course. Notably, Haley can be a spirited GOP partisan in her attacks on Democratic leaders and proposals (though in the legislature and as governor, she sharply criticized fellow Republicans at times, as well). Even so, it seems plausible that at least one reason Haley is relatively popular with Democrats and independents is that her self-presentation as a woman effectively activates certain perceptions about women in politics—responsiveness and coalition-building, for example—whether or not her issue positions and policy record actually reflect these supposed gender traits.

In 2009, the year before Haley ran for governor, she was one of just 17 women in the 170-member South Carolina legislature (46 senators and 124 representatives).[16] She has spoken and written about the state legislature, especially, as a kind of proving ground. Media coverage of Haley as candidate and officeholder has sometimes tended toward the gendered stereotypes journalists use when describing women in politics. Haley herself has remarked on her frequent characterization as "ambitious" —pointing out that when the word is used to describe men in politics, it is generally in a positive sense, whereas for women the implication is often quite negative.

Media profiles have been particularly interested in exploring Haley's Indian American heritage and getting her to talk about her background; it is not clear that a man in her position would be so continuously solicited on this subject. Even so, Haley appears to approach discussions of her ethnicity and heritage with conviction and enthusiasm, and not (only) as a performative requirement. Moreover, unlike, say, Louisiana's former governor Bobby Jindal, Nikki Haley has never distanced herself from an Indian American identity. Her frequent formulation, when discussing her self-identification, is "the proud daughter of Indian immigrants" who "grew up a brown girl in a black-and-white world" in 1970s small-town South Carolina.[17]

The comparison with Jindal is instructive. Jindal, also of Punjabi heritage and raised in a South Asian faith tradition (in his case, Hinduism), was the first Indian American governor in the United States, elected in 2008: another conservative Republican leading a former Confederate state. Jindal was more outspoken than Haley about his conversion to Christianity (in his case, evangelical Catholicism), and during his ill-fated presidential campaign in 2015, he told an audience his parents had come to the US from India "to become Americans, not Indian-Americans." This statement was a source of disappointment to some Indian Americans who had looked to Jindal as a standard-bearer. As Suresh Gupta, a former fundraiser for Jindal (and a Democrat living in Maryland) responded, "So what if he's Republican? So what if he's Christian? I don't care about those things. . . . But you can't forget about your heritage. You can't forget about your roots."[18] (Within its first year, Haley's governorship had become similarly nationalized, with around two-thirds of contributions to her reelection campaign coming from out-of-state sources.)[19]

Haley acknowledges, and in her own way affirms, an Indian American identity. As well, she seems to perceive that other Americans—and not only Indian Americans—expect such acknowledgment and affirmation from someone in her position. What Haley does not acknowledge—and seems not to perceive—is any contradiction between her conservative governing philosophy and GOP star status on the one hand, and her heritage and identity as an Indian American woman on the other.

David Brooks, a conservative commentator at the *New York Times* and the founding senior editor at the *Weekly Standard*, recently surveyed the state of ideas in the Republican Party in 2020 as it headed into an uncertain presidential election—with Donald Trump as the incumbent, and amid the spiraling COVID-19 pandemic and continuing protests in American cities over anti-Black racism in policing, structural inequality, and other grievances. Brooks wagered that even if Trump were to lose the election (as many polls suggested he might), Trumpism—the basic Trump worldview on immigration, trade, foreign policy—"will shape the GOP for decades, the way the basic Reagan worldview did for decades." Looking back at that earlier outlook and ethos, Brooks offered a brief outline that could have described Nikki Haley's political thought perfectly:

If you came of age with conservative values and around Republican politics in the 1980s and 1990s, you lived within a certain Ronald Reagan–Margaret Thatcher paradigm. It was about limiting government, spreading democracy abroad, building dynamic free markets at home and cultivating people with vigorous virtues—people who are energetic, upright, entrepreneurial, independent-minded, loyal to friends and strong against foes.[20]

Brooks's premise was that Reaganism largely had run its course, as "many came to see its limits" and American conservatism had fragmented into various strands, each trying "to create a new, updated conservative paradigm." Meanwhile, he observed, "most actual Republican politicians" rejected new intellectual possibilities, and "stuck, mostly through dumb inertia, to an anti-government zombie Reaganism decades after Reagan was dead and even though the nation's problems were utterly different from what they were when he was alive." Globalization and deindustrialization had made working class lives increasingly insecure, destabilizing communities. Trump's campaign of "class-based ethnic nationalism" radically "overturned the Reagan paradigm"; his actual presidency, Brooks lamented, went on to deliver "bigotry, incompetence and tax cuts for the wealthy" as he "handed power to [son-in-law] Jared Kushner and a bunch of old men locked in the Reagan paradigm."[21]

Brooks looked to younger men—and only men—for the "intellectual ferment" that might offer a path forward from Trump's "brain-dead" paradigm. He rifled through the sometimes competing visions of "a small group of Republican senators in their 30s and 40s"—Marco Rubio, Josh Hawley, Tom Cotton, Ben Sasse—searching for clues. Brooks had only half a thought for "the former UN ambassador Nicki [sic] Haley," whom he lumped together with Senator Pat Toomey of Pennsylvania as "staunch defenders of Minimal-Government Conservatism": essentially, the Reagan paradigm.[22]

Brooks theorized that whatever the rising men's brain trust might come up with for its intellectual underpinnings, the long-term future would see some version of working-class Republicanism, because "when push comes to shove, Republican politicians are going to choose their voters over their donor class." Almost as an afterthought, he added, "None of this works unless Republicans can deracialize their appeal . . . [and] stop presenting themselves as the party of white people."[23]

What if it isn't so much the earlier message but the messenger that the next-phase Republican Party will seek to change? Could the GOP rebuild a broad Reaganite electoral coalition to replace the base strategy of Trumpism, repackaging it for a more diverse twenty-first-century America—even if such rebooted Reaganism does not, as Brooks suggests, really respond to economic and social problems facing the country today?

Nikki Haley ran on a neo-Reaganite message and won—twice—in South Carolina before going to New York and casting her UN ambassadorship in the mold of Jeane Kirkpatrick, Reagan's formidable envoy. When campaigns can be framed around identities and personalities as much as ideas and policies (with Barack Obama's 2008 run as a particularly successful example), an Indian American woman from South Carolina, carrying the torch for Reagan and Kirkpatrick (with a dash of Thatcher?) could be the GOP's own Hope and Change.

According to data from the progressive Women Donors Network's Reflective Democracy Campaign, in 2016 some 97 percent of all Republican elected officials were white and 76 percent were male identified, even though white men comprised just 31 percent of the US population.[24] Back in 2010, when Haley was first elected governor, a *New York Times*/CBS poll found that "only 3 percent of Tea Partiers were Hispanic, while a meager 1 percent were black and 1 percent were Asian."[25] As scholar Ian Haney López has put it, an Indian American with a southern governorship on the résumé is a chance to "at once highlight the antiracist credentials of the GOP and to appeal for support among a growing South Asian population."[26]

In fact, Haley's much broader appeal has reached far across ethnic and political lines: in April 2017, early in her UN ambassadorship, a Quinnipiac University poll found her approval rating to be 75 percent among Republicans, 55 percent among Democrats, and 63 percent among Independents (with disapproval rates of 9 percent, 23 percent, and 19 percent, respectively). In the same poll, President Donald Trump's approval/disapproval was 84/11 among Republicans, 05/92 among Democrats, and 34/58 among Independents.[27] In December 2017, Haley made her first appearance on a list of "most admired women in the world" according to a Gallup poll, joining former US secretaries of state Hillary Clinton (who Haley has credited as an inspiration, despite significant policy disagreements) and Condoleezza Rice, First Lady Melania Trump, Duchess Kate Middleton, and singer Beyoncé Knowles.[28]

Haley thus stands out as more than an exceptional figure in the top party ranks. She is a symbol of the mere *potential* of greater GOP diversity (or a token, by one's interpretation) and the unusual if not singular position she occupies in the party firmament has made her a significant and powerful figure in American politics. Her "structural" position, in the academic lingo, is only enhanced by the "agency" Haley brings to the equation in telling a unique but relatable personal story, and through her charisma and political skills.

This book seeks to understand how Haley's combination of political talents and her intersectional identity as an Indian American woman—and a Republican, Christian, and southern one—have given her power and influence in her party, in her state, in the Trump cabinet, in American politics, and at times, on the world stage. How is it that Nikki Haley has maintained a basically consistent leadership identity and "brand" for the last decade, even as so much in American politics and international relations seems to have changed? What did Haley's six-year governorship and two-year ambassadorship mean to various American and global audiences? What assumptions, dreams, expectations, fears, hopes, and prejudices have been projected onto the canvas of her political career? Where have her own ideas and achievements aligned with these various images, and where have imaginations and the record diverged? How have her actions (and inactions) in responding to events engendered new expectations, disappointments, projections, and meanings?

From lowering a flag on South Carolina's past to flying the flag of her South Asian American heritage, from broadening the Republican Party's electoral appeal to representing America to the world, admirers and critics—Black, brown, and white—have looked to Nikki Haley for many things. Can there be any through line connecting Haley's background in South Carolina to her rapprochement with Trump and Trumpism as forces in American politics and international relations?

These questions and frames inspire the remainder of this introductory chapter, and the five chapters that follow. Here, in chapter 1, "This Land Is Your Land," the book sets a wide framework for contextualizing Haley's rise in American politics, briefly invoking relevant and complementary (but basically separate) scholarly literatures in Asian American political participation and race and religion in American politics. The chapter also briefly fills in some of the biographical details sketched above, from Haley's South Carolina roots to key episodes and issues in her first term as governor that seem especially significant in light of events in South Carolina she would confront in 2015, and the turn her political career would take the following year.

Chapter 2, "Charleston: 'We Are at War with Ourselves,'" is mainly about the hate crime at Mother Emanuel AME Church in June 2015 that resulted in the murder of nine Black Americans, including a prominent minister and state lawmaker, and that led to the state's decision, following Haley's call, to take down the Confederate battle flag for good. By striking coincidence, the very week of the Mother Emanuel murders, Donald Trump announced his campaign for the presidency from the lobby of Trump Tower in New York.

Chapter 3, "UN-Likely Ambassador," traces the remarkable path that Nikki Haley traveled from outspoken Trump critic to Trump cabinet member, in less than a year, after her delivery of the GOP response to President Barack Obama's final State of the Union address in January 2016. Haley denounced "the siren call of the angriest voices" (which surely included Trump), later endorsed Marco Rubio for president before her state's GOP primary, and fired back at Trump's criticisms of her over Twitter with that incomparable southern saying: "Bless his heart." But come November, Haley would interview with Trump for secretary of state (she withdrew before an offer was made) and by the end of the year she would be the president-elect's nominee for UN ambassador. She would also be prepping to join the cabinet and the National Security Council (NSC), having insisted on both privileges as conditions of her nomination.

In chapter 4, "Taking Names," the book chronicles roughly the first year of Haley's ambassadorship, moving forward somewhat into spring 2018 to contain several storylines and themes within a single chapter. During this period, Haley appeared at times as Trump's leading foreign policy spokesperson—an unusual role for a UN ambassador, but made possible by Haley's cabinet and NSC positions and especially by the ineffectiveness of Trump's first secretary of state, former Exxon-Mobil CEO Rex Tillerson. During a fast-paced first fifteen or so months at the United Nations, Haley was often uncompromising in her defense of the Trump administration's unilateral impulses, yet she managed to earn the respectful reviews of fellow diplomats and even some congressional Democrats as she led UN efforts to tighten multilateral sanctions targeting North Korea's nuclear and missile programs. In other issue areas, such as the

Iran nuclear deal and the Israeli-Palestinian conflict, Haley was unable to build broad international support for Trump's policies. Perhaps most strikingly, she positioned herself as a human rights champion (if a selective one) in the American internationalist tradition. She was singularly outspoken at the UN Security Council in condemning chemical weapons atrocities in Syria, an issue that had bedeviled the Obama administration. She also maintained a hard-line stance against Syria's patron Russia, even as President Trump voiced unorthodox admiration for its president Vladimir Putin, and as US intelligence reports and investigations examined Russian interference in the 2016 election.

Chapter 5, "Hedging Bets," finds Ambassador Haley in a somewhat different place in her second year on the job, amid significant personnel changes in the administration. She was still "taking names" and generally holding her own, but with fewer openings to distinguish herself from the secretary of state, especially after the feckless Tillerson's replacement by Mike Pompeo. Even so, Haley found and made opportunities to continue speaking as a unique kind of Trump surrogate. She made an unusually high number of media appearances for a UN ambassador. She seemed particularly interested in speaking to American audiences, both through TV and through numerous speeches at universities and to conservative groups. She exhibited an increasingly sharp sense of how to cultivate media coverage, which remained largely favorable (and always *intrigued*) even as she began to be criticized more directly and more often. She defended the administration's policies of migrant detentions and family separations at the US-Mexico border, even as she announced American withdrawal from the UN's Human Rights Council (somewhat undermining the principled human rights reasons she gave for the exit). She continued to defend Israel and made a high-profile visit to India, effectively standing in for Pompeo after a last-minute change of plans put him in North Korea. She seemed fully engaged in the job.

Chapter 6, "Citizen Haley," begins with the ambassador's surprise announcement in October 2018—at Trump's side in the Oval Office—that she would be stepping down the following January. The brief final phase of Haley's ambassadorship saw efforts at tying up some of the issues she had engaged over her two-year tenure, but there was no grand finale. This concluding chapter of the book offers some assessments of Haley's UN legacy, and briefly (and with only limited speculation) considers how her more circumscribed public life since stepping down may be laying groundwork for a future campaign—particularly after the 2020 US presidential election rendered a verdict on Trump, if not necessarily on the future of Trumpism.

✦ ✦ ✦

With Barack Obama's historic election to the presidency in 2008, some observers suggested the United States had arrived at a new "post-racial" politics.[29] Many scholars were immediately skeptical of this notion, with some seeing a new racialization of white Americans' political views on policy issues such as health care.[30] Other scholars saw a continuing divide between "*color-blind* advocates [who] contend that they stand for judging people not on the color of their skin but on the content of their character, as the Reverend Martin Luther King Jr. called for in his 1963 'I have a dream' speech that culminated the March on Washington . . . [and] *race-conscious* proponents [who] maintain that they stand for cashing America's 'promissory note' to give the nation's racial minorities 'the riches of freedom and the security of justice,' as King also called for in that speech."[31]

Nikki Haley's leadership and representation style may offer a glimpse into the future, as demographic trends portend a "majority minority" America by the mid-twenty-first century.[32] Far from ushering in a halcyon age of "multiculturalism, antiracism, racial reconciliation, and cultural diversity," some scholars argue that racial and ethnic divisions are not so much being erased as reconfigured. The political profiles and sociocultural identities of Asian Americans, Hispanic and Latino Americans, and other groups may be undergoing a "whitening" process, not unlike that of earlier Irish, Jewish, and other immigrants.[33] We also may be seeing a "new black/nonblack divide," where Black Americans continue to "experience a degree of alienation unlike that of other groups"[34]—though recent anti-immigrant demagoguery, directed especially at Central Americans and Muslims, is a forewarning that leadership choices, and not only demographic forces, will shape what kind of country the coming America will be.

The US Census category of "Asian Indians" accounted for more than 2.8 million Americans, around 1 percent of the US population, in 2010 (coincidentally, the year of Nikki Haley's election as governor). But in South Carolina, Asian Indians numbered just under sixteen thousand, or 0.34 percent of the state's population—and this was an 80 percent increase since 2000. Haley's margin of victory in the 2010 gubernatorial race was almost six times the size of South Carolina's entire Indian American population: thus, whatever support she received from the community was hardly decisive from an electoral perspective. But fundamentally, when Nikki Haley discusses her Indian American heritage, the close-knit South Carolina community is her frame of reference.

Haley in 2010 was not a "national" Indian American candidate according to Sanjay Puri, chairman of the Washington, DC–based US-India Political Action Committee. USINPAC supports Indian American candidates of both parties, as an auxiliary to its original focus on US-India relations. Unlike Jindal (whose Louisiana gubernatorial campaigns saw fundraising by Indian Americans in Texas and along the Gulf Coast), Puri said, Haley had fewer connections outside South Carolina, where the Indian American community was attuned to her developing career.[35] But Haley would soon be a nationalized candidate, full stop.

Nimrata Nikki Randhawa (always called Nikki) was born January 20, 1972, in Bamberg city, the seat of Bamberg County, in the south-central part of South Carolina where the Sandhills meet the Lowcountry coastal plain. Inside the book jacket for Haley's 2012 memoir, *Can't Is Not an Option: My American Story*, behind a soft-focus portrait of the governor, the family story begins: "Ajit and Raj Randhawa were well-educated, well-off Sikhs in the Punjab region of India. But despite their high social status, the Randhawas wanted more for their family—the opportunities that only America could offer."

The Randhawas left India with infant son Harmeet ("Mitti") in 1962, heading first for Vancouver, Canada, where Ajit completed a PhD in biology at the University of British Columbia. Raj worked at a post office, sold Avon products, and cared for another family's special-needs child. The Randhawas moved to South Carolina in 1969, now with a second child, daughter Simran ("Simmi"), when Dr. Randhawa accepted a faculty position at historically Black, Episcopal Church–affiliated Voorhees College in the town of Denmark, near Bamberg. Nimrata Nikki was born three years later. With a younger brother, Gogi, rounding out the household, the family took to calling themselves "the original six"—the first Indians in town. (The Original Six is also the name of a foundation Governor Haley started in 2011.)[36]

Bamberg is a small town; its population was around 2,500 in the 1970s and a little over 3,600 in the 2010 Census. The Randhawas may have been the only Indian family starting out, but there were others in nearby Orangeburg, where Nikki later would attend preparatory high school. A childhood acquaintance, also from the small Punjabi Sikh community, described South Carolina's Indian American community at that time as close-knit: Hindus, Muslims, and Christians coming together with Sikhs, like the Randhawas, across religious differences.[37] In her first memoir, Haley also recalls getting together with other Sikh families at someone's home, about one weekend every month, for "three-day-long rituals of prayer followed by copious amounts of wonderful food."[38]

The future governor ventured upstate to Clemson University for a BS in accounting; her first job after graduating in 1994 was with a regional company specializing in waste management and recycling, which put her in Charlotte, North Carolina, for a couple of years. (In *With All Due Respect*, Haley writes that it was the farthest north she'd ever lived, until moving with her family to New York for her UN ambassadorship.)

When she met her future husband on her first weekend at Clemson, he went by Bill Haley, and went to another school. After they'd been dating for a little while, she writes in *Can't Is Not an Option*, Nikki told him, "You just don't look like a Bill. What's your whole name?" He told her, "William Michael," and she started calling him Michael. She writes, "When he transferred to Clemson his sophomore year, my friends became his friends, and before we knew it, he was universally known as Michael," though older friends still call him Bill. Concluding the illuminating passage, she writes, "He looks like a Michael."[39]

The intercultural couple "had many heartfelt conversations about religion," she recalls. In those conversations, Michael Haley (who is white) touched "a lot on the circumstances of his birth, savior, and upbringing." She writes, "When I attended Sikh worship services as a young person, I gained an appreciation for God's presence, but because the ceremony was conducted in Punjabi, I never truly understood the message. . . . I converted to Christianity because the teachings of Christ spoke to me in a way that I could understand and that would help me live my life—the life I wanted in mine and Michael's marriage and in the raising of our children."[40]

They were married at the Haley family church, Saint Andrew By-the-Sea United Methodist, in Hilton Head in 1996. Nikki Haley then came home to a job she had first held at age thirteen: bookkeeping for the family's "upscale fashion" company, Exotica International, now in Lexington. Founded in Bamberg by Raj while Ajit taught biology, Exotica was originally run "out of the living room" of the family's home.

Moving upstate widened the Randhawas' community and put the family in a new socioeconomic setting. Bamberg and Lexington, about sixty-five miles apart, exhibit very different sides of South Carolina. Median income for a family in Bamberg is about $28,000; in Lexington it is around $66,000 (putting the former well below the state average, the latter appreciably above). Bamberg is around 54 percent Black or African American and 45 percent white, with very small Hispanic, Asian, and Native American populations of under 1 percent each (2010 Census). Lexington is almost 84 percent white and about 13 percent Black, with Asian and Hispanic populations each of about 2 percent.

In her writings and in interviews, Haley talks more about Bamberg than about the Lexington area, of "finding the similarities and avoiding the differences" during her childhood encounters with the racial divisions that continued to order everyday life a decade after the civil rights movement's major court victories and legislative achievements. Haley also talks candidly about encountering discrimination, particularly toward her father, who wears a turban and beard in the Sikh tradition.

In *Can't Is Not an Option*, Haley recalls a playground encounter in third grade that shaped her awareness of race relations and how to define her place:

> I walked over and noticed that [the children] were divided into two groups, a black group and a white group. One of the kids in the black group was holding the ball. . . . I walked over and said, "Are we playing today?" And one girl said, "We are. You're not."
>
> I was stunned. "Why?" I asked. She replied, "You can play with us, but you have to pick a side. Are you white or are you black?" she replied. I was in a panic. Which side could I choose? What was I? Then I saw a solution: change the subject. I grabbed the ball from the girl and ran as fast as I could to the field. "I'm neither!" I yelled. "I'm brown!" Before I knew it, we were all playing kickball on the playground.[41]

She had "dodged the issue," she writes, but she knew it wouldn't be the last time. Haley's account of another story, about her experience as a four-year-old in the Wee Miss Bamberg pageant, is more ambivalent. Certainly, the anecdote affords less agency to her younger self, in a social structure upheld by adults. The *New York Times* had reported it during the 2010 campaign. She writes, "It quickly became one of the stories the media most liked to repeat about me. . . . It confirmed their preconceived notions of life in the South, particularly in the small-town, rural South of Bamberg, South Carolina."

In Haley's telling, her talent, "such as it was, was singing." Her selection: Woody Guthrie's "This Land Is Your Land." But there was a problem:

> After all the little girls had performed, they lined us all up on the stage. The little white girls were on one side, the little black girls were on the other, Simmi and I were in the middle. The pageant traditionally had two winners, a black queen and a white queen. But before they revealed who the winners were, the organizers of the pageant said they had an announcement to make. They called Simmi and me out of line and said, "We don't have a place for you."[42]

She received a beach ball—"a disqualification gift." Haley explains, "I didn't fit into either of the categories (black and white) by which the pageant judged the winners." Even so, she concludes, "What matters isn't the stories themselves; it's how the stories end. . . . Over time that town, Bamberg, adopted us as its own."[43]

And yet she also observes of her gubernatorial run: "My dad would always stand in the corner at events he attended." She wanted everyone to see her parents and how proud she was of them. But her father "was always concerned that the fact that he looked different would hurt my chances in the campaign," she explains. "And while it's true that some tried to make our difference a disqualifying issue, they didn't succeed."[44]

Though Haley does not mention it, in the 2010 gubernatorial general election, Bamberg County voters favored her Democratic opponent (by more than 10 percent), while Lexington County voters overwhelmingly favored her (by more than 30 percent).[45] As a considerable body of political science literature attests, party identification is the single strongest predictor of voting behavior. Depending on where they lived, it is safe to surmise, many South Carolinians voted for or against Nikki Haley simply because she is a Republican.[46]

Haley's account of how she came to identify as a Republican, after growing up in what she describes as an essentially nonpolitical household, is straightforward. After becoming more involved at Exotica as bookkeeper and seeing how much went to taxes, she said, she started to take an interest in politics. A prominent businesswoman in the community asked her party affiliation. She said she didn't know, but described her budding political views. The mentor pronounced her "clearly a Republican."[47]

★ ★ ★

On opposite sides of tranquil Lake Murray, a reservoir in Lexington County, sit two houses of worship that offer different windows into Nikki Randhawa Haley's intersecting worlds. Mt. Horeb United Methodist Church in Lexington, which the Haley family attended during her governorship, is a relatively large congregation offering both traditional and contemporary Sunday worship services. On an October morning in 2013, at the casual-dress contemporary service, the governor was not in attendance. Apart from a Black member on stage with the praise band, playing bass guitar and wearing Washington Redskins ball cap, white faces filled the sanctuary. The pastor was engaging but informal and conversational in his invocations of scripture. A new member of the church gave his testimony from a recent men's retreat, filled with Bible study and skeet shooting.

A fourteen-mile drive north and over the 7,800-foot-long Saluda Dam, the Sikh Religious Society of South Carolina held worship at the Gurdwara Guru Nanaksar, in the bedroom community of Chapin. Set along a two-lane highway among single-family subdivisions, the temple is surrounded by tended gardens and a high chain-link fence. Its congregation was welcoming. Ajit Randhawa, the governor's father, held open the door to the main hall, which smelled of fresh carpet. Men and women sat in separate groups, heads covered, for incantations from the Guru Granth, the Sikh holy book. Later, chai and a vegetarian meal were served in a separate building.[48]

Haley attended an inauguration of the Gurdwara's new hall as governor, and for several years was pictured on the society's website, wearing the traditional salwar kameez and head scarf.[49] The governor's father and mother were among the society's most active members, serving on its board at the time of the author's visit.

There is a rich scholarly literature on Indian immigration to the United States and on the diverse experiences of Indian Americans.[50] It is often said of Black and brown Americans leading major US institutions that their stories "wouldn't have been possible" in an earlier America. In the case of Indian Americans, the journey from explicit exclusion to hard-won (if still contested) inclusion has been particularly dramatic.

As historian Mark Noll puts it, "Religion has always been crucial for the workings of race in American politics. Together, race and religion make up not only the nation's deepest and most enduring moral problem, but also its broadest and most enduring political influence."[51] This has been particularly true for Indian and South Asian Americans, and particularly for the majorities who do not identify as Christian.

In 1918, Bhagat Singh Thind, a Sikh from Punjab (described as "Hindoo" in some contemporaneous accounts) and a US Army Veteran, filed in Oregon and Washington (state) for American citizenship under the Naturalization Act of 1906. Thind's citizenship was approved, only to be rescinded four days later by the Immigration and Naturalization Service. Thind applied again the following year, again with initial success, but an INS objection to the Oregon federal judge's ruling in Thind's favor sent his case to the Ninth Circuit Court of Appeals and ultimately to the US Supreme Court in 1923.

Thind did not challenge the constitutionality of the act's exclusion of Asians from American citizenship. Rather, he told the court that as a high-caste Indian he was a member of the "Aryan" race, therefore Caucasian or white, and thus eligible for citizenship. The court decided unanimously against Thind, making him ineligible for naturalization. After *United States v. Bhagat Singh Thind*, other previously naturalized citizens of Indian origin had their American citizenships stripped, until the Luce-Celler Act of 1946 allowed for naturalization and permitted just one hundred new Indian immigrants into the country each year.

The Immigration and Nationality Act (Hart-Celler Act) of 1965 phased out national origin quotas. This landmark legislation was brought by Democratic leaders in the US Congress and signed by President Lyndon Johnson, over opposition from southern Democrats. The Hart-Celler Act effectively established a new immigration regime, based on attracting skilled labor and reuniting immigrant families, thus beginning an era of continuous growth in immigration from India especially, which surpassed all other non-European countries.[52] By 2014, India was the largest source of new immigrants to the United States at 147,000, ahead of China (132,000) and Mexico (130,000), and the second-largest country of origin cumulatively.[53]

Thind's legal claim of whiteness failed. But scholars have recorded other pathways by which Indian (and other South Asian) immigrants negotiated their places in the racial and religious structures of twentieth-century America.[54] Some, taking the opposite tack from Thind, embraced Blackness, moving into Black neighborhoods in Northeastern and West Coast cities and "melting" into Black communities through intermarriage and cultural assimilation. Some traveled to the Jim Crow South—ironically, to escape the harassment often encountered in exclusivist ethnic neighborhoods in the North.[55] A few even sought to challenge the South's own racial caste system through the ambiguity of their positions. The literature includes colorful examples of South Asians in the American South donning turbans and other "Asiatic" effects, in efforts to confound white segregationists and transgress the signs reading, "No Coloreds Allowed." As one southern sojourner wrote in 1952, "A turban makes anyone an Indian."[56] In the post–civil rights movement era, Indian and South Asian Americans have continued to define their places amid and across the Black-and-white lines that continue to divide communities, and not only the South, in the twenty-first century.[57]

Anthropologist Ajantha Subramanian, who has studied Indian American experiences in North Carolina, notes a "superseding of race by culture as the definitive characteristic of Indian immigrant identity," particularly among the entrepreneurial and professional sections of the population that have contributed to the image of a "model minority." But, Subramanian adds,

> we must ask to what extent the racial hierarchies of the early twentieth century have been dismantled or whether they continue to structure American society and Indian American politics. . . .
>
> The affluence of Indian professionals has ensured their segregation from other nonwhite populations and their entry into previously white-dominated social spaces of the university, the corporation, the research institution, and the gated community.[58]

Indian Americans represent the highest-educated and highest-income population in the United States, surpassing white Americans and other Asian American subgroups on both dimensions.[59] This has given rise to a "model minority" stereotype, which often obscures significant class, cultural, regional, and religious diversity among Indian Americans.

The *political* lives of South Asian Americans have received relatively little scholarly attention until recently. Political scientist Sangay Mishra offers the most systematic analysis of how divisions and identities among Indian Americans—by class, religion, place of origin, language, caste, gender, and sexuality—all inform how Indian Americans experience and participate in American political life, leading to multiple pathways of political inclusion and exclusion that defy almost any effort to describe a united group experience.[60]

Similarly, Prema Kurien has analyzed different patterns of Indian and South Asian American political identification and behavior, often around "homeland and domestic issues" (that is, issues in India and other South Asian countries of heritage). There are differences across religious communities, and between "parents' generation" and "second-generation" South Asian Americans. The differences, Kurien finds, "can be explained by the ways in which race and religion intertwine with the characteristics of groups and political opportunity structures in the United States."[61]

Some scholars have documented a reracialization of Indian American and other South Asian American identities after September 11, 2001, as "people of South Asian ancestry, so easily mistaken as terrorists" were confronted anew with "the reality of racism and profiling."[62] Sikh men in particular—traditionally turbaned and bearded—have been subject to law enforcement profiling and hate crimes.[63]

The several non-Christian faiths widely practiced by Indian and South Asian Americans remain unfamiliar to many Americans, with receptions sometimes ranging from fawning exoticization to fearful suspicion and hostile confrontation. The 2008 National Asian American Survey found 77 percent of respondents whose national origin was India identify as Hindus. The community's Sikh, Muslim, Christian, Buddhist, "Other non-Christian," agnostic, and atheist sections each accounted for single-digit percentages. At 6 percent, Sikhs were the largest of these groups.[64]

Notably, Pew Research finds that only one-third of Indian Americans say that the "freedom to practice their religion" is better in the United States than in India, compared to 52 percent for Asian Americans over-all.[65] This comes at a time when there is some evidence that Americans are becoming more receptive to the Vedic notion that "Truth is One, but the sages speak of it by many names." A Pew Forum survey in 2008 found that while 76 percent of Americans identified as Christian, 65 percent also agreed with the statement "Many religions can lead to eternal life." Among white evangelical Christians, however, that statement found only 37 percent support.[66]

The identification of white evangelicals with the Republican Party has grown closer in recent years: the Pew Religion and Public Life Project found that in 2008, 65 percent of white evangelical Protestant voters identified as Republican or leaned toward the party; by 2011, the figure was 70 percent—with only 24 percent identifying or leaning Democratic.[67] Polls also suggest that evangelicals make up the single largest bloc in the Republican Party, followed by (at the time of Haley's governorship in 2013) Tea Party identifiers, with "moderates" accounting for just one-fourth of the party base.[68]

In South Carolina, white evangelicals represent an estimated 40 to 50 percent of primary voters in the Republican Party.[69] Though such voters have shown some willingness to support "non-Christian" candidates—this is how many Southern Baptists, for example, describe Mormonism, Mitt Romney's faith—it seems fair to surmise that a South Asian American candidate who presented herself to voters as something other than Christian would face a harder road to nomination and winning elections.

In a 2014 survey-based experiment through the Elon University Poll, this book's author and a colleague asked North Carolina respondents to evaluate profiles for fictional Indian American candidates for an elected state-wide office (state treasurer, a real position).[70] We varied the hypothetical office-seekers by party, gender, religious identification (Christian, Hindu, or Sikh), and use of an "Indian-sounding" first name or "Americanized" nickname (a Mr. Jagdish Singh, a Mr. Jack Singh, a Ms. Jamila Singh, and a Ms. Jamie Singh). The survey asked respondents to rate (1–10) a randomly selected profile according to "how likely would you be to vote for the candidate?" and "do you think the candidate will understand voters like you?"

The strongest correlation the survey found was around party: Democrats were more likely to rate a Democratic Indian American candidate highly, likewise for Republicans evaluating a Republican Indian American candidate. Most other differences were not statistically significant. Our male and female Indian American candidates fared about the same; both rated generally favorably across respondent demographics. Our "Indian" and "Americanized" names essentially made no difference (though other research suggests that nicknames do benefit Indian American candidates).[71] Our survey did find, however, that Republican respondents rated the hypothetical Hindu and Sikh candidates less favorably than the Christian ones, a statistically significant result. Democratic and Independent respondents did not exhibit the same result.

None of this means, or is meant to imply, that successful Indian American candidates strategically craft their biographies—changing religions, adopting nicknames—to win over American voters. The findings do suggest, however, that the political process may *select* for candidates who exhibit certain characteristics and tell personal stories that make them more relatable to voters. And these effects may be particularly true among Republicans (North Carolinians, at least) when comparing Christian and non-Christian candidates.

★ ★ ★

In 2004, while running for the South Carolina legislature, Nikki Haley told an interviewer, "I was born and raised with the Sikh faith, my husband and I were married in the Methodist Church, our children have been baptized in the Methodist Church, and currently we attend both [Methodist and Sikh religious functions]."[72] A campaign brochure from the period said, "Nikki was proudly raised with her Indian traditions and her husband, Michael, was brought up in the Methodist faith." (The brochure did not specify Sikhism as the tradition she was raised in.) "Together they lovingly raise both of their children the way they were raised; appreciating the blessings of God, the values of family, and respect for all people."[73]

Six years later, Haley's gubernatorial campaign website at first described her faith in "Almighty God," later changing to "faith in Christ" and "living for Christ every day."[74] In reporting on the website revision, just before the June 2010 South Carolina GOP primary, David Brody of the Christian Broadcasting Network said it was "a legitimate question" to ask whether Haley now was "making a political decision by playing up her Christian faith . . . and LOSING the Sikh emphasis."[75] But when Haley became the party's nominee, Brody offered his strong endorsement and unequivocally characterized her as a "Christian, Indian-American woman." He added, "For the GOP, this is a best case scenario. . . . Folks, from a PR perspective, it doesn't get any better."[76]

In July 2011, six months into Haley's first term, Charleston's *Post and Courier* reported she had "listed her race as white on her voter registration card" ten years earlier. This was discovered by state Democrats through a public records search.[77] Not long before this was reported, critics pointed out, Haley had signed voter ID legislation proposed by state Republicans, requiring voters to present photo identification at polling stations. A South Asian American writer for liberal *Mother Jones* suggested, "Her self-race-mis-classification seems to undermine her credibility as someone who wants to prevent people from lying on their way to the voting booth."[78] Scholar Vijay Prashad suggested that Haley "was born Nimrata Randhawa in South Carolina to Sikh parents, but washed that away" to follow the "twenty-five percent of Indian Americans [who] put themselves down as 'white' in the 1990 Census."[79]

These are harsh judgments of Nikki Haley, and of many other Indian Americans. They are also, by extension, harsh judgments of American society. On this terrain, it is easy to moralize about brown immigrants, and brown children of immigrants, who stand ready to subordinate their identities to "whitewashing" and therefore to be complicit in cultural erasure. But equally, we must remember that those who have moved halfway around the world in pursuit of better lives for themselves and their families are, almost by definition, "exceptional people" as migration scholars Ian Goldin, Geoffrey Cameron, and Meera Balarajan have written.[80] Race is an especially fraught subject in America, and the US Census itself is an imposing, ordering, and non-neutral machinery of state. It forces categorical choices, without contextualizing their implications for respondents. Perhaps some understanding can be extended for how people choose to self-identify, without treating "wrong" choices as crimes against culture.

"This land is your land, this land is my land," sang Woody Guthrie, and later Nikki Randhawa, invoking an egalitarian American ideal and aspiration. More darkly, as Guthrie's musical progeny Bob Dylan (née Robert Zimmerman) recorded in "Things Have Changed" at the end of the twentieth century, "Some things are too hot to touch. The human mind can only stand so much." The singer could have been talking about America's racial baggage.[81]

Historians of southern culture have analyzed the reactionary "politics of whiteness" and "pattern of defensiveness that shaped the region's political and cultural conservatism" in the face of pervasive national criticism, across the post-Reconstruction twentieth century to the present day.[82] In this light "new groups, such as the Tea Party protestors, the Birthers who challenge the constitutionality of Barack Obama's presidency, and the anti-environmentalists, among others, are not new, but are old spirits that will not die" and that "predominate in the South."[83]

And yet. There is another, forward-looking South, in which anthropologist James Peacock sees a "grounded globalism" where "the rest of the nation is no longer the dominant framework; the world is."[84] Peacock sees in this southern cultural development the potential to "emancipate at various levels" the mental habits, social relationships, and sense of place in the region, and at its best, sustains a distinct identity even as it absorbs new immigrants, cultures, religions, and foods, and even as it adjusts to both job losses to other countries (mostly in the wider "global South") and to new and different economic opportunities brought by globalization. It may be tempting to write off as romanticism the notion that the American South exhibits Peacock's notion of "grounded globalism"—and to point out that when BMW came to South Carolina in the mid-1990s, it was for the region's low wages and non-union workers not its world famous hospitality. But immigrants from across the world have made their homes in the "*Nuevo* New South,"[85] and a political leader like Nikki Haley may be part of the region's broader process of diversifying and enduring while transforming.

Even if, at times, that process can feel like two steps forward, one step back.

★ ★ ★

As she embarked on a political career, beginning with a successful 2004 run for the South Carolina House of Representatives, Nikki Haley drew on her family's small-business story and crafted a fairly standard Republican campaign around low taxes and family values. But she also presented herself as a reformer against the state's "good old boys' club," advocating legislative transparency, financial disclosure, and term limits. The transparency crusade did not endear her to everyone in the state's political establishment, including in her own party.

Picking up on an "outsider" theme during her gubernatorial run later on, the *New York Times* titled a June 2010 profile "All Her Life, Nikki Haley Was the Different One."[86] The gubernatorial contest was ugly, even by the rough standards of South Carolina campaigns. Haley entered the race as a protégé of the two-term incumbent, Mark Sanford, who had sparred with the "old boys" himself and had appeared to have a bright future as a reformist Republican. But Sanford had let his personal life unravel in mid-2009 when he disappeared for a week to "hike the Appalachian Trail"—which turned out to run through the Buenos Aires bedroom of an Argentine journalist.

Haley thought her campaign might become a "casualty" of the "Sanford implosion," but it drew her closer to the governor's suddenly estranged wife, Jenny, whose endorsement proved to be an asset.[87] In the weeks leading up to the June 2010 primary election, Haley herself had to fight off unsubstantiated allegations of past infidelity—first from a former

Sanford press secretary, and then from a paid consultant to the incumbent lieutenant governor, a campaign rival and fellow Republican.

Then came a racist remark by another fellow Republican, state senator Jake Knotts of Lexington, a white man, on a webcast called *Pub Politics*:

> Her daddy wears a turban around Lexington. And her momma wears a ruby between her head [*jabbing his forehead*]. And she is a Sikh [*pronouncing it* "Sheek"], and trying to be a Methodist. And it gets to Greenville, around the Bob Jones University people, they're not gonna like that.
>
> We got a raghead in Washington, we don't need a raghead in the State House.[88]

At least Knotts, invoking the "Barack Obama is a closeted Muslim" canard, was somewhat better informed of Haley's heritage. (An anonymous flyer that circulated during her 2004 run for the SC House had warned voters not to elect "a Hindu.")

Haley lagged behind three Republican rivals in 2010 polls, before the Palin endorsement helped put her on top heading into the primary. The Tea Party was at the height of its cultural and political impact. At the same time, Haley may have benefited from at least one form of Republican establishment support. Former Massachusetts governor Mitt Romney had run for the presidency in 2008 (and would, of course, do so again in 2012). According to journalists Mark Halperin and John Heilemann in their book *Double Down* about the 2012 presidential campaign, Romney "tapped his donor network" for Republican candidates ahead of the 2010 midterms. Using his PAC's "offshoots in New Hampshire and Iowa that allowed him to tiptoe around donations to local officials, he hit the trail on behalf of congressional and state-level candidates, handing out hundreds of thousands of dollars to the likes of future governors Nikki Haley, in South Carolina, and Terry Branstad, in Iowa."[89] (As noted previously, Haley met Romney when he sought her endorsement in 2012; Halperin and Heilemann also report that after he became the Republican nominee, Haley would be one of a select group of "war councilors" to Romney as he prepared to debate President Obama.)[90]

On June 8, Haley finished first in the four-way Republican primary, but her 49 percent share fell just short of the threshold to win. On June 22, she won the runoff with 65 percent of the vote, defeating US representative Gresham Barrett, a four-term Republican congressman who had drawn

Tea Party criticism for his vote favoring the 2008 Wall Street bailout. South Carolina Republican voters also chose Tim Scott (who, as noted, Governor Haley would later appoint as the state's first Black US senator) for nomination to the US House of Representatives over Paul Thurmond, son of Strom Thurmond, the white segregationist Dixiecrat presidential candidate of 1948 and the state's US senator for forty-eight years.

National Public Radio called the Haley-Scott twofer "a break from the state's racist legacy" and said their primary victories "offered clear signs of racial progress in the South."[91] Newsweek's July 12 cover story called Haley "earthy, attractive, articulate—and the GOP's newest star in a fast-changing South." National Republicans, "eager to shed their image as the party of old white men," were "salivating," the magazine reported, quoting Nick Ayers, executive director of the Republican Governors Association. Ayers said Haley represented "a big chance for us to bring ethnic minorities into the party." Ayers praised Haley's "unwavering" commitment to core Republican principles, adding, "I thought it would be icing on the cake that she had darker skin and was Indian American."[92] Conservative columnist Kyle Wingfield, writing for the Atlanta Journal-Constitution, agreed. Haley's success, he said, showed "signs of color-blindness" among Republican voters (to which one reader commented, "If the party is color blind, then why does this column exist?").[93]

Haley was circumspect in addressing "talk of breaking racial and gender barriers." She told Newsweek, "Everybody else is looking at this to be something special, [but] there was actually nothing special about this at all." She allowed, "The fact that I happen to be an Indian female, of course that brings a new dynamic. But what I hope it does is cause a conversation in this state where we no longer live by labels, but we live by philosophies."[94]

Even so, in her acceptance speech—from outside the South Carolina Confederate Relic Room and Military Museum in Columbia—the nominee said, "South Carolina just showed the rest of the country what we're made of. It's a new day in our state, and I am very blessed to be a part of it." She also said, "To our friends in the media across this state and across this country who are analyzing what this victory means and what barriers this may have broken, I will tell you there might be some truth to that. But this is so much more than that. This is a movement about the idea of government being open and accountable to the people."[95]

Beyond South Carolina, reactions to Haley's election were mixed, particularly among some Indian and other South Asian Americans wary of having her as a symbol. Adding curiosity and inviting comparisons, her governorship now joined Jindal's in Louisiana (the first in the country by an Indian American) in what struck some observers an emerging template. Writer-activist Bilal Ahmed pulled no punches in calling Haley and Jindal "two deeply conservative and opportunistic politicians" who "emphasize their immigrant roots in order to lend desperately needed token diversity to Republican policies that otherwise verge on white supremacy."[96]

More equivocally, Aseem Shukla, co-founder of the Hindu American Foundation, responded to Haley's sudden emergence into national visibility in his religion column for the *Washington Post*. "A credible argument could be made that in politics, at least, a post-racial South is emerging," Shukla suggested. The Indian American community, he said, "may be politically mature enough to realize that Indian Americans in high office necessarily serve their constituency and not the ethnic community from whence they came." But it still was "unnerving," Shukla said, that Haley and Jindal seemed to feel that they had to "prove" their Christian "fidelity" to voters.[97] Another national columnist called Haley's victory "a win for assimilation, not acceptance."[98]

Conservative pundit Reihan Salam, who is a second-generation Bangladeshi American, asked, "How ethnic can our politicians be?" He suggested, "Let's keep the fact that some of our citizens are too exotic for leadership roles in mind before we congratulate ourselves on our tolerance and our embrace of diversity."[99] But in an admiring *Wall Street Journal* blog, Prashant Agrawal proclaimed: "An Indian-American will enter the White House this decade. That's my prediction." Haley and Jindal, he said, "have shown that Indian-Americans can succeed anywhere in the U.S."[100]

At the *Daily Beast*, Tunku Varadarajan, an Indian Briton, asked, "What explains the success of Jindal and Haley in their respective states? In posing this question, I hint, of course at the South's lingering reputation for racial intolerance." He suggested, "One answer is that these two politicians are consummate conservatives in a milieu that rewards political conservatism, and their success is a validation of their ideology and intelligence. Their ethnicity, in other words, is an irrelevance."[101] But he also offered another possibility: "I do wonder, sometimes, whether America's toxic black-white history and its legacy create a need for a 'third way'—for emblems of the Other that are not part of the toxic mix, especially in the South. Indians, here, offer a great political convenience. They have an irrefutable profile as strivers and self-starters."

Interestingly, Varadarajan and fellow *Daily Beast* writer Peter Beinhart both imagined a Democratic version of Nikki Haley, from which they drew different conclusions about identity politics and the parties. Varadarajan asked, "Could it be that since Democrats put more of an emphasis on identity politics, an Indian-American Democrat would have to contend with other ethnic constituencies that might think that it's 'their turn' first?"[102] But Beinhart contended, "The GOP's basic problem is that many Republicans equate Christianity, or at least Judeo-Christianity, with Americanism. . . . It's less likely that Haley would have had to hide her Sikh heritage had she been running in, say, a Democratic primary in California."

Though Beinhart said there was "no reason to doubt the sincerity of [Haley's] conversion," he saw constraints on her ability to represent her faith in a more nuanced way: "Is it good that the South Carolina GOP has embraced a South Asian woman? Of course. When that woman can practice whatever religion she wants, without fear that it will wreck her political career, then Republicans will truly deserve to crow."[103]

After Mitt Romney's loss in 2012, the Republican National Committee prepared its *Growth and Opportunity Project* report, widely known as the "autopsy" for its post-mortem message for the Grand Old Party's future. The report, published in early 2013, outlined a path to broadening the Republican electoral coalition by appealing to nonwhite voters. The authors, who included a former George W. Bush press secretary and Jeb Bush's 2016 campaign advisor, wrote, "[By] 2050, whites will be 47 percent of the country while Hispanics will grow to 29 percent and Asians to 9 percent. If we want ethnic minority voters to support Republicans, we have to engage them and show our sincerity."[104]

The report also said the GOP should find better ways of communicating with women voters, including "develop[ing] a surrogate list of women based upon areas of policy and political expertise." The RNC's media affairs team "should be focused on booking more women on TV on behalf of the party and be given metrics to ensure that we aren't just using the same old talking heads." The report mentioned Governor Nikki Haley as one of a half-dozen women "among many other excellent surrogates" who were "outstanding national surrogates."

★ ★ ★

Political scientist Alan Rosenthal calls being a governor "the best job in politics."[105] Most governors, he argues, get what they want, in policies and budgets. Historically, South Carolina's governor has been regarded as "relatively powerless and subordinate to the state's legislature," though in recent decades various changes "have strengthened gubernatorial authority and the office's capacity for shaping public opinion."[106] As governor, Haley led with Republican majorities in both chambers of the legislature. Though she occasionally sparred with her former colleagues on transparency, taxes, and budget issues, policy-wise she and the GOP majorities were more often simpatico. Haley seemed to know how to use the symbolism of her heritage to advance conservative talking points for GOP legislation on issues like voter identification and immigration.

Haley gave strong support to the passage of a South Carolina voter ID law in 2011, similar to Arizona's 2004 law requiring voters to present photo identification at polling places. (At least thirty other states at the time required some form of identification in order to vote, with some of the strictest requirements found in the South.) Proponents argued that identification was needed to prevent voter fraud, while opponents countered that actual fraud was negligibly low and that the requirements disproportionately and systematically disenfranchised Black and other minority voters. Political scientists saw evidence of discriminatory intent behind such legislation.[107]

In signing the law, Haley acknowledged but waved off concerns about "voter suppression," noting that the state took measures to ensure ID access: an 800 phone number, a ride to Motor Vehicles to register. Ultimately, she offered exactly the kind of "common sense" claim that other conservative Republicans advanced: "If you have to show a picture ID to buy Sudafed, and if you have to show a picture ID to get on a plane, then you should have to show a picture ID to do the one thing that's so important to us which is that right to vote."[108]

The US Department of Justice rejected South Carolina's law, on the grounds that it discriminated against minority voters. But in October 2012, the US Court of Appeals for the DC Circuit found no discriminatory intent behind the law, though it blocked its implementation until the following year, citing the "potential for chaos" in the November election. The three-judge panel found that "South Carolina's new voter ID law is significantly more friendly to voters without qualifying photo IDs than several other contemporary state laws that have passed legal muster," particularly because of a "reasonable impediment" caveat in the law that "allows voters to cast a ballot after signing an affidavit to explain why they did not obtain an ID."[109]

South Carolina Republicans also followed the lead of the Arizona GOP in passing restrictive immigration legislation. As a state representative, Haley had cosponsored "strong illegal immigration reform," applauding the Arizona law in a 2010 gubernatorial campaign video—and adding, "My parents are immigrants, they came here legally, they put in the time, they put in the money, they did what they were supposed to. It makes them mad when they see illegal immigrants come into this state."[110]

South Carolina is not a US-Mexico border state, of course. Its Hispanic population in 2010—around 235,000, or 2.4 percent of the state population—was considerably less than that of neighbors Georgia and North Carolina. The Palmetto State did, however, experience the fastest Hispanic population growth of any American state between 2000 and 2010, at nearly 150 percent.

In June 2011, Haley signed a bill modeled after the controversial Arizona SB 1070, portions of which were later struck down by the US Supreme Court. The bill required police to check the immigration status of any person whom they suspected of being undocumented when arrested or stopped for any reason and made it a misdemeanor for any adult in the state not to carry official identification while traveling. Opponents called it racial profiling.

This legislation did not fare as well in court as the state's voter ID law. In early 2014, South Carolina settled in a lawsuit brought by a coalition of groups—including the American Civil Liberties Union, League of Women Voters, and NAACP—and agreed that police could not detain stopped motorists while checking their immigration status.

It was a defeat. But Haley stood her ground. The governor said through a spokesperson, "Illegal immigration is still a serious issue in this state, and this settlement doesn't change that.... The fact is, the federal government has completely failed to address this problem and, until they do, South Carolina will continue doing what is necessary to uphold the laws of our state."[111]

Haley also joined other conservative governors in opposition to the Obama administration's efforts at Medicaid expansion for low-income Americans. A signature Obama initiative, the Affordable Care Act ("Obamacare") had passed along strictly partisan lines in the US Congress and was signed by the president in early 2010. But Tea Party-supported GOP victories in the fall midterm elections had empowered opponents at the federal and state levels, including Haley.

Haley wrote in an op-ed for the *Post and Courier* that the "price tag to South Carolina taxpayers" would be "an extra $1.1 to $2.3 billion" over six years. "We simply can't support this," she said.[112]

Standing to benefit from Medicaid expansion were 344,000 mostly nonwhite South Carolinians, according to the Kaiser Commission. The Kaiser Commission on Medicaid and the Uninsured, a non-partisan not-for-profit organization, estimated the actual cost at between $470 and $615 million, depending on enrollment patterns. In the first six years of expansion, the federal government would pay for more than 95 percent of total costs. Haley said the state also had to consider the costs in the out-years.

Revising the state's tax code to eliminate a generous capital gains deduction, according to the non-partisan Institute on Taxation and Economic Policy in Washington, DC, would have more than covered the cost of Medicaid expansion.[113]

That solution would not be part of her agenda.

2 ⋆ Charleston
"We Are at War with Ourselves"

ON AUGUST 5, 2012, A WHITE GUNMAN ATTACKED THE SIKH TEMPLE of Wisconsin, located in Oak Creek near Milwaukee. He killed six people—Paramjit Kaur, 41; Satwant Singh Kaleka, 65, and the gurdwara's founder; Prakash Singh, 39; Sita Singh, 41; Ranjit Singh, 49; and Suveg Singh, 84—and wounded four others. Five of the victims were men and wore customary turbans. Four were Indian nationals. A seventh victim, Baba Punjab Singh, a priest, was shot in the head, partially paralyzed, and suffered prolonged complications. (When he died in 2020, the cause was listed as homicide.) A responding police officer shot the gunman in the hip. The perpetrator then shot himself in the head and died. Investigators said forty-year-old Wade Michael Page, a former US Army psyops specialist, had ties to several white supremacist and neo-Nazi groups, but he had acted alone.

From South Carolina, Governor Nikki Haley posted a statement on her Facebook page, saying, "It's very sad to see something like this happen to a peaceful place of worship. Our prayers and condolences go out to the families of the innocent victims and the family of the heroic officer in this senseless tragedy."[1]

The governor's father, Ajit Randhawa, was now the president of the Sikh Religious Society of South Carolina, with its own gurdwara in Chapin. When first asked for a comment on the day of the mass shooting, he said he was waiting for more information. The next day, he told a reporter, "This is senseless, and of course this shows this person was not at all familiar with what this place is and what goes on." Randhawa explained the Sikh tenets of focusing on God's word, living ethically, working hard, and sharing earnings with those in need. "If he had only known where he was going, he would've gotten a free meal at lunch time. Because that's a tradition. His thoughts may have changed after that."[2]

The Wisconsin gurdwara mass shooting was reported to be the deadliest hate crime in US history at an American house of worship. That was before Charleston.

★ ★ ★

Marjory Wentworth, South Carolina's poet laureate since 2003, has written poems for three gubernatorial inaugurations. Wentworth's 2011 work "The Weight It Takes," published in the *Post and Courier* of Charleston, carries the dedication: "For Nikki Randhawa Haley, on the Occasion of her inauguration as Governor of South Carolina." The poem closes with a benediction:

> Now your life belongs to the world.
> Hold fast to everything
> beating with sunlight.
> Pull us together, like water.
> Be the weight that grounds us
> Through swirling hours of each day.
> When voices shout without ceasing,
> be the stillness we hear ringing in our hearts.[3]

In 2014 Wentworth wrote a poem to speak to the times, amid the national Black Lives Matter protests that followed the August shooting in Ferguson, Missouri, of Michael Brown, an eighteen-year-old Black man, by white police officer Darren Wilson.

Her intended second inaugural poem for Haley, "One River, One Boat," likens South Carolina's own racial history to "a knot we try to unravel, while others try to tighten it." The cord binding the state "is a slow moving river . . . splintering near the sea"—in Charleston.

> It is not about asking for forgiveness.
> It is not about bowing our heads in shame;
> because it all begins and ends here:
> while workers unearth trenches
> at Gadsden's Wharf, where 100,000
> Africans were imprisoned within brick walls

awaiting auction, death, or worse.

Where the dead were thrown into the water,

and the river clogged with corpses

has kept centuries of silence.

It is time to gather at the edge of the sea,

and toss wreaths into this watery grave.

Wentworth's panorama briefly sweeps west to Columbia before returning to Charleston, linking the two cities in way that would later seem tragically prophetic.

Here, where the confederate flag still flies

beside the Statehouse, haunted by our past,

conflicted about our future; at the heart

of it, we are at war with ourselves

huddled together on this boat

handed down to us – stuck

at the last bend of a wide river

splintering near the sea.[4]

No one at Haley's second inauguration heard Wentworth's new poem. Haley's staff cut the poet from the January 14, 2015, ceremony; they claimed not to have seen the new work and that there simply wasn't time for a two-minute poetry reading.

Wentworth (who is white) told news media she believed the cut was about priorities and not content, noting that the governor's office had previously ended a $1,500 annual earmark that funded her travel around the state. "Governor Haley inherited me," she told *Statehouse Report*. "I don't take it personally, that's for sure. It certainly is a statement about their ideology. The arts are of no value. It's a Tea Party thing, I guess."[5] The Mount Pleasant resident told the *Post and Courier*, "It wasn't anything like, 'We don't like your poem.' It's not personal. It's not something that is on their radar."[6]

National and even international media picked up the story of the snub. The details didn't really matter; the story was rendered in *The State*'s headline: "SC's Official Poet Silenced at Haley Inaugural."[7] In Washington, DC, shortly after noon on the Wednesday of Haley's inauguration, US representative James Clyburn, a Black Democrat representing South

Carolina's Sixth Congressional District, read "One River, One Boat" into the Congressional Record—"in keeping with the tradition of the First Amendment" protection of free speech, he said.

Wentworth said she had hoped the poem could help South Carolinians confront the issue of race. Referring to the Confederate flag on the capitol grounds in Columbia, she said, "Every time I go to the Statehouse, I'm like, 'Really? I mean really?' It should be under glass at a museum, that's where it belongs. There's a lot of pain associated with that flag."[8]

In their October 2014 gubernatorial debate, Democratic challenger Vincent Sheheen had sought to press the governor on the issue of the Confederate flag at the State House. He said, "I believe it's time that we retire the Confederate flag to a place of respect, where the history of this great state can be told, and we all rally together under a flag that unites us all—the American flag—that looks toward the future, not the past."

Governor Haley responded, "What I can tell you is over the last three and a half years, I spent a lot of my days on the phones with CEOs and recruiting jobs to this state. I can honestly say I have not had one conversation with a single CEO about the Confederate flag."

Then she added, "But we really kind of fixed all that when you elected the first Indian-American female governor. When we appointed the first African-American U.S. senator [Tim Scott, the first from South Carolina], that sent a huge message."[9]

If Haley had not immediately followed it with the more serious comment about Senator Scott, "the fix" might have been more widely taken as a lighthearted, even frivolous remark—the kind of thing a popular politician says to get an applause reaction in the moment. In any case, the line would not wear well. To be sure, Haley easily won reelection. Six months after her second, poetry-free inauguration, South Carolina would experience one of the most heinous hate crimes in recent national memory: the river splintering in Charleston.

★ ★ ★

But before Charleston there was North Charleston. The adjacent, separate city sits between the Ashley and Cooper Rivers, above Charleston where their waters merge and flow on, past Fort Sumter and Sullivan's Island, into the Atlantic. All one river, as the poet wrote.

On April 4, 2015, in North Charleston a white police officer shot and killed Walter Scott, a fifty-year-old Black man, following a daytime traffic stop for a nonworking third brake light. Scott had just bought the car, a 1991 Mercedes, from a neighbor; his brother told reporters he planned to stop by an auto parts store that very morning to take care of the light. Officer Michael Slager, thirty-three, shot Scott in the back while Scott was running away from him. (A warrant for Scott's arrest was outstanding over a child support matter, leading to speculation that this was why he fled the traffic stop.) Slager claimed he "felt threatened" by Scott's attempt to grab his Taser shock weapon, but this testimony was contradicted by video evidence from an eyewitness. The incident sparked national outrage and was seen by many as part of a pattern around the country in which white police were killing Black and brown Americans during routine encounters.

Slager was charged with murder. On April 8, Gov. Haley released a statement, saying, "We have many good law enforcement officers in the field. What happened in this case is not acceptable in South Carolina, nor is it reflective of our values or of the way most of our law enforcement officials act."

In June, Governor Haley signed into law a bill named for Walter Scott that purported "to require all state and local officers to implement the use of body-worn cameras pursuant to guidelines"—and here was the crucial caveat—"established by the Law Enforcement Training Council." The council is an eleven-member body, consisting of the South Carolina attorney general and various state, county, and local officials—representing almost entirely law enforcement and corrections agencies, departments, or divisions. While Haley and others supporters celebrated the law as a vital step to provide greater transparency in policing practices, skeptics pointed out that the overwhelming influence of law enforcement authorities in its implementation would severely weaken the intended oversight—a concern that appears to have been warranted.

In signing the legislation Gov. Haley said, "This is going to strengthen the people of South Carolina, this is going to strengthen law enforcement, and this is going to make sure that Walter Scott did not die without us realizing we had a problem."[10]

Unlike in Ferguson, and after other similar incidents, residents of North Charleston did not "riot" or engage in civil unrest after the killing of Walter Scott (or later, after Slager's initial mistrial in December 2016, when Governor Haley, with only weeks left in the job, pleaded for calm).[11] Haley urged all South Carolinians "to continue along the path we have walked these last two years—a path of grace, faith, love and understanding. That is who we are and who I know we will continue to be."[12]

☆ ☆ ☆

The young man announced his intentions online, but no one was listening. On June 17, 2015, Dylann Roof, who is white and whose bowl haircut made him look younger than his age of twenty-one, drove nearly one hundred miles from Eastover, a mostly Black community southeast of Columbia, to Charleston. He came for a Wednesday evening Bible study at Emanuel African Methodist Episcopal Church. Roof may have known that "Mother Emanuel" AME, in its ninety-ninth year, was one of America's most storied Black churches. He certainly did know that its pastor was the Reverend Clementa C. Pinckney, also a Democratic member of the state senate. Roof asked for Pinckney by name and took a seat beside him, joining a group of fifteen clergy and congregants.

Roof listened quietly for most of the hour. Then, according to witnesses, he spoke, argumentatively. He stood up, opened a waist pack he had brought with him, took out a handgun, and aimed it at eighty-seven-year-old Susie Jackson, a member of the church choir. Her nephew, Tywanza Sanders, asked why. He was killed first, the youngest victim protecting the oldest. Roof murdered pastors, church members, and educators. All nine victims were Black Americans:

> Sharonda Coleman-Singleton, 45, pastor, speech therapist, and
>   track coach
> Cynthia Marie Graham Hurd, 54, Bible study member and
>   public library manager
> Susie Jackson, 87, Bible study and church choir member
> Ethel Lee Lance, 70, church sexton
> Depayne Middleton-Doctor, 49, pastor and university admis-
>   sions coordinator
> Clementa C. Pinckney, 41, pastor and state senator
> Tywanza Sanders, 26, Bible study member, grandnephew of
>   Susie Jackson
> Daniel L. Simmons, 74, pastor at Greater Zion AME Church in
>   Awendaw
> Myra Thompson, 59, Bible study teacher

Roof, an unemployed high-school dropout with recent arrests for trespassing and narcotics possession, reportedly told one of his pleading victims, "No, you've raped our women and you are taking over the country. . . . I have to do what I have to do."[13] He stood over a witness to say he needed someone to survive and tell what had happened, since he intended to kill himself. Then Roof walked out into the night and drove away. Five people survived, including Sanders's mother and five-year-old niece, who pretended to be dead.

★ ★ ★

The next morning, the nation awoke to news of the tragedy. Dylann "Storm" Roof's manifesto traced his "awakening" to the 2012 Trayvon Martin case, viewing the acquitted Hispanic white vigilante George Zimmerman, not the slain Black high schooler carrying a pack of Skittles candy, as the victim. A photograph posted by the *New York Times* and other media showed Roof leaning on the hood of his black 2000 Hyundai, his black pants legs and black boots straddling a decorative front plate reading "Confederate States of America" and picturing Confederate flags.

Police apprehended Roof in Shelby, North Carolina, nearly 250 miles away, thirteen hours after he left Charleston. A local florist on her way to work had recognized his car from the television news and trailed it, coming close enough to identify him by his bowl haircut.

The national media discovered Roof's white-supremacist writings on his personal web page, Last Rhodesian. In a rambling, racist diatribe, he explained, "I have no choice. I am not in the position, alone, to go into the ghetto and fight. I chose Charleston because it is the most historic city in my state, and at one time had the highest ratio of blacks to Whites [*sic*] in the country. We have no skinheads, no real KKK, no one doing anything but talking on the internet. Well someone has to have the bravery to take it to the real world, and I guess that has to be me."[14] A photograph depicted Roof crouching in cutoff jeans, brandishing a handgun and a small Confederate flag on a wooden stick. Roof's manifesto (later read in court) also said, "I hate the sight of the American flag" and said "modern American patriotism" was "an absolute joke."[15]

Shortly after Roof's capture, Governor Haley made a brief statement to the media. "We woke up today, and the heart and soul of South Carolina was broken," she said, laying bare her own grief as her voice faltered briefly. She appeared to be fighting tears. But, she maintained, "We love our state, we love our country, but most importantly, we love each other." She spoke of grief and faith, of the families of the victims, and of families across the state with "parents having to explain to their kids how they can go to church and feel safe." She did not speak of Dylann Roof. (In her second memoir, Haley maintains that she has never said his name aloud.)[16]

At half past nine the night before, within minutes of the Charleston police response, Haley had posted a statement on Facebook. Naming her husband, daughter, and son, she said, "Michael, Rena, Nalin and I are praying for the victims and families touched by tonight's senseless tragedy. . . . While we do not yet know all of the details, we do know that we'll never understand what motivates anyone to enter one of our places of worship and take the life of another." (It was later reported that Michael Haley was away at Army National Guard training exercises when the governor learned of the murders.)

By morning's light, her earlier statement's suggestion of a mystery motive struck some observers as not quite right. The motive was manifest: Dylann Roof's hateful worldview had led him to murder nine Black Americans in a church—the first such hate crime in an American house of worship since the Wisconsin gurdwara mass shooting in 2012.[17] A *Huffington Post* columnist called Haley's statement "strangely obtuse" and "defensive," noting that the state's senior US senator, Lindsey Graham, "showed no similar confusion" in saying, "There are bad people in this world who are motivated by hate."[18]

The next day, Haley told NBC's *Today* show that Roof was "a person filled with hate," and that the state would "absolutely want him to have the death penalty."[19]

Haley later said her first impulse on hearing that Mother Emanuel had been struck was to call Rev. Pinckney directly. She left a voicemail he never heard: "This is Nikki. I've heard about the shooting. I'm sending my full SLED team down there. Call me." Throughout the night, until 4:30 a.m., she received "kick in the gut" updates from South Carolina Law Enforcement Division (SLED) chief Mark Keel, including that Pinckney was among the dead. Haley said she did not know Pinckney well, but that she knew him as a respected state senator.[20] At dawn, she woke her two children to tell them where she was going—and why—and boarded the governor's plane for Charleston.[21]

★ ★ ★

The afternoon after the shootings, Haley ordered all US and South Carolina flags statewide to fly at half-staff for nine days, in memory of each of the nine victims. Her authority did not extend to the Confederate battle flag at the capitol, however, which could only be lowered by a two-thirds majority vote in both chambers of the legislature—an unusual provision detailed in the exacting legislation passed amid the compromise that, fifteen years earlier, had removed the flag from the State House dome.[22]

In fact, the flag could not be "lowered" to half-staff at all—its attachment was fixed, the flagpole lacking a pulley—and therefore it could only fly at full staff or not fly at all. Thus, a Confederate battle flag, a square banner bearing that blue X-shaped St. Andrew's Cross and thirteen white stars over a scarlet background, continued to fly high, oblivious to the events in Charleston and to emotional pleas from leaders and citizens in the state and across the country, again.

As a report in the *Washington Post* put it, "This looked bad."[23]

Others went further. *The Atlantic*'s Ta-Nehisi Coates wrote, "Roof's crime cannot be divorced from the ideology of white supremacy which long animated his state nor from its potent symbol—the confederate flag. . . . More than any individual actor, in recent history, Roof honored his flag in exactly the way it always demanded—with human sacrifice." Coates exhorted:

> Take down the flag. Take it down now.
>   Put it in a museum. Inscribe beneath it the years 1861–2015. Move forward. Abandon this charlatanism. Drive out this cult of death and chains. Save your lovely souls. Move forward. Do it now.[24]

In November 2014, Winthrop University's Winthrop poll "conducted one of its periodic surveys asking people if they favored flying the flag over the Confederate memorial on the State House grounds." In all, 65 percent of South Carolinians did. But responses were starkly divided by race, with 77 percent of whites supporting the flag flying and 69 percent of Blacks opposed.[25]

Haley at first appeared hesitant to change her position on the flag. She recalled the state's past "conversation" and explained the "consensus" behind the flag's particular display to *CBS This Morning*, adding, "I think the state will start talking about that again, and we'll see where it goes."[26] But for the moment, the governor sought to keep the focus on the victims and their families, saying, "There will be a time and a place where we talk policy. . . . I'm not going to have these conversations [now]."[27]

State Rep. Todd Rutherford, the leader of the Democratic minority in the House and an African American, called the banner a "racist symbol." He said, "The flag needs to come down—it's time."[28]

Leading Republicans shared Haley's hesitancy. On MSNBC's *Morning Joe*, US representative Mark Sanford, Republican for South Carolina's First District and Haley's immediate predecessor as governor, said that he had attended a prayer vigil where talk turned to "how each one of us could be part of racial reconciliation . . . of healing a community through little acts of kindness."

NBC's Chuck Todd asked:

> Congressman, you just talked about racial reconciliation. A symbolic move could be something like, "You know what? Enough of this putting the Confederate flag on any part of state property" —that maybe it's time to retire that debate, trying to find compromises of how that flag still flies on government property. Is it time to, sort of, bury the Confederate flag?

Sanford responded:

> I don't know, I mean, that's opening up Pandora's box. So what you have with the Confederate flag is a political compromise, and as we both know with any political compromise you do not have perfection. Both sides end up a little bit unhappy. . . .
> And so in the wake of this, 24 hours after, to say, "You know, the solution here is moving that flag." . . .
> So it's a very, very complicated issue within our state, and I don't think that should be the immediate solution because it's one that would take, frankly, some time. It's not going to come down immediately, would be my political take.[29]

Veteran analysts shared Sanford's "political take" on the issue. David Woodard, a Clemson University political scientist and Republican consultant, doubted that Governor Haley would enter the fray. "It's a total lose-lose issue," Woodard said. "You're not going to make any friends by doing it, so you just leave it be. . . . I don't see anyone who's willing to take it on. There's no politician who's powerful enough to take it on."[30]

US senator Lindsey Graham, who had announced his presidential candidacy just three weeks earlier, said that to revisit the decision about the flag would be "fine" with him. Still, he maintained, "This is part of who we are." Squinting in the sunlight at the Charleston waterfront, he told CNN that the compromise of the Confederate memorial and a separate

African American memorial on the capitol grounds in Columbia "works here."[31]

But state senator Tom Davis, District Forty-Six (Beaufort), saw that the ground had shifted; the river had bent. Davis—who is white and has been a Republican member of the state senate since 2009—called for the flag's removal, saying it would be a mistake to avoid the issue. While Haley deserved high marks for her immediate response to the shootings, he said, "What role she plays in this conversation—the jury is out on that."[32]

As the conversation about the Confederate flag unfolded, Haley sought as much as possible to keep the focus on the Emanuel Nine. She went to every one of the funerals.[33]

☆ ☆ ☆

On Monday, June 22, 2015, Governor Haley stood before the cameras in the lobby of the State House flanked by more than thirty political leaders—Democratic and Republican, Black and white—and called for the flag to come down.[34] Haley praised the state's people for their calm after Walter Scott's police shooting death in North Charleston. She said that, while the state had changed so much in recent years, bigotry remained, and nobody needed to be reminded of it. She said supporters of the Confederate flag had every right to honor it on their private property—it would always be part of South Carolina's air and soil. "But the State House is different," she said. "And the events of this past week call upon us to look at this in a different way."

When the words came, they came quickly and directly. "It is time to remove the flag from the Capitol grounds. We are not going to allow this symbol to divide us any longer," she said, to bipartisan applause.

The governor said she had asked state legislators to take up the matter during their soon-to-adjourn session and would call a session extending their work further into the summer if necessary. The state's US senators were with the governor: Lindsey Graham now supported the flag's removal, and Tim Scott—the only Black Republican in the US Senate—said, "There are so many who see the flag through the prism of racism." He stood shoulder-by-shoulder with Haley during her statement.[35]

The next day, three other governors—Democrat Terry McAuliffe of Virginia, Republican Pat McCrory of North Carolina, and Republican Larry Hogan of Maryland—each announced that their states would no longer offer specialty license plates with Confederate symbols.[36] Then Alabama's Republican governor, Robert Bentley, ordered a Confederate flag removed from a memorial on his state's capitol grounds, saying he did not want it to become "a distraction."

Haley said her surprising reversal followed a late-night conversation with her husband, still away for Army National Guard training. "I told him what I was thinking and he told me I was right and that's all I needed," she told an interviewer. "That next day I called the staff in."[37] Over the weekend, Haley's office began to hear from concerned business leaders who had on their minds the recent civil unrest in Ferguson, Baltimore, and elsewhere.

That Saturday, several thousand people gathered outside the State House. Most came to protest the flag, some to defend it. There were reports that white supremacist and Black nationalist groups were planning to bring in people from outside the state for dueling demonstrations. The president of the state chamber of commerce sent a text to one of Haley's aides to ask what was going to happen with the flag's display on the State House grounds.[38]

On the morning of her Monday announcement, Haley met separately with Democratic and Republican state leaders, with the state's US congressional delegation, and with business and civic leaders to inform them of her decision to call for removing the flag. She later said she gave each group the same message: "I'm going to have a press conference at four. If you would stand with me, I would be forever grateful. And if you choose not to stand with me, I hold no ill will, and I respect you, and I will never let anybody know that you were in this room." After her announcement, a spokesman for Boeing Company, which has an aircraft assembly plant in North Charleston, told the *Wall Street Journal* that the company supported the governor's call.[39]

The major state and national papers reported on Haley's new position in generally positive tones, casting it as her "calling for" or "joining calls for" the flag's removal. At liberal *Salon*, editor-at-large Joan Walsh refused to credit Haley with taking a principled position, arguing that the move was really about partisan self-preservation. "Haley certainly deserves the GOP's thanks for rescuing the party's presidential field from its own cowardice about the issue," she said, noting that the presence of Republican National Committee chair Reince Priebus at the announcement "was the tell that Haley's move was about politics" (and that Democratic National Committee chair Debbie Wasserman Schultz "received no such invitation").

Walsh conceded, "Of course, Haley deserves some credit for the move." But she noted, "The South Carolina governor is getting entirely too much credit from the media for doing something she should have done long ago."[40]

From the opposite direction, conservative provocateur Ann Coulter told Fox Business that she was "appalled" by the flag debate, which she considered irrelevant to the "sick, horrible, evil" murders in Charleston. She said, "I really like to like Nikki Haley since she is a Republican," but added—falsely—"on the other hand, she is an immigrant and does not understand America's history."[41]

Rush Limbaugh told listeners that that the flag debate was "so classic of what the left does. They take an event—a horrible sad event, this kid killing nine people in a church—and they turn it into something entirely different; they turn it into something it is not about." He, too, argued, "It was a Democrat governor that raised the flag," similarly eliding the intervening history of party realignment in the South to lodge an overwrought protest: "The Republican Party has nothing to do with the flag flying. The flag was hoisted by Democrat governors. The flag was believed in and sworn to by Democrats. They were the segregationists. What this has become is a political opportunity to once again blame it on the Republicans, blame it on Southern culture."[42]

It was a specious argument: segregationists from the Democratic Party indeed had been responsible for flying the flag a half century earlier—it went up ceremonially to mark the Civil War centennial in 1961, but it *stayed* up to defy the civil rights movement—and by Limbaugh's own confused lights, that should have been ample justification to remove the flag now ("I'm not arguing to keep it," he somehow also said).[43]

★ ★ ★

Haley hoped to see the flag come down before Independence Day on July 4. She said, "It will be fitting [that] our state will soon fly the flags of our country, of our state, and no other." She had to postpone that symbolism, however, as she waited for the legislature to act, amid a backlash from the Confederate flag's defenders. Some lawmakers gave voice to their constituents' staunchest sentiments about "Southern heritage." Given the sometimes strained relationship between the governor and the legislature, it seemed possible that some might resist Haley's call simply to deny her a political victory. One unnamed House Republican—who actually supported removing the flag—called Haley a "cyber-bully" for her social media gibes at the legislature.[44]

At Pinckney's packed funeral at the College of Charleston's TD Arena on June 26, President Barack Obama gave the eulogy and led five thousand voices in a spontaneous singing of "Amazing Grace." (National media reported that another five thousand mourners had been turned away for lack of space.) The president praised Governor Haley's "recent eloquence" in her call to remove the flag.

"It's true," Obama said. "A flag did not cause these murders. But as we all have to acknowledge, the flag has always represented more than ancestral pride. For many, black and white, that flag was a reminder of systematic oppression and racial subjugation. We see that now." Taking down the flag, he said, "would not be an act of political correctness," but rather "an expression of God's grace." He added, "I don't think God wants us to stop there."[45]

The momentum to start, at least, had gathered quickly. The day after Haley's June 22 call, the General Assembly added discussion of the flag to its agenda by broad bipartisan votes in both chambers: by 103–10 in the House, and by voice vote in the Senate, where Pinckney's desk was covered by black cloth and a single white rose. Still, a handful of lawmakers were determined to resist change.

The *Washington Post*'s Amber Phillips blogged from the Senate debate on July 6, calling it "strikingly blunt," "incredibly honest," and "powerful." It was expected that lawmakers would muster the two-thirds vote necessary to advance to the House a bill to bring down the flag, but with "much of the legislative contention out of the way, lawmakers spent their Monday reflecting on the flag's place in the state's history—and just how much healing on race the state has left to do."[46]

Advocates for removing the flag set the tone. State senator Vincent Sheheen, Democrat for the Twenty-Seventh District (Kershaw) and Haley's two-time gubernatorial opponent, introduced the bill. He recalled a "heated debate" during a campaign event, a year earlier, at the Confederate war memorial. After Sheheen had called for the flag's removal, a white woman walked up to him and said, "All you care about is black people and Mexicans." Sheheen also read an email he had received from a constituent after the Charleston shootings: "It's not about the Confederate flag. It's about the entitlement given to minorities, and folks are getting tired of it." Sheheen used it to make a point: "That's days after nine people are murdered because their skin was dark. What happened, happened in our state. There's a quiet bigotry that still exists, and if those of us who are white don't say anything . . . then we're part of the problem."[47]

From the Republican side, Sen. Larry Martin, Second District (Pickens), said he had heard from constituents who feared that removing the flag would be but the first step in a broader campaign to erase Confederate history. Would the renaming of buildings and roads be next? But Martin said that South Carolinians had to be honest with themselves about the flag's symbolism across the decades. The white fifty-eight-year-old said he "remembered well" what the adults in his life had to say about public school integration, "and it wasn't pleasant. You couldn't repeat it today . . . what was being said about the fact that we were going to be going to school with Black children. And the adults in my life didn't want to hear it. In my view, that's the reason the flag stayed up." Martin said that before the Charleston shootings, he hadn't "thought twice" about the implications of flying the flag on the State House grounds, but now he saw the matter differently. "It isn't part of our future," he said. "It's part of our past. And I think we need to leave it at that."

Sen. George "Chip" Campsen, Republican for the Forty-Third District (Charleston), said he experienced a similar conversion after the Emanuel AME tragedy. "I'm going to vote to relocate it, to pursue peace and mutual affection like Paul preaches us to do," he said. "I hate that it took a tragedy like this for me to really, fully understand it. But I do fully understand it, and it is utterly amazing. It is one of the greatest testimonies of Christian faith that I have experienced in my life."

But Sen. Lee Bright, Republican for the Twelfth District (Spartanburg), said it was a mistake to assume that the actions of one individual with a gun meant that South Carolina suffered from pervasive racism. "I am more against taking [the flag] down in this environment than at any other time," he said. "We're placing blame on what one deranged lunatic did on people who hold their Southern heritage high, and I don't think that's fair." He called for a statewide referendum on the issue.

Sen. Paul Thurmond—whose father, Strom Thurmond, had brandished the Confederate flag as a white segregationist Dixiecrat presidential candidate in 1948—told colleagues, "Our ancestors were literally fighting to keep human beings as slaves, and to continue the unimaginable acts that occur when someone is held against their will. I am not proud of this heritage." The thirty-nine-year-old Republican senator for the Forty-First District (Charleston) said he would vote to remove the flag.[48]

Haley and staff had thought the Senate might be the more difficult chamber because of the possibility of a filibuster.[49] But the 37–3 vote easily cleared the two-thirds threshold needed to advance the bill.

★ ★ ★

Next came the state's House of Representatives, whose members voted 93–18 on July 7 to bypass committee review and send the bill straight to floor debate. Representative Mike Pitts, Republican for the Fourteenth District (Laurens), filed some twenty amendments aimed at striking a new "compromise" and halting the momentum to bring down the flag. One included a provision that would have required the US flag to be flown upside down atop the capitol dome, a traditional distress signal (and, presumably, a poison pill to taint the bill). At a midweek meeting of the Republican caucus, Haley rejected another proposed amendment that would have kept the memorial's flagpole but replaced the Confederate battle flag with a different flag—a less recognized flag associated with the state's secession-era history, or even the current South Carolina flag—and simply said, "No flag, no pole."[50]

Replacing the Confederate flag with the South Carolina state flag on the existing pole at the Confederate war memorial was a curious and not really objectionable proposal—House leaders thought it stood a good chance of passing—but if members had voted for such an amendment, it would have sent the matter to committee (on technicalities) and thus killed the momentum for action. The Confederate flag might have continued to fly for six months or longer, until the next legislative session in January.

In the state Republican caucus, Haley told a story about a time growing up when she and her turban-wearing father drove from Bamberg to Columbia. On the way home, they visited a roadside fruit and vegetable seller and loaded a basket with produce. Two police pulled up as they went to pay: the seller had called to report suspicious activity. Ajit Randhawa paid and thanked the farmer. He said nothing about the incident on the drive back. But Haley said she never forgot it. It was one of the governor's go-to stories, previously told in her memoir, though she added a new detail: she said she still had to pass by that farmer's stand every time she drove to the airport, and it was always a painful experience. She understood that for many, the flag at the State House was a continuing source of a similar pain.

State representative Mike Pitts wasn't listening: he told reporters that he sat in the back of the room and removed his hearing aids while the governor spoke.[51] Pitts and other House holdouts did not have the Senate's filibuster at their disposal, but since they attempted more than sixty amendments to the bill, and since each one required twenty minutes of debate, it amounted to the same thing—prompting minority leader Todd Rutherford, Democrat for the Seventy-Fourth District (Richland), to call their tactics "filibuster by amendment."

The bill went to the House floor at midday on Wednesday, July 8. Per the Senate's language, the bill provided for the removal of the flag and pole from the capitol grounds within twenty-four hours of its becoming law. This meant that a swift passage could bring the flag down by Friday— and avoid a weekend of escalating protests. But as debate dragged on for hours, it looked like Pitts and his faction might win the day, if only to postpone the inevitable.

Governor Haley and aides sat in a conference room downstairs from the drama. The governor sent texts to House members to whip votes— telling supporters, "Please hold. Don't flip." Aides shuttled up and down a private staircase connecting the conference room to the House floor to reinforce the message.[52]

Shortly before midnight, Pitts played his last card—the proposal involving the state flag—and several members stepped forward to support it. Wearing a suit that the *Washington Post* described as "dapper white," the very image of southern gentry, majority leader James Merrill, Republican for the Ninety-Ninth District (Berkeley), said, "A clear majority of people in this body want to take down the Confederate battle flag. We have figured out that it is going to be moved. It is going to come down, there is no doubt about it. . . . But I just don't understand why we can't support putting the South Carolina flag up there."[53]

Then Rep. Jenny Horne, Republican for the Ninety-Fourth District (Dorchester), came forward to weigh in on the largely male-dominated proceedings. As the *Post* reported, "The 42-year-old lawyer from Summerville stepped up to the podium and delivered words so raw and impassioned they would immediately go viral on the Internet."

With her fingers piercing the space between her and her colleagues, her voice tremulous but powerful, Horne said,

> I cannot believe that we do not have the heart in this body to do something meaningful such as take a symbol of hate off these grounds on Friday. And if any of you vote to amend, you are

ensuring that this flag will fly beyond Friday. For the widow of Senator Pinckney and his two young daughters, that would be adding insult to injury.

I'm sorry, I have heard enough about heritage. I have a heritage. I am a lifelong South Carolinian. I am a descendent of Jefferson Davis, okay? But that does not matter. It's not about Jenny Horne. . . . It's about the people of South Carolina who have demanded that this symbol of hate come off of the State House grounds.

Thus, "a descendant of the president of the Confederacy helped vanquish his flag," as the *Washington Post* put it in a headline. "Horne's fiery speech injected new energy into what appeared to be a flagging take-down-the-flag faction and paved the way for a 1:00 a.m. vote to remove the flag from the state capitol," the reporter recorded.[54] In the end, the House voted 94–20 in favor of the proposal.

Even before the final vote was taken, Governor Haley went on Facebook to praise the state's lower chamber for following the Senate's lead, saying it had "served the State of South Carolina and her people with great dignity."

Comments from Facebook followers were mostly critical, including one from a young woman who warned, "You have set SC on fire and it is clear to see the lines are drawn." Some praised the governor for her courage to challenge the symbol that had so divided the state, but others accused her and fellow Republicans of capitulating to pressure from the "left wing national media" and "demonizing regional identity."

One Amber Blakes replied in support of the governor's post:

> I'm proud to raise my son in this state, and will one day show him our statehouse without having to explain the shame behind that symbol: the shame that includes the work my ancestors did as slaves in this state, and the scars my great grandmother had from being assaulted by KKK members as she walked home from work in this state. My sister and husband serve at military bases in this great state while this symbol flew insult in our faces when its meaning should have been enjoyed in a museum. Those grounds now represent all, and not just some. Thank you![55]

On July 9—five days after her Independence Day goal, fifteen years after the compromise that moved the flag, and 150 years after Lee's Army of Northern Virginia surrendered to Grant's Union Army at Appomattox

Court House—"a beaming Gov. Nikki Haley signed a bill paving the way for the flag's removal."[56]

Invoking the motto she had state employees use when answering phones, Haley said, "Today, I am very proud to say, 'It's a great day in South Carolina.'"

She signed the bill with nine pens—one for each of the departed—while three former governors looked over her shoulders, surrounded by state officials and community leaders. Haley had reached out to her predecessors to help bridge the divide between the governor's office and the legislature. One of those former governors was David Beasley, the Republican who had reversed his earlier defense of the flag to call for its removal from the capitol dome in 1996, only to lose his 1998 reelection bid.[57] He told reporters, "I'm the last living casualty of the Civil War."[58]

On Friday, July 10, fellow and former leaders again flanked Haley as she stood among thousands of citizens outside the State House. A South Carolina Highway Patrol honor guard donned white gloves and "carefully folded and furled the square banner, bound it with white string and marched it to the Statehouse [sic] steps," where "they handed it to an archivist, who transported it to a state museum, where it [would] be ensconced in the Confederate Relic Room."[59] Before the ceremony, "a few gray-haired white men at the front of the crowd waved confederate flags." But "many more, both black and white, waved the U.S. flag."[60]

★ ★ ★

After the ceremony, Haley sat with CNN's Don Lemon for an interview at the State House. A tri-folded and framed US flag sat on a shelf behind Lemon's shoulder as he asked the governor about what had just taken place. Behind her stood the South Carolina state flag and a second American flag.

Haley told Lemon, "It should have never been there." She said, "These grounds are a place that everyone should feel a part of. What I realized now more than ever is people were driving by and felt hurt and pain. No one should feel pain."[61]

She told a personal story:

> We grew up an Indian family in a small town in South Carolina.
> My father wears a turban. My mother, at the time, wore a sari.
> It was hard growing up in South Carolina. But what I've always
> been proud of, and what I've worked towards, is to make sure

that today is better than yesterday, and that my kids don't go through what we went through. And now I feel good because now I know my kids can look up and there won't be a flag. And it will be one less reason to divide, and it will be more reasons for us to come together.

Lemon, who is Black, noted that a new CNN/Opinion Research Corporation poll found that 57 percent of Americans viewed the Confederate flag as a symbol of southern pride and not racism. (Though he did not say so, the same poll also found that 55 percent supported removing the flag from government property that isn't part of a museum.)[62]

"Is that surprising to you?" Lemon asked.

Haley responded, "No. Because a lot of the people—and if you had heard the debate in the State House, so many of them look at it as honoring ancestors who fought and died for their state. That's the way they look at it. You look at people—and this really is, Confederate proponents, they're not haters. They're not, you know—you've got people who will hijack it—"

Lemon interjected, "Who use this flag as a symbol of hate, right?"

Haley continued, "Right. And so—what we have to remember is that people *are* using it as a symbol of hate. And it is something that causes people pain, because it's a reminder of a time that was painful. So, you know, what we have to do is remind the pro-Confederate citizens, 'Look, we're not trying to take away your heritage. We're not trying to take away the family members that sacrificed.' But what we are trying to do is not give people reason to hurt, and we all are responsible for that. We all have to play a role in that."

Haley told Lemon she planned to extend her "anti-bullying tour" of state schools now to talk about race, the "Emanuel Nine," and "why we brought the flag down."

Lemon asked whether that meant that Haley was now taking on race as part of her platform.

The governor replied, "I'm going to take bringing South Carolina together as part of my platform—that this should not be one day in time. That this should be the start of a conversation, which is why South Carolina handled it so gracefully. Why did the citizens come together, and not protest? What made South Carolina so special, across this country, that people said 'Wow.' I want those kids to know that, because they've got to carry it on."[63]

That Sunday, Haley appeared on NBC's *Meet the Press*. She told host Chuck Todd "it felt like a massive weight had been lifted off South Carolina" to see the flag come down. "To say, 'You know, we're not that state that everybody thinks we are. We actually are a state where we love our God, we love our country, we love our state, but we love each other.'"

Todd, who is white, asked Haley if her reflection on race relations after Charleston might lead her to see something like voter ID laws "in a different light," particularly given Clementa Pinckney's opposition to the state's policy that "some African Americans" saw as "a way to single out or disenfranchise them."

Haley said, "The flag coming down was a moment that I thought needed to happen. That doesn't mean that I philosophically changed the way I think about other things. I've never seen the voter ID as a racial issue, for whites, for Blacks, for Asians, for anyone." She repeated a favorite formulation: "Having to show a picture ID when you get on a plane, and having to buy a picture ID when you buy Sudafed, you absolutely should show a picture ID to vote."

Haley's leadership in removing the flag had earned her more national media attention than at any time since her ascendance as a gubernatorial candidate, five years earlier. Todd asked her what she made of "the extra political attention" she'd been getting, including speculation that Americans might see her name "on a national ticket [in 2016] or down the road."

Haley responded, "It's painful. Because nine people died. . . . That's what I want people talking about, the Emanuel Nine that forever changed South Carolina, and changed this country and showed what love and forgiveness looks like."[64]

★ ★ ★

The Emanuel Nine may have changed how Nikki Haley looked at the flag, but not everyone was ready to change their assessments of her leadership. For some, the flag's final folding merely reinforced competing narratives—of the trailblazing nature of Haley's governorship, or of its calculated service to Republican party interests.

At the *Post and Courier* in Charleston, Jennifer Berry Hawes observed that the tragedy's impact on Haley "would force her to shift from a publicly guarded, often rehearsed, on-message partisan to a very human, deeply grieving governor trying to heal a diverse and wounded flock."[65]

The morning the flag came down, Doug Heye, a past communications director for the RNC and deputy chief of staff to the US House majority leader, praised Haley's leadership in an online commentary for the *Wall Street Journal*. "Her words were careful, balanced, and smart," he wrote. "They recognized the seriousness and sincerity with which many view the flag as an important part of their heritage, while still making clear that, although those feelings were valid, keeping the flag on the capitol grounds would keep South Carolina on the wrong side of history." He noted that the NAACP had already lifted its boycott, and the NCAA ended its post-season ban, yielding "tangible benefits" for the state. He noted that speculation had increased about her potential as a 2016 vice-presidential nominee.

"But perhaps more important," Heye concluded, "she appears to have done something that has long eluded Republicans: she has pointed a positive path forward on the issue of race that elected officials throughout the nation and, frankly, all candidates can follow."[66]

James C. Cobb, a southern historian at the University of Georgia, saw it differently in an essay published by *Time*. Removing the divisive symbol was not really about ideas, he said, but was simply good for business. "It is tempting to see Haley's rise as personal triumph and regional redemption," he said. "Yet contrary to liberal presumptions, Nikki Haley has proven to be anything but the empathetic, compassionate champion of minorities, women, and immigrants that her background seemed almost to mandate."

Cobb said Haley's conversion on the flag issue followed a well-worn trajectory for Deep South governors, going back to the mid-1960s, of simply recognizing when a tipping point had been reached over "the potentially harmful effects of racial tensions on business development." In South Carolina, he said, "that flag might still be flying atop the state capitol had a torrent of threatened economic and tourist boycotts and pressure from the state's business community not forced the legislature 15 years ago to at least move it to the capitol grounds. Governor Haley had shown no inclination to move it until the slaughter of nine African-Americans in Charleston by a Rebel-flag-worshipping gunman became both catalyst and premise for a step that southern political leaders had been at once eager but too timid to take."

Still, the historian could see that to make virtue out of necessity was still to make virtue: "Albeit 150 years too late, the move by Haley and other southern leaders to finally furl the Confederate flag is a welcome one nonetheless. History, after all, offers too few examples of right things done for precisely the right reasons to afford us the luxury of being picky."[67]

From the moment Haley called for its removal, as Charleston reporter Jennifer Berry Hawes details in her book *Grace Will Lead Us Home*, defenders of the flag "assailed the governor," flooding her inbox with thousands of emails. While some were more measured, others accused Haley of betrayal and "linked her actions to her Indian heritage and her purported exotic faith." As Hawes describes it, "Their message was clear: Nikki Haley wasn't white enough, southern enough, or Christian enough to understand the flag's proper place in South Carolina."[68]

Some of the messages were filled with obscenities; one poison missive from Georgia said, "The fact that someone like you can be born to 1st generation immigrants who came to this country from a 3rd World hell hole, only to have their daughter take a steaming dump on the ancestors of the residents of her new host country is truly pathetic."[69] The notion was chilling: Haley had been born in America—right there in South Carolina—but it was her "host country." (The language was also remarkably similar to a remark that Donald Trump, as president, would make two and a half years later, in meeting with a bipartisan group of senators at the White House, in which he reportedly referred to a group of African countries, Haiti, and El Salvador as "shithole countries.")[70]

But overall, in the second half of 2015, Haley enjoyed the highest approval ratings of her governorship. South Carolina's extraordinarily challenging year—Walter Scott's killing in North Charleston in April, the Mother Emanuel mass shooting in June, a hurricane causing devasting flooding and widespread property losses in October—also brought renewed national attention to the governor at the start of her second term.

In April 2016, *Time* named Haley one of the "100 Most Influential People" in the world. The magazine's brief essay about Haley was written by Sen. Lindsey Graham, who recalled how the governor had responded to the events of 2015, "one of the most challenging years on record" for the state. Haley, Graham said, "led with determination, grace and compassion" through these tragedies and "put a face on South Carolina that we were all extremely proud of." Though he credited the governor with "shaking up the system"—her brand since her time in the state legislature— the examples Graham cited were all responses to events, in which Haley had shown "kindness and understanding to the individuals and families affected by these tragedies." Graham concluded, "It is during challenging times when you really learn the mettle of a leader, and in the case of Nikki Haley, she excelled to the lasting benefit of our state."[71]

Over twenty-four days in the late spring and early summer of 2015, Charleston had touched the country and had changed minds in Columbia. A chapter in South Carolina's history was closed.

But already that summer, a new story was being written—for South Carolina's governor and for America. Another American on *Time*'s list, Donald Trump, would be its leading author.

3 ★ UN-Likely Ambassador

DONALD TRUMP HAD FIRST LAID THE GROUNDWORK FOR HIS insurgent 2016 presidential campaign on cable TV, by promoting the so-called "birther" conspiracy that Barack Obama was not born in the United States and had somehow faked his birth certificate. The real-estate developer, naming-rights licenser, reality-TV star, and all-around self-promoter declared his candidacy on June 16, 2015, descending a grand escalator and giving a speech from the gilded lobby of the Trump Tower building in New York. In remarks shown repeatedly on the networks and shared widely on social media, Trump characterized Mexican immigrants as criminals, drug dealers, and rapists—along with "some," he "assumed," "good people." It was the day before the Mother Emanuel murders in Charleston.

In the months that followed, Trump's promise to "build a great wall" along the US-Mexico border (and to make Mexico pay for it) became a through line of his "Make America Great Again" campaign. The billionaire New Yorker turned out to have a strong instinct for getting across a consistent if not always coherent message to working-class Americans who felt left behind by economic globalization and alienated from a popular culture mediated by "politically correct" elites. Trump's populist nationalism venerated a vaguely postwar, pre-civil-rights-era America at its moment of "great"-ness, and portrayed immigration as an economic and national security threat.

Trump visited South Carolina on December 7 for a Pearl Harbor Day rally on the USS *Yorktown* in Mount Pleasant. Five days earlier, there had been a fatal mass shooting and attempted bombing in San Bernardino, California, at a workplace Christmas party by a local married couple, both radicalized Islamists. The candidate read out a blunt statement: "Donald J. Trump is calling for a total and complete shutdown of Muslims entering the United States until our country's representatives can figure out what the hell is going on." (An FBI investigation later concluded that the couple, a US-born citizen of Pakistani descent and a Pakistan-born green card holder, were "homegrown violent extremists," inspired by foreign terrorist groups through social media but not affiliated with any, though they had traveled to Pakistan and Saudi Arabia.)

In January 2016, Governor Nikki Haley gave the Republican Party's response to President Barack Obama's final State of the Union address. Her remarks seemed aimed at Trump as much as the outgoing president, though she did not mention the candidate by name. On immigration, in particular, she implicitly rejected Trump's rhetoric, beginning with her own family's story:

> Growing up in the rural South, my family didn't look like our neighbors, and we didn't have much. There were times that were tough, but we had each other, and we had the opportunity to do anything, to be anything, as long as we were willing to work for it.
>
> My story is really not much different from millions of other Americans. Immigrants have been coming to our shores for generations to live the dream that is America. They wanted better for their children than for themselves. That remains the dream of all of us, and in this country we have seen time and again that that dream is achievable.

Haley drew a line between lawful and unlawful immigration, in an implicit contrast with Trump:

> Today we live in a time of threats like few others in recent memory. During anxious times, it can be tempting to follow the siren call of the angriest voices. We must resist that temptation.
>
> No one who is willing to work hard, abide by our laws, and love our traditions should ever feel unwelcome in this country.
>
> At the same time, that does not mean we just flat out open our borders. We can't do that. We cannot continue to allow immigrants to come here illegally. And in this age of terrorism, we must not let in refugees whose intentions cannot be determined.
>
> We must fix our broken immigration system. That means stopping illegal immigration. And it means welcoming properly vetted legal immigrants, regardless of their race or religion. Just like we have for centuries.
>
> I have no doubt that if we act with proper focus, we can

protect our borders, our sovereignty, and our citizens, all while remaining true to America's noblest legacies.

Finally, the governor invoked the Emanuel Nine to repudiate that angry "siren call":

This past summer, South Carolina was dealt a tragic blow. On an otherwise ordinary Wednesday evening in June, at the historic Mother Emanuel church in Charleston, twelve faithful men and women, young and old, went to Bible study.

That night, someone new joined them. He didn't look like them, didn't act like them, didn't sound like them. They didn't throw him out. They didn't call the police. Instead, they pulled up a chair and prayed with him. For an hour.

We lost nine incredible souls that night.

What happened after the tragedy is worth pausing to think about.

Our state was struck with shock, pain, and fear. But our people would not allow hate to win. We didn't have violence, we had vigils. We didn't have riots, we had hugs.

We didn't turn against each other's race or religion. We turned toward God, and to the values that have long made our country the freest and the greatest in the world.

We removed a symbol that was being used to divide us, and we found a strength that united us against a domestic terrorist and the hate that filled him.

There's an important lesson in this. In many parts of society today, whether in popular culture, academia, the media, or politics, there's a tendency to falsely equate noise with results.

Some people think that you have to be the loudest voice in the room to make a difference. That is just not true. Often, the best thing we can do is turn down the volume. When the sound is quieter, you can actually hear what someone else is saying. And that can make a world of difference.

Of course that doesn't mean we won't have strong disagreements. We will. And as we usher in this new era, Republicans will stand up for our beliefs.[1]

But reactions to Haley's State of the Union response pointed to the emerging rifts among conservatives that would shake up the Republican Party in the months that followed. Commentator Ann Coulter, who in criticizing Haley's shift on the Confederate flag had called the governor "an immigrant" who didn't understand American history, now tweeted "Trump should deport Nikki Haley" over what she saw as a too-soft GOP message on immigration.

The *Wall Street Journal*'s editorial board strongly objected to Coulter's comment (though its headline, "Deport Nikki Haley," amplified Coulter's noxious othering of the governor). "It's a sign of the GOP's distemper that some conservatives denounced her because she didn't denounce *legal* immigration," the newspaper said. "The attacks on Ms. Haley show that many on the right these days oppose any immigrants, even those who arrive legally. They also want to make opposition to immigration a GOP litmus test. A party that rejects Nikki Haley as a spokeswoman is one that doesn't really want to build a governing majority."[2]

Writing for the *New York Times Magazine*, Anand Giridharadas was ambivalent about Haley's high-profile response as a signifier of Indian American political visibility. Giridharadas (who dryly described himself as sitting in Brooklyn, wearing a hoodie, and typing "some online-only essay") said that many Indian Americans he knew nursed "some resentment" toward Haley, and similarly, toward Governor Bobby Jindal in Louisiana. "Part of it is the generic loathing of inauthenticity that bedevils many leaders," he said, "like Hillary Clinton or Jeb Bush."

But in this case, he said, "the feeling is deeper":

> When Nimrata Randhawa, born to Sikhs, becomes the Methodist politician Nikki Haley . . . it confirms unuttered suspicions: that the road to brown political success is not via colorblindness but rather via the simulation of whiteness. You worry that certain correlates of whiteness—Methodism, guns, the name Nikki—are needed to compensate for your lack of the actual thing.[3]

Even so, Giridharadas credited Haley for rejecting Trump's bigoted rhetoric toward immigrants. "It was when Haley spoke as 'the proud daughter of Indian immigrants' that she most shone. . . . She spoke of the communal closeness that helped them to weather tough times and the dream of self-invention that propelled her climb. And then she trumped Trump, and those others with similar ideas but less instinct for virality."[4]

Trump's candidacy had by now roiled the Republican primary campaign, from which many had once imagined that Florida's Spanish-speaking former governor Jeb Bush would emerge as the moderate conservative nominee—gesturing toward diversity while mainly promising continuity. Just days before South Carolina's Republican primary election in February, Nikki Haley endorsed Marco Rubio. Like the South Carolina governor, the junior US senator from Florida had been elected in 2010 on the Tea Party wave. Haley and Rubio, both forty-four in 2016, were widely regarded as rising stars in the party, who brought needed diversity (Rubio's parents are from Cuba) to the GOP starting lineup.

Haley's surprise endorsement sparked speculation that a Rubio-Haley ticket could be formidable in the general election. Writing for the *Washington Post*, Janell Ross called the prospect "a fantasy dream ticket of young, brown or faintly tan Americans with governing experience and strong Republican principles."[5] The University of Virginia's Larry Sabato, a prominent elections analyst, said, "It would blow apart most people's image of the GOP as a home for aging white people—and I say that as an aging white person."[6]

Trump, who would be seventy on Inauguration Day, won South Carolina easily, beating Rubio by 10 points. He continued to bash Republican leaders who didn't support him, using Twitter's 140-character-limited tweets as his platform. On March 3, Mitt Romney pronounced Trump "a phony, a fraud"—an unprecedented criticism by a prior nominee. Trump excoriated Romney as a failed "establishment" politician, deploying the same trope of emasculated power with which he attacked Bush ("Low Energy Jeb") and Rubio ("Little Marco"). Along with US Senator Ted Cruz of Texas ("Lyin' Ted") and his late-stage ally John Kasich ("1 for 38 Kasich," for the Ohio governor's single primary win), the GOP men lined up to take Trump's puerile but effective blows. (When Rubio dropped out of the race in mid-March, Haley informally supported Cruz, who stayed in the race until May.)

Haley lent her voice to the rearguard Republican efforts to derail Trump's nomination, making her critique more explicit. Already in January, on the morning after her State of the Union response, on NBC's *Today*, Haley had taken the opportunity to call out Trump directly, saying, "Mr. Trump has definitely contributed to what I think is just irresponsible talk." Trump fired back that Haley was "weak" on immigration, on accepting Syrian refugees, and on the possible transfer of prisoners to her state from the US detention facility at Guantánamo Bay in Cuba.

Haley responded, "When you have a candidate that comes in and goes against a governor, it's everything a governor doesn't want in a president. Because we don't want a president that's just going to bash and sit there and tell us what we're not doing right. We want a president that is going to help us fight, help us win and help us explain why we don't want Syrian refugees and why prisoners at Guantanamo Bay don't need to come to South Carolina."[7]

Trump held his grudge over Haley's endorsement of Rubio for more than a week after winning the South Carolina primary. He sought to portray Haley's high-mindedness as hypocritical, pointing on Twitter to a 2012 video in which Haley, when asked whether then-candidate Romney should release his tax returns, had responded, "I think those are distractions." (Trump, famously, did not release his tax returns.) Trump retweeted his excitable campaign manager Corey Lewandowski, calling Haley, for some reason, "a liability" for Rubio in light of the old video. Apropos of nothing else, apparently, Trump tweeted on March 1: "The people of South Carolina are embarrassed by Nikki Haley!"

Twenty-two minutes later, the governor tweeted back: "Bless your heart."

It was an early sign of the self-described "grit and grace" that Haley would bring to the public performance of her relationship with Trump, recognizing his takeover of the GOP and his resetting of American political norms and policy debates. Southern, saccharine, and sincere in its insincerity, it was a sharper rejoinder than anything Trump's primary opponents had been able to land previously.

For his part, Trump's taunting of Haley was issue-oriented; he notably did not deploy the vulgar misogyny of his recent attacks on other prominent conservative women, such as Fox News anchor Megyn Kelly or former Hewlett-Packard CEO Carly Fiorina, an early primary opponent. Whatever his strategy or impulse, Trump seemed to take Nikki Haley seriously.

In July, Governor Haley attended the Republican National Convention in Cleveland. *USA Today* reported that Haley, speaking to South Carolina delegates over a bacon-and-eggs breakfast, "never uttered Trump's name. But she urged the Republican Party faithful to vote for him by vilifying his likely Democratic foe, Hillary Clinton."

Governor Haley told her state's delegates, "President Obama was awful the last eight years—a President Clinton would be disastrous." She urged them to help get out the message that "a no vote [for Trump] in November is a vote for Hillary Clinton."

Katon Dawson, a former chair of the South Carolina Republican Party and a state delegate in Cleveland, told the newspaper, "That was an endorsement, as best as Nikki could do." Clemson University political scientist David Woodard was more blunt. "She is holding her nose. She doesn't particularly like him, but he's won [the nomination] fair and square."[8]

Indeed, once Trump secured the GOP nomination, Haley muted her criticisms. In late October, she said at a news conference that she would vote for the party nominee despite his attacks on her record. "That doesn't mean it's an easy vote," she said. "I think I've been really clear. This election has turned my stomach upside down. It has been embarrassing for both parties. It's not something that the country deserves, but it's what we've got," she said.

"Having said that," she confessed, "what I will tell you is that this is no longer a choice for me on personalities because I'm not a fan of either one," referring to Trump and Clinton, by then the Democratic nominee. Adding that Trump would be the better choice for his political appointments, conservative Supreme Court nominations, and other issues, she concluded, "What it is about is policy."[9]

How far could a Republican southern woman governor go with the line that the election was "about policy"? Could she acknowledge deeper cultural and structural forces at work in the electorate? That deindustrialization, growing income disparities, and public health crises—including opioid addiction and high rates of suicide—contributed to open hostility toward institutions American and global, and toward elites across party lines? Could Haley's "It's a Great Day in South Carolina" be squared with Trump's scorched-earth rhetoric—which held immigrants, America's traditional allies, and Republican incumbents as much as Democrats all to be hostile enemies of "America First"?

As historian Timothy Snyder records,

> Inequality of income and wealth grew drastically from the 1980s through the 2010s. In 1978, the top 0.1% of the population, about 160,000 families, controlled 7% of American wealth. By 2012, the position of this tiny elite was even stronger: it controlled about 22% of American wealth. At the very top, the total wealth of the top 0.01%, about 16,000 families, increased by a factor of more than six over the same period. In 1978, a family in the top 0.01% was about 222 times as rich as the average American family. By 2012, such a family was about 1,120 times richer. Since 1980, 90% of the American population has gained essentially nothing, either in wealth or income. All gains have gone to the top 10%—and within the top 10%, most to the top 1%; and within

the top 1%, most to the top 0.1%, and within the top 0.1% most to the top 0.01%.[10]

Haley and Rubio, who both came of age during these decades, embodied a kind of can-do Reaganism that seemed suddenly out of step with national mood. As Snyder observes, "During the presidential campaign, Trump asked Americans to remember when America was great: what his supporters had in mind were the 1940s, 1950s, 1960s, and 1970s, decades when the gap between the wealthiest and the rest was shrinking."[11] Not that Trump was talking about inequality per se, but the pledge to "the forgotten men and women of this country" that he would be "your voice" and the repeated attacks on "elites" were a rough approximation. To supporters, he seemed to come by his own resentments of the old money and Washington beltway insiders naturally enough. Since Trump would not release his tax returns, it was impossible to know just where he ranked in terms of personal wealth. But he offered up a vision of the American political economy as a "rigged system," which he "alone" could fix, as a "smart and successful" businessman who understood how it all worked.

★ ★ ★

The X factor in 2016 was Russia. Just weeks before Election Day, seventeen US intelligence and law enforcement agencies would announce, impotently, that the Russian government sought to influence the American election through an elaborate cyber campaign of espionage and psychological influence. Russia's authoritarian president, Vladimir Putin, disdained Hillary Clinton for her support as US secretary of state of opposition forces in Russia's rigged 2012 election. President Obama was wary of appearing to put his thumb on the scales for candidate Clinton, though he ultimately took up the Russian interference with the congressional leaders of both parties. Obama aides later claimed that efforts to mount a strong bipartisan response were watered down by the Senate majority leader, Republican Mitch McConnell of Kentucky, who said he would regard the administration's pushback at Russia as a partisan effort to help Clinton.[12]

Trump praised Putin's "strong" leadership. His blistering criticisms, meanwhile, were mostly reserved for America's longtime democratic allies and trading partners, which he said were "taking advantage" of the United States and its "stupid" leaders. There was, however, one important exception. Trump's ascendance in the Republican field followed the successful "Brexit" campaign to vote Britain out of the European Union in a June 2016 referendum, and he and leading Brexiteer Nigel Farage expressed mutual admiration. The Kremlin had good reason to prefer Trump's candidacy. The cohesiveness of a US-led international order, and American commitment to multilateral institutions like the United Nations and the NATO alliance, seemed more in doubt than at any time since their creation.

Given Trump's unorthodox foreign-policy positions and the questions about Russian interference in the election, the formation of his foreign policy team would be followed with more than the usual media interest during the transition. For the key position of secretary of state, Trump seemed to relish the chance to let it be known that Republicans who had so recently and publicly criticized his campaign were now willing to curry favor.

Just eight days after Trump's victory over Hillary Clinton, a transition source told CNN that Nikki Haley was under consideration for secretary of state and other cabinet positions, as part of a first wave of interviews on November 17 at Trump Tower. A later account by CNN's Elise Labott, based on an interview with Ambassador Haley eight months into the Trump administration, confirmed that then-governor Haley "was under consideration to become secretary of state when she flew to New York to meet the President-elect for the first time since his election victory." Haley was "torn," Labott reported, and "the baggage from the 2016 campaign . . . didn't suddenly evaporate for Trump, who never forgets a slight." Haley told Labott she did not think she had sufficient foreign policy experience to lead the State Department.

"She told Trump no," was how Labott reported on Haley's exchange with the president-elect. It wasn't intended to be a direct quotation. The in-so-many-words formulation may have been intended to underscore Haley's independence, but it was potentially misleading: Trump hadn't actually offered Haley the job of secretary of state. In fact, Haley told Labott that she ruled herself out, and withdrew from consideration. "I'm very aware of when things are right and when they are not. I just thought he could find someone better," Haley said.[13]

Also riding the Trump elevator that day were Alabama's senator Jeff Sessions, who would be Trump's choice for US attorney general, and former New York mayor Rudy Giuliani, another reported prospect for secretary of state. Both had supported Trump's candidacy.[14] Lending his mannered gravitas to the revolving-door atmosphere was Henry Kissinger, the ninety-three-year-old former national security advisor and secretary of state to Richard Nixon, who used a side entrance to avoid Trump Tower's media-packed lobby (and its actual revolving doors).[15]

Haley may have been glad she withdrew. Trump seemed to regard the selection process for secretary of state as a reality-TV show, especially when former critic Mitt Romney showed interest. In late November, Trump and Romney dined together at a white tablecloth New York restaurant in view of the media. A press photographer captured the indelible image of Trump grinning widely, head hunkered conspiratorially, and Romney arching his eyebrows, seeming to be in on the joke. Their wine glasses are filled with water (as has been widely reported, neither man drinks alcohol). Trump associate Roger Stone said that the president-elect was interviewing Romney "in order to torture him."[16]

The Haley-Trump rapprochement would be neither public nor humiliating to the governor. In fact, compared to the circus atmosphere that Trump seemed keen to promote, their discussions were unusually discreet, with the details of Haley declining the position emerging only months later. At the time, Haley remained quiet about the meeting, putting out only a statement that she "had a good discussion, and [was] very encouraged about the coming administration and the new direction it will bring to Washington." Before their meeting, Trump campaign manager Kellyanne Conway said, "We're just happy to have her here for her advice and counsel to hear about the great success story of South Carolina." After the meeting, Trump's team offered no comment.[17]

★ ★ ★

On November 23, Trump announced Nikki Haley as his choice for UN ambassador, formally the "Permanent Representative of the United States of America to the United Nations, with rank of status of Ambassador Extraordinary and Plenipotentiary, and Representative of the United States of America in the Security Council of the United Nations"—quite a brief for a governor who had declined consideration for the top State Department job citing lack of foreign policy experience.

The selection was first reported by the *Post and Courier* in Charleston. The *New York Times*'s Maggie Haberman wrote, "The news of Ms. Haley's selection came after days of criticism of Mr. Trump's early picks as a homogeneous bloc of older, white men."[18] The *Washington Post*'s Philip Rucker and Carol Leonnig later wrote in their bestselling book *A Very Stable Genius* that while Trump "gravitated toward generals" for national security positions, "for public-facing communications roles, he wanted attractive women." Haley was "typecast for the UN in part because she was a daughter of Indian American immigrants," they said.[19]

As Haley would later tell CNN's Elise Labott, the UN job offer came days after she returned to South Carolina from the Trump Tower meeting. She first received a call from Trump's incoming chief of staff, Reince Priebus, the chair of the RNC and a bridge between the insurgent president-elect and the party establishment. As RNC chair, Priebus had a hand in the GOP's post-2012 "autopsy" report (the *Growth and Opportunity Project*), which had counseled a need to appeal to a broader electorate through diversifying the candidate field. Priebus had set up Haley's visit to Trump Tower to discuss the secretary post.

Trump may have had reasons other than diversity for offering Haley a position. *Vanity Fair*'s Abigail Tracy suggested that Haley "may have been the beneficiary of a political bankshot involving her lieutenant governor, Henry McMaster," an early Trump supporter. As this theory went, "not only did this make McMaster the front-runner should he seek re-election in 2018 as the incumbent, it also placed a top Trump supporter in a key state during presidential cycles," which could help Trump if he ran again in 2020. After Trump's win in the state's 2016 primary, he said of McMaster, "I will take him over the governor anytime, because we won."[20]

For Haley, withdrawing from consideration for the State position but accepting the UN job made sense politically. Trump's GOP takeover had upended the conventional wisdom, following Romney's inability to unseat Obama in 2012, that the party's future lay in broadening its appeal to a younger and more diverse set of voters. Haley's political future had looked bright under that light. Now she would be a term-limited, outgoing governor in the 2018 midterm electoral cycle, with Trump in the White House for two or six more years (barring any wild cards). Her prospects for working with the state legislature to achieve an agenda in her remaining two years looked reasonably good, but Haley seemed to be looking past that horizon. Just the week before her meeting with Trump, she was elected vice chair of the Republican Governors Association at the group's annual conference, setting her up for a key fundraising role ahead of the 2018 midterms.

If Haley could make peace with Trump (and his voters) while stepping up to a national stage and gaining foreign-policy experience, she might yet emerge as a Republican standard bearer, whenever the dust settled. Given uncertainties about Trump's actual foreign-policy prospects—however directly he had telegraphed intentions—UN ambassadorship might also be preferable to secretary of state. Leading the State Department bureaucracy in Washington, DC, and across embassies worldwide—13,000 Foreign Service employees, 11,000 Civil Service employees, and 45,000 local staff employees—is an enormous job, even under a normal presidency. But Trump's secretary of state would be expected to translate his impulses—to blow up agreements, alliances, and institutions—into real policies, with uncertain consequences. Haley's career in South Carolina had shown her to be a boundary pusher, but one who first sought to understand where the boundaries lie and how the system works.

A benefit of the ambassadorship was that in the United Nations, such lines were reasonably well established. Country positions are often predictable, if not entrenched. This can make it hard to coordinate action, especially when the veto-holding great powers on the Security Council see their interests as coming into conflict. But if an American ambassador can manage to help lead the UN to consensus on some of the world's most vexing problems, she can be hailed as a great statesperson. On the other hand, failure to do so can be pinned on the refusal of others—often permanent members Security Council members China and Russia—to see the rightness of the American position, and this may have its own appeal for a neophyte diplomat eager to be seen as standing on principle.

Haley told CNN's Labott that she had presented Trump with three conditions for accepting the job: first, that she be granted the same cabinet-rank status her Obama administration predecessors held (breaking with recent Republican practice); second, that she be seated on the president's National Security Council, with a hand in shaping administration policy, as have some previous UN ambassadors; and third, that she would be free to speak her mind.

As Haley recalled her direct conversation with Trump, in which she set forth her conditions:

> I said, "I am a policy girl, I want to be part of the decision-making process." . . . He said, "Done." And I said, "I don't want to be a wallflower or a talking head. I want to be able to speak my mind." He said, "That is why I asked you to do this." In all honesty, I didn't think [Priebus and Trump] were going to take me up on everything I asked for. And they gave me all that. So how do you turn that down?[21]

During his administration, President Dwight Eisenhower first raised the UN post to cabinet level so that his ambassador, Henry Cabot Lodge Jr., could have direct access to him without going through the domineering secretary of state, John Foster Dulles. President George H. W. Bush broke with the tradition, and the position has see-sawed in status ever since—with Bill Clinton restoring it to the cabinet, George W. Bush removing it, and Barack Obama reinstating it again. Jeane Kirkpatrick, Reagan's UN ambassador, is the only other woman in a Republican administration to have held the post with cabinet rank. (Kirkpatrick, formerly a conservative Democrat, switched parties in 1985.) Haley would later cite Kirkpatrick as an inspiration to her as UN ambassador.

As UN scholar David Bosco observed during hearings for Haley's immediate predecessor Samantha Power (a Pulitzer Prize–winning reporter and Harvard University professor), the cabinet-inclusion practice is unique to the US among the major powers. He explained, "In bureaucratic terms, the U.N. ambassador—like any ambassador—serves under the secretary of state and executes policy ordered by the secretary. But the ambassador's presence in the cabinet confuses that chain of command."[22] Haley's cabinet status was noteworthy not only for breaking with recent Republican tradition, but also for the potential lack of clarity it created for her relationship to the new leadership at the State Department, not yet identified.

Establishment reactions to Trump's selection of Haley were mostly polite but somewhat bewildered, as few knew what to say about her foreign-policy leanings. The *New York Times* tried to glean Haley's views by reviewing the relatively few positions on high-profile international issues she had taken as governor: signing legislation opposing a disinvestment campaign targeting Israel, arguing for stronger security checks for Syrian refugees entering South Carolina (but ultimately not joining other governors in a lawsuit against the Obama administration to block resettlement), and describing herself as "pro-life," which was relevant insofar as it suggested she might favor reinstating a Republican ban on funding international family-planning organizations that provide abortion access.[23] A primer on Haley in the *Washington Post* simply said, "She has virtually no foreign policy experience: Her views on foreign policy and the military tend to fall in line with hawkish Republicans."[24]

Lindsey Graham, South Carolina's senior senator and one of those hawks, praised Haley in a statement telegraphing his hopes for her appointment: "As Governor of South Carolina she has recruited and dealt with some of the largest international business firms in the world. Her husband was a member of the South Carolina [Army] National Guard who served a tour of duty in Afghanistan. Governor Haley and her family fully understand what is at stake in the war against radical Islam. I know she will be a valuable ally to President-elect Trump as our nation tries to reengage the world and lead from the front, not behind."[25] On Twitter, Graham added, "I'm confident @nikkihaley will be a strong voice for UN reform and stand for American interests throughout the world."[26]

Back home, Haley's pastor at Mt. Horeb United Methodist Church in Lexington, Reverend Jeff Kersey, told the Columbia newspaper *The State*, "I think God's hand is upon her. . . . She has a chance to change the world through serving there. I think her experience with the flooding and the Charleston church shooting have all prepared her to solve problems on a bigger scale." From the Democratic side, former South Carolina representative, CNN contributor, and Bamberg native Bakari Sellers told *The State* that Haley would be "going into the job with the least experience of any UN ambassador in the history of the U.S.," but that the "statesman" governor was "more than competent" to serve. "Count me as someone who has really low expectations for Donald Trump," Sellers said. "We're praising people he nominates just for not being xenophobic. She's going to balance Trump out. She does not want to start World War III, and Trump might start World War III by accident."[27]

UN insiders, and close observers of the organization, were generally unimpressed. On *Devex*, a "UN civil society insider who did not want to be named for diplomatic reasons" said, "If you ask [Haley] how many UN agencies there are she would say, 'I have no idea,' and if you ask her what the SDGs are she might say, 'What's that?'"[28] The acronym refers to seventeen Sustainable Development Goals set by the UN in 2015, spanning climate change, education, gender equality, health, hunger, poverty, social justice, and other areas. (Few non-specialists would know this).

Not everyone was so patronizing. On Twitter, Nicholas Kristof, the global affairs columnist for the *New York Times*, took a question from a follower, who asked, "Curious: you feel the 'UN issues' are so complex it's unlearnable? If that's the case maybe the problem is with the UN." Kristof wrote back, "No, UN issues are not unlearnable. Nikki Haley is smart and may end up doing well, but she won't hit the ground running."

Three weeks after the announcement that Haley would be headed to the United Nations, Trump finally named his choice for secretary of state: Rex Tillerson, a sixty-four-year-old Texan and formerly the CEO of ExxonMobil, the American multinational oil and gas corporation. Like Trump and unlike Haley, Tillerson had no prior experience in government. His company's global operations were extensive, and so often intertwined with local politics in countries that journalist Steve Coll titled his 2012 book about the corporation *Private Empire: ExxonMobil and American Power.*

Did any of that qualify Tillerson to serve as secretary of state? Fewer were asking that question. For some critics on the left, Tillerson's association with ExxonMobil seemed to suggest sinister possibilities, a Trump foreign policy by and for American oil and gas interests. Tillerson's work in Russia, for which Putin awarded him the Russian Order of Friendship following a 2011 oil deal, also added to the Russian intrigue around the incoming administration. As Coll's book pointed out, ExxonMobil at times openly disdained US diplomatic goals (as when it dealt directly with Iraq's semi-autonomous Kurdistan region during the Obama administration, while officially Baghdad and Washington sought to hold Iraq together amid its internal tensions).[29] But that wasn't quite the same as asking if Tillerson was actually up to the job.

Haley told Trump she didn't have the foreign policy background to lead the State Department. If Tillerson was inclined to similar introspection, he didn't let on. He had been CEO of a major corporation that knew its way around governments; how hard could government be?

★ ★ ★

Haley's US Senate confirmation hearing took place in mid-January, shortly after Tillerson's contentious hearing. Democratic senators had regarded Tillerson warily and even hostilely, and even some leading Republicans seemed skeptical. The testiest exchanges were over Russia. Senator Rubio pressed Tillerson to label Putin a war criminal over Russia's past actions in Chechnya and ongoing support of the Bashar al-Assad regime in Syria's civil war. Tillerson responded, "I would not use that term." Tillerson also would not commit to continuing Obama administration sanctions against Russia over its interference in the election. (Trump had boasted that his relationship with Russia would be so good, sanctions would not be necessary.) Tillerson did, however, criticize Russia's seizure of Crimea and interference in Ukraine following its 2014 Maidan Revolution.

Nikki Haley's January 18 US Senate hearing, by contrast, was the kind of gracious bipartisan affair seldom seen in the modern Congress, with members of both parties seeming to genuinely respect and even trust the South Carolina governor, even if some Democrats seriously chal-lenged her on issues. The Foreign Relations Committee chair, Senator Bob Corker (R-Tennessee), hailed Haley as an "outstanding nominee,"[30] and it quickly became clear that Haley's confirmation essentially was a foregone conclusion. The smiling governor was flanked by her state's two senators, Lindsey Graham and Tim Scott, who each offered warm introductions. Behind them sat the governor's son Nalin, husband Michael, mother Raj Kaur Randhawa, father Ajit Singh Randhawa, and older brother Mitti Randhawa.

The Haley-Randhawa family tableau was a backdrop to the gover-nor's assertively upbeat performance. Over her left shoulder, her father's crimson turban featured prominently throughout the C-SPAN telecast, sometimes filling the frame while the governor spoke. It was a reminder of what Graham, in his introduction, called Haley's "uniquely American story." It was also a poignant visual aid to Haley's statement, during the hearing, that she continued to believe that blocking entry to the United States based on a person's religion was unconstitutional. (Nine days later, Trump, as promised, would issue a Muslim ban, in an executive order blocking persons entering the US from seven majority-Muslim coun-tries.) Haley said she planned to focus on human rights at the UN, and linked that focus to her love of her family's and America's "immigrant heritage" and her experience as governor with removing the Confederate flag from the State House.

The committee's ranking member, Senator Ben Cardin (D-Maryland), expressed "concern" about Haley's "lack of foreign policy experience," but turned almost immediately to the governor's previous big moment in the national spotlight and praised her leadership in the Confederate flag removal in South Carolina. This showed her ability to forge coali-tions around difficult issues, he said, and that would be a valuable skill at the UN.

Haley faced some tough questions about a range of issues she would confront as ambassador, but compared to Tillerson, she seemed significantly more willing to acknowledge that Trump's rhetoric made American allies uneasy. In particular, she seemed to grasp the danger to the incoming administration in appearing too soft on Russia. Asked by Senator Ed Markey (D-Massachusetts) whether she agreed with Trump that NATO was "obsolete" or with General James Mattis, Trump's pick for Secretary of Defense, that the alliance was "vital," she said, "I think NATO is an important alliance for us to have, and now we need more allies than ever, and we need more alliances than we've ever had. I think it's one that we need to strengthen." Senator Jeanne Shaheen (D–New Hampshire), the only woman on the committee, cited Trump's recent comment saying Vladimir Putin was a "stronger leader" than Germany's Angela Merkel and asked Haley if that was not an unproductive way to relate to an important US ally. Haley agreed that it was not good diplomacy.

When asked by Senator Robert Menendez (D–New Jersey) if she agreed that Russia had "committed war crimes when it ultimately, indiscriminately bombed" civilians and hospitals in Aleppo, Syria, Haley said, "Yes, I do." She said that the United States should "stand up to any country that interfered in its elections." And when asked what her message to her Russian counterpart on the UN Security Council would be with regard to Russian interference in 2016, Haley said, "That we are aware that it has happened, that we don't find it acceptable, and that we are going to fight back." She said that Moscow would have to show "positive actions before we lift any sanctions on Russia." Regarding other big issues she expected to face as ambassador, Haley said, "I think North Korea is definitely one to watch. I think we are going to have to work closely with China to show the threat of what is happening [with North Korea's nuclear weapons and missile capabilities] and we can't let up on North Korea."

On US-Israel relations and the Israel-Palestine conflict, she tried to walk a fine line. Prompted by a friendly Rubio, she said the United States should "never have abstained" from a recent vote in the Security Council on a resolution condemning Israeli settlement expansion in the Palestinian territories. Fourteen countries had voted for the resolution and none against, with only the US abstaining. Haley said, "I think that was the moment when we should have told the world how we stand with Israel, and it was a kick in the gut that we didn't." On the other hand, when Senator Tom Udall (D–New Mexico) pointed out that even President Ronald Reagan had called on Israel to freeze settlement expansion, and asked her if she supported that policy, she said, "Yes." She attempted to clarify her position by saying, "And so we can think what we want to think on settlements, but you have to think that the U.S. abstention . . . was wrong."

On climate change, Udall asked Haley if she agreed "that the United States is indispensable and must maintain its leadership in the Paris Agreement in order to ensure that countries abide by their climate obligations." The governor was less than committal, allowing that "the climate change situation should always be on the table, should always be one of the issues that we look at." If she didn't echo Trump's contemptuous scorn for the 195-nation 2016 agreement, part of the United Nations Framework Convention on Climate Change, neither did her anondyne statement affirm the accord: "I do think that when we look at the Paris Agreement, we should acknowledge what we do believe is right"—whatever that was—"but we don't want to do it at the peril of our industries and our business along the way."

Asked by Senator Ron Johnson (R-Wisconsin) if she had a "game plan" for "reforming a UN that has been unreformable," Haley asserted, "It is what I have done all my life. I love to fix things. And I see a UN that can absolutely be fixed." She continued, "We've seen fraud, we've seen sexual exploitation"—referring to numerous credible allegations against UN peacekeeping forces in conflict zones—"we've seen corruption of all kinds, and the whistleblower protections are not strong enough. People are still too afraid to speak up. We need to make sure that the countries that are contributing troops hold those troops accountable when they go and they make these violations." But Haley said she didn't believe in a "slash-and-burn" strategy of cutting US funding to the United Nations and looked forward to communicating to Trump the importance of building coalitions to secure US objectives.

Haley told the committee of her conversation with Trump, "When this position came up, he said that he wanted me to have a very strong voice in the UN, and he wanted us to have a higher profile in the UN, and to really use it to work. And so I do think that obviously, you know, any comments that the president-elect has made, those are his comments."

Two days after Haley's confirmation hearing, on January 20, 2017, Donald John Trump was inaugurated forty-fifth president of the United States, vowing to end the "American carnage" of "mothers and children trapped in poverty in our inner cities; rusted out factories scattered like tombstones across the landscape of our nation; an education system flush with cash, but which leaves our young and beautiful students deprived of all knowledge; and the crime and the gangs and the drugs that have stolen too many lives and robbed our country of so much unrealized potential."

Nikki Haley, who told a different American story, turned forty-five the same day.

The Senate voted 96–4 in favor of Haley's confirmation on January 24, with the "no" votes coming from Senators Chris Coons (D-Delaware) and Bernie Sanders (Independent-Vermont), along with Senators Martin Heinrich and Tom Udall, New Mexico's two Democrats. Coons explained his opposition to Haley in a statement, saying, "She did not convince me that she understands and embraces the foreign policy principles that the United States has championed over the past seventy years to serve effectively. . . . The position of US ambassador to the United Nations requires a high level of expertise on international affairs, not someone who will be learning on the job."[31]

The "no" votes notwithstanding, Haley's easy passage stood out as a rare show of bipartisan support for a Trump nominee amid Republican accusations of Democratic obstructionism. Notably, Tillerson's confirmation vote split across party lines, with only three Democratic senators joining the narrow Republican majority to approve the former energy CEO by a 56–43 margin. It was the most opposition that any secretary of state nominee had ever encountered, setting up an uncertain dynamic between an embattled secretary and a UN ambassador enjoying broad bipartisan support.

Haley's broad acceptability was not the only distinction she brought to the cabinet. She was also the least wealthy person in an administration consisting largely of multi-millionaires (and at least one billionaire in secretary of education Betsy DeVos). The *New York Times* estimated the value of assets held by various top officials, based on financial disclosure filings, at the time they joined the administration. Out of three dozen cabinet secretaries, senior advisors, and other top officials listed by the newspaper, Haley ranked last, with between $66,003 and $165,000 in estimated assets. (The next-lowest were Sebastian Gorka, a deputy assistant to the president for foreign affairs, with assets of $101,010 to $353,000, and Mike Pompeo, the CIA director, with $77,021 to $456,000.) The wide estimate ranges attest to the inexact nature of this kind of reporting, but Haley's modest means starkly contrasted the fortunes of the president's son-in-law and senior advisor Jared Kushner, Commerce Secretary Wilbur Ross, National Economic Council Director Gary Cohn, Treasury Secretary Steven Mnuchin, and Tillerson—each worth hundreds of millions.[32]

Haley took a salary cut as ambassador, starting at an annual $185,101, after earning $203,316 as governor. The UN post did, however, come with benefits, including a rented penthouse condominium at 50 United Nations Plaza valued at $58,000 a month and a budget for housekeeping and entertaining. While certainly tony, Haley's living expenses were less than half the cost of the UN ambassador's usual residence at the Waldorf Astoria New York, which was undergoing renovations.[33]

In early March 2017, Haley would speak to NBC's Matt Lauer about her family's transition to New York. "Certainly living in a city like this is very different, but we've all adjusted well and my son loves it. He's decided he's a city boy and Bentley [the family dog] has gotten used to the fact that there's no grass. It's been great," she said. Haley's husband Michael and son Nalin moved into the UN Plaza condo, while daughter Rena attended Clemson University as a first-year student. Haley's mother and father also moved to New York—the next chapter in the family's American story.

4 ✶ Taking Names

ON JANUARY 27, 2017, HER FIRST DAY ON THE JOB, HALEY WALKED into the UN headquarters and told reporters that a "new US UN" was at hand. Looking out at the assembled media, she said, "Our goal with the administration is to show value at the UN, and the way to show value is to show our strength, show our full voice. Have the backs of our allies and make sure our allies have our backs as well." She added, "For those who don't have our backs, we're taking names, and we will make points to respond to that accordingly."

"Taking names" was a formulation Haley had sometimes used as governor, and one she would return to when defending unpopular US positions at the UN. She did not, however, take questions that morning, leaving it for speculation whether the Trump administration planned major UN agency and staff reductions—and a decrease in the US financial contribution to the organization—as press reports had it. She took leave of the press pool to present her ambassadorial credentials to new UN Secretary-General António Guterres, as France's UN envoy François Delattre told reporters he had "only good things to say" about his new US counterpart. The French official, previously ambassador to the United States during the Obama presidency, now said, "Our main message to the American administration is, 'Please stay committed to world affairs, because we need America.'"[1]

Haley wasted no time in distinguishing herself from Trump on the defining Russia issue. Just two weeks into Trump's presidency, she used her first open address at the Security Council, on February 2, to say that the United States still considered Russia's 2014 annexation of Crimea and ongoing military interference in eastern Ukraine to be illegitimate, and that US sanctions against Russia from the Obama administration would remain in place. This was during a week that saw Ukraine lose a dozen soldiers in fighting between its forces and Russian-backed separatists (clandestinely augmented by Russian forces), leading Ukrainian president Petro Poroshenko to call for a referendum on bringing his country into NATO. Haley seemed to grasp the moment's magnitude in speaking both to Russia and America's NATO allies on the Security Council—coincidentally, during a session chaired by Ukraine's representative, who held the monthly rotating presidency of the Security Council.

"This is my first appearance in this chamber," Haley said. "The United States is determined to push for action. There is no time to waste. I must condemn the aggressive actions of Russia." She said that, while the US would seek improved relations with Russia, "the dire situation in eastern Ukraine is one that demands clear and strong condemnation of Russian actions. The sudden increase in fighting in eastern Ukraine has trapped thousands of civilians and has destroyed vital infrastructure." She added, "The United States stands with the people of Ukraine, who have suffered for nearly three years under Russian occupation. Until Russia and the separatists it supports respects Ukraine's sovereignty and territorial integrity, this crisis will continue. This escalation of violence must stop."

With this, Haley set a tone she would maintain: criticizing Russia in strong and specific terms, and in the pre-Trump American foreign-policy tradition. When asked repeatedly by the media, she would support the US inter-agency consensus that Russia had interfered in the 2016 election. That consensus—newly detailed in a declassified January 2017 report by the Office of the Director of National Intelligence, based on intelligence gathered by the CIA, FBI, and NSA—held that Putin had ordered the multi-pronged cyberattack and influence campaign, with the goal of hurting Clinton and helping Trump.

Haley held firm even as Trump's Russia intrigue built to a full-blown scandal that dominated headlines and cast a cloud over his presidency. Trump himself repeatedly claimed that there had been "no collusion" between his campaign and Russia. He seemed unable or unwilling to distinguish the question of active "collusion" or conspiracy from the official finding that Russia *had* interfered in the election to help his campaign. But the firing of Michael Flynn, the national security advisor, for lying to the FBI and to Vice President Mike Pence about Russian contacts, coupled with Attorney General Jeff Sessions's recusal from overseeing the investigation into Russia's election interference (this, too, over Russian contacts) were problems even for a president who seemed impervious to embarrassment.

On March 29, Ambassador Haley spoke to the Council on Foreign Relations in New York and took questions from its president, Richard Haass. If the confirmation hearing had been the audition for the UN job, this was something like a preliminary exam in an advanced seminar in multilateral diplomacy, proctored by a seasoned veteran of the foreign policy establishment. Haass, a career diplomat, director of policy planning in the State Department in the George W. Bush administration, and prolific author, gave a business-like introduction; his only gesture toward Haley's background was a quip asking her prediction for the Final Four of the NCAA men's college basketball tournament. (The University of South Carolina Gamecocks had won the East Regional Final three days earlier.)

Haass introduced Haley's main themes for the conversation as highlighting human rights and assessing current UN peacekeeping missions, but they weren't necessarily the most interesting part of her remarks. Haley, who only four months earlier had professed to know hardly anything about the UN, offered her early assessments of the institution:

> Being at the UN has reminded me, in powerful ways, of my early days in the state government in South Carolina. The UN Security Council, just like the South Carolina legislature, is basically a club. And the thing about clubs is that they have rules and they have a culture. There is a constant pressure to comply with this culture. And soon enough, members are doing things a certain way because that's the way they've always done them. And then the club becomes stale. Its members forget that being responsive and changing with the times are needed to show value to the people that they serve.

The ambassador said she approached her job at the UN the same way she did in South Carolina, where she had brought to institutions "an outsider's perspective" as "the first minority governor and—a real shock to the state—the first girl governor as well." She said her perspective allowed her to see the ways the legislature, and now the UN, had become complacent.

> We've put accountability front and center. . . . My team is about action, reliability, and results. We demand that of ourselves and we expect it of others. We're also having the backs of our allies, and we're not afraid to call out the governments that don't have our backs. We will deal fairly with the people who are fair with us. If not, all bets are off.

Don't get me wrong. I don't have illusions about how easily an institution the size and complexity of the United Nations can be changed. Still, with the support of the new secretary general [Guterres] and many of my colleagues on the Security Council, we've already started to make some progress.[2]

Then Donald Trump's UN ambassador said, "The United States is the moral conscience of the world. We will not walk away from this role, but we will insist that our participation in the UN honor and reflect this role." Winding up her prepared remarks, Haley concluded,

> This is a moment of great responsibility for those who believe in peace and security through international cooperation. Countries all over the world are turning inward. People are questioning the value of interactions with other nations and with international institutions. Some of those questions are good and are long overdue, but there's also a danger. Hanging in the balance is the very relevance of the United Nations. This is a time, in short, to show the people reasons to support the UN. Even in these cynical times, I believe we all carry in our hearts a bit of [the] idealism that inspired the creation of the United Nations. I know we all want those ideals to succeed in the world—I know I do.

In the question-and-answer period, Haass pressed Ambassador Haley on something Secretary Tillerson had said, about putting on the table the possibility of American withdrawal from the UN's Human Rights Council, which Republican administrations in particular had long criticized for perverting human rights principles by protecting human rights abusers and disproportionately focusing its criticisms on Israel.

Haley responded, "I mean, the Human Rights Council is so corrupt." After briefly elaborating on its flaws, she said, "I'm trying to find value in the Human Rights Council. If I find it, I'll let you know."

Haass asked if not, then was she was prepared to recommend that the United States leave the Council?

Haley said, "I am."

The CFR president also wanted to know Ambassador Haley's perspective on President Trump's harsh criticisms of multilateral institutions more broadly:

> HAASS: Let me ask you one last question, then I'll open up to our members. You work for an administration that has in several

areas staked out a position that's quite hostile to multilateralism. It's pulled the United States out of the Trans-Pacific Partnership [a pending trade agreement linking American and Asian economies and excluding China]. It has raised as recently as yesterday fundamental questions about American participation in global climate change efforts. It's raised certain questions about American alliances. It has supported Brexit, the president has done that. So do you feel in a sense that you're out there on a limb here? I mean, what is the relationship do you feel of this administration with the—with the United Nations?

HALEY: It's like you want me to answer it a certain way. That was too funny in the way you worded that. You go, this is—(laughter).

This is what I will tell you is, look, you have an administration that very much wants to see what opportunities are out there. So they for the first time are going out there with fresh eyes and saying, let's take a step back. What can we fix? What is broken? What can we do differently? And the beauty of this administration is all bets are off. We're not going to look at how things were done in the past. We're going to look at things in the future. So the president's going to make the decisions he's going to make. And he is our president. Whether, you know, people agree or disagree, he's going to make those. My job is to make sure that at the United Nations I'm making the negotiations I need to make, I'm making sure that everyone understands where the US stands.[3]

When Haass circled back to basketball at the end of the hour, Ambassador Haley said, "So I got to tell you, I mean, loving South Carolina, first of all I'm a Clemson girl." She then ran quickly through the state's recent national championships (Clemson for football, again) and tournament runs by several other schools. She reminded Haass that the University of South Carolina women's team had also just made the Final Four. (They beat Mississippi State to win the women's championship the following week.)

That March Madness season and into the spring, depending on which network you watched after all the basketball, President Trump was either hurtling off the rails or seizing control of a runaway conspiracy theory that threatened to undermine his presidency. On May 9, he fired FBI director James Comey. Initially, the reason the president gave for the firing was that Comey had botched the investigation into Hillary Clinton's unsecured emails. Two days later, Trump told NBC's Lester Holt that he was thinking of "this Russia thing with Trump" (referring to himself in the third person) when he decided to fire Comey. In the interval between these different accounts, the president had also met with Russian officials at the White House, barring US journalists (but permitting a Russian photographer) and telling Foreign Minister Sergey Lavrov and Ambassador Sergey Kislyak that by firing Comey he had removed "great pressure because of Russia."[4] In the same meeting, according to alarmed US sources who informed the *New York Times*, the president had shared classified Israeli intelligence with the Russians.[5]

Trump's firing of Comey, far from taking pressure off, led to an expanded investigation into Russian involvement in the election, with the appointment of Special Counsel Robert Mueller (Comey's predecessor as FBI director and a veteran of Republican administrations) by the acting attorney general in the matter, Rod Rosenstein. Trump called the widening probe a "witch hunt," but his firing of Comey also handed investigators a new angle: obstruction of justice.

The disarray in Washington made Haley's decision to put herself in New York look prescient, and the relative constancy of her efforts at the United Nations made for a clear juxtaposition to Trump's erraticism. The media took notice, and Haley became a regular presence on the Sunday morning network talk shows and on cable news. She wrote editorials on policy issues and sat for profile interviews that furthered the intrigue around her role in the administration—and her presumed ambition for higher office.

Some saw Ambassador Haley creating problems for herself by being so far out in front: a kind of celebrity-diplomat, working for a celebrity-president unwilling to share the spotlight, even as she ruffled the feathers of the very foreign policy "elites" Trump regularly derided. In her April 2017 *Vanity Fair* profile, Abigail Tracy quoted a "George W. Bush–era State Department official" who said, "She is not only trying to make policy from the podium at the UN, she is in danger of alienating the entire State Department." This person added, "Although you will get press attention and you will get on *Meet the Press*, the danger is that, inside the Security Council, diplomats will know that you don't speak for the president and you are going to be an ineffective advocate for the United

States government." Tracy observed that Haley's outspokenness (on Syria, in particular) showed that she was "a gifted politician at the UN," adding, "But what looks like a policy victory and an example of leadership for Haley has put her in bureaucratic peril."

Tracy quoted "a senior State Department staffer" who remarked on "barely disguised political ambitions in the post Trump Republican Party." Another State Department source said, "With what must be lofty ambitions, [Haley's] perch in [New York] gives her a platform to engage in international policy and strengthen her street cred while remaining far from the ever-erratic Trump vortex. Indeed she gets high marks for growing into the position and has now earned the respect of her colleagues in Foggy Bottom." A spokesperson for Haley declined to comment on the matter.[6]

Politico's Eliana Johnson reported that "with Rex Tillerson conducting his job almost entirely out of public view, Haley has improbably eclipsed the secretary of state as the country's leading voice on foreign affairs." She also quoted a George W. Bush–era State Department official who told her, "I think in [Haley's] mind, the key issue that would normally exist—her relationship with the secretary of state—does not exist. She thinks she's operating completely independently of him." There was even speculation that Ambassador Haley might get Secretary Tillerson's job when he left it, which seemed inevitable at some point. Johnson reported "buzz among Republican operatives that she may be Tillerson's heir apparent and a future presidential candidate."[7]

In an April 14 interview, CNN's Jamie Gangel asked Haley about her ambassadorial statements: "How much of it is coordinated with the White House and the State Department?"

"Well, it's always coordinated with the White House," Haley said, tellingly.

"You're not going rogue," Gangel prompted.

"No," Haley said. "I would never go rogue, because I'm very aware of who I work for. But what I'll tell you is, it's a sign of how this president works. It's not uncommon for him to pick up the phone and tell me what he feels on an issue, it's not uncommon for him to say, 'Make sure you say this, don't be afraid to say this.' He's given me a lot of leeway to just say what I think, and interpret what he thinks. I'm a strong voice by nature, I'm sometimes a bull in a china shop, and you know, he allows me to do that."[8]

Contributing to the sense that Haley was "being political" was her reliance on what CNN's Labott described as "a small group of trusted aides who worked with her in South Carolina." Haley's longtime political strategist Jon Lerner, a former GOP pollster, was put in charge of her Washington office. David Glaccum, Haley's former deputy chief of staff in South Carolina and former chief counsel to Senator Lindsey Graham, was reported to be "almost always at her side at the UN."[9] In August, Haley's chief of staff Steven Groves and director of communications Jonathan Wachtel both resigned. Both were newer to Haley's circle, Groves having come from the Heritage Foundation and "known to be deeply skeptical of international institutions and multilateral agreements," and Wachtel from Fox News, where he reported on the United Nations. A source told *Politico* that Groves never really broke into Haley's inner circle.[10]

Haley may have seen little point in coordinating with the State Department. With some four dozen ambassadorships worldwide as yet unfilled by Trump eight months in, and 21 of the 23 assistant secretary positions either vacant or tended by provisional staff, reports of low morale were widespread. Sharp budget cuts proposed rank-and-file reductions across the bureaucracy. Though Tillerson's focus on shrinking the department seemed aligned with Trump's "America first" agenda, rumors that he was on his way out became the working assumption.

In October, Dexter Filkins reported in an extensive essay for the *New Yorker* that the State Department was breaking down and that Tillerson was struggling to do his job. Alarmingly, there was no Assistant Secretary for East Asian and Pacific Affairs, and no ambassador to South Korea had been confirmed. One Asian official said to Filkins, "Why call the [US] Embassy when the only thing that matters is what the president tweets?"

Filkins cited a senior Trump administration official who had traveled to northeast Asia, who said that Ambassador Haley was widely seen as the most effective diplomat in the crisis. This person said, "Nikki's getting it done. She's bringing home the bacon." According to the official, this perception of Haley's diplomatic skill displeased Tillerson. "Rex hates her," the official said—adding, in strikingly undiplomatic language, "he fucking hates her."[11]

Questions remained about Haley's ability to match tough talk with substantive and sustained impact. But even the more critical coverage attested to Haley's unusual prominence as UN ambassador, and to the interest in her positions (and in her personally) amid the upheaval of Trump's presidency. The website *PassBlue*—offering "independent coverage of the UN," and affiliated with the New School's Graduate Program in International Affairs in New York—started a *Nikki Haley Watch* blog section featuring in-depth analysis of the ambassador's diplomacy, with writing by veteran journalists such as Barbara Crossette and Irwin Arieff. There were no *Susan Rice Watch* or *Samantha Power Watch* blogs during the Obama administration, even though both women cut intriguing profiles. On the contrary, a *PassBlue* headline from 2015 had inquired of the former journalist, "Where's Samantha Power? Her Rare Appearances Rankle the Press Corps at the UN."[12] During her first seven months in the job, Power sat for exactly one TV interview.

In the same amount of time, between January and August 2017, Haley racked up at least twenty-three appearances on American TV news programs. No previous UN ambassador had ever appeared on TV so frequently. Haley's interviews ran the spectrum of broadcast and cable news networks; interestingly, she made fewer appearances on Fox News, Trump's favored network, than on CNN, which the president frequently derided as "fake news." (She appeared once on left-leaning MSNBC.) Haley's appearances, *PassBlue*'s Kacie Candela observed, tended to be of three types: profile interviews, policy discussions, and responses to Trump comments. In order of airtime, Haley's main topics were North Korea, Russia, Trump's comments, the conflict in Syria, and criticisms of Iran and its "nuclear deal," the Joint Comprehensive Plan of Action between Iran and the five permanent members of the Security Council (China, France, Russia, the UK, and the US) along with Germany and the European Union.

Candela described Haley as "appearing on many channels in the same polished, Jackie Kennedy–style suit or sheath dress," sometimes doing multiple rounds on the same day.[13] Haley seemed to prioritize reaching Americans over speaking to foreign audiences, which she could have done through the international press corps based at the UN. *PassBlue*'s Irwin Arieff suggested that Haley's TV appearances were good for her "personal brand," since "she does not hesitate to speak out on matters on which [Trump] or Tillerson, the president's bizarrely reclusive secretary of state, have maintained silence or expressed a different view."[14]

Haley's high visibility (and relative effectiveness) did little to ease the inherent tension in her ill-defined relationship to Tillerson's State Department. But month by month, her footing looked more secure, and she seemed to have the upper hand in any bureaucratic infighting. Writing for CNN's *The State* in September, Elise Labott reported, "Some in the State Department describe Haley as playing for her own team in an effort to further future political ambitions." According to Tillerson aides,

Haley did not see herself as reporting to him, and used her cabinet rank to deal directly with the White House. One State Department source told Labott, "There have been times when her outside freelancing has hurt the process, but when she takes the time to learn the plan and play from the playbook, she has done a great job and added value to the situation." This person added, "She is figuring out now how to be part of the team and part of the process and be political at the same time instead of just being political."[15]

Ambassador Haley's highly intentional engagement with the press was revealing for what it suggested about how she saw her role, and how she wanted to be seen. Nine months into the job, Labott's CNN interview gave her an opportunity to share the details of how she had withdrawn from consideration for the top State Department job and negotiated the terms of her UN post. As described by Labott, Haley's office overlooking the East River seemed to offered further clues: mementos from South Carolina—Clemson football memorabilia, a picture of Emanuel AME Church in Charleston—and a picture of Ambassador Jeane Kirkpatrick.[16]

Haley was also a prolific poster on social media, curating a work-hard-play-hard persona that seemed to strive for a perfect balance of mission-driven professional and fun-loving family woman. On June 28, 2017, Haley tweeted, "Just 5 months into our time here, we've cut over half a billion $$$ from the UN peacekeeping budget & we're only getting started." At *PassBlue*, Arieff wondered, "Was this a tweet for the other 192 members of the UN? Or for her personal fan clubs in Washington and South Carolina?"[17]

Haley's use of social media drew an official rebuke that same month, when the US Office of Special Counsel (a permanent federal investigative agency, unrelated to Special Counsel Robert Mueller's Russia probe) said she had violated the 1939 Hatch Act, which prohibits executive branch employees from engaging in certain types of political activity. The offense was Ambassador Haley's retweet of President Trump's endorsement of a South Carolina congressional candidate. (The act does not restrict the president or vice president from such endorsements.) Haley was given a warning, and she deleted the offending tweet. The Special Counsel's office followed with a letter stating that, because Haley's personal Twitter account included so much information about her work as ambassador, including an official headshot and listing of her office in her bio, it "gave the impression that she was acting in her official capacity." The letter further noted that many of Haley's "posts and photographs were about and of official matters." Haley changed her profile photo and dropped her official title from her Twitter bio. She continued to post regularly about her UN work.[18]

By using the personal Twitter account she had kept since South Carolina, Haley diverted attention from the State Department's official public diplomacy channels, and amassed new followers she potentially could take with her whenever she moved on from the UN post. Between January 2017 and May 2018, Haley's Twitter followers increased more than eightfold, to 1.6 million—more than four times the followers of the US Mission to the United Nations' official Twitter handle, @USUN. A former diplomat who helped craft State Department guidelines for using social media told *Politico*, "Taxpayer dollars shouldn't be used to fund someone's social media stardom for political or business purposes. It doesn't take a savvy political mind to identify that Haley is trying to attract American voters for 2024." (By contrast, predecessor Samantha Power used the Twitter handle @AmbPower44, which was archived at the end of her service, before launching a new personal account @SamanthaJPower.)[19]

Haley's personal Twitter account was heavy on UN-related tweets, many featuring shots with VIPs from overseas trips. Interspersed were seemingly every milestone in the ambassador's family life, including canine Bentley's latest adventures. @NikkiHaley attended staff weddings and UN movie nights. @NikkiHaley couldn't wait for Clemson's football season to start. @NikkiHaley went to baseball games and a Billy Joel concert. @NikkiHaley rubbed shoulders with rock stars, tweeting a picture of herself with Bono, her hand over her heart, captioned and hashtagged, "And this just happened . . . #Starstruck #Bono #DidIEvenMakeSense." (Haley would also reveal herself as a big fan of Joan Jett, an "inspiration" who she had previously met in New York during a gubernatorial visit, when she appeared in a 2018 documentary about the eighties rocker.)[20]

A review of Haley's Instagram summarized its oeuvre: "Challenging job? Check. Family? Check. Social life? Check. Dog Instagram? Check." Yes, ambassador_bentley had an account, and *Slate*'s Rob Dozier had something to say about it: "The fact that Haley would make an Instagram account, presumably run by herself and her family, for her labradoodle in February 2017, a month after being confirmed as ambassador, and continue to maintain it throughout her tenure at the UN underscores exactly what makes Nikki Haley so interesting and frustrating as a public figure." (As metacommentary, "the fact" of the review itself clearly underscored the media's fascination with Haley.) Dozier called Haley "an extremely charming and politically savvy woman . . . who also happens to be serving a critical role in an administration that is changing American foreign policy dramatically." Finally, he got to the heart of the matter: "Her double Instagrams—her own and her dog's—deliver consistently cheerful messaging that obviates the impact of her political actions but also largely just raise the question: Where does Nikki Haley find the time?"[21]

Even the Kremlin-affiliated *Sputnik News* reported on Ambassador Haley's breaking with protocol in her use of social media, including a tweet from February 23, 2018, that must have irritated Russian officials: "Unbelievable that Russia is stalling a vote on a ceasefire allowing humanitarian access in Syria. How many more people will die before the The Security Council agrees to take up this vote? Let's do this tonight. The Syrian people can't wait."[22]

★ ★ ★

The administration's Russia policy could seem confused, particular given Trump's peculiarly pro-Putin positions. But tensions with Russia more broadly, and over Syria in particular, had been building for months. On April 5, 2017, not quite three months into her term, Haley spoke at the Security Council to condemn a chemical bomb attack in the Syrian town of Khan Shaykhun the day before that killed nearly one hundred. The ambassador held up large photographs of small Syrian children. One was a close-up of a dead boy, belly up, arms and fingers splayed open. She warned of unilateral US action if the Security Council did not respond.

It was not the first chemical weapons attack in the six-year-old conflict, which already had taken some four hundred thousand lives. But it was a particularly gruesome assault on civilians that again crossed a "red line" that had haunted the Obama administration. After a 2013 attack involving the deadly nerve agent sarin in a Damascus suburb that killed over fourteen hundred (by US estimate), Obama made the decision not to follow through on his prior warning against chemical weapons use, instead accepting a Russian-negotiated deal for the surrender of Syria's chemical weapons stockpiles. Just after the attack, Obama had sought US congressional authorization for the use of military force in Syria— wanting buy-in for another intervention in the Middle East—but majorities in both political parties were opposed.

The United States, France, and Britain all accused the Bashar al-Assad government of responsibility for the latest attack involving sarin and criticized its ally Russia for blocking a resolution they drafted to condemn it. Russia supported Assad's line that Syrian rebels could have been responsible for the chemical attack. UN Secretary-General Guterres declared that "war crimes are going on in Syria" and called for "a very clear investigation to remove all doubts" about responsibility.[23]

Haley went further. "Time and time again, Russia uses the same false narrative to deflect attention from their allies in Damascus," she said. "How many more children have to die before Russia cares?" She closed with a warning: "When the United Nations consistently fails in its duty to act collectively, there are times in the life of states that we are compelled to take our own action." Haley told CNN she did not clear with the White House or State Department the idea to hold up pictures of dead Syrian children, instead making the decision on her own and at the "last minute."[24]

Trump's prior statements about Syria were often linked to his seeking better relations with Russia. He wanted Russian help in achieving the only real US interest at stake in Syria, as he saw it: defeating the international terrorist organization known as the Islamic State of Iraq and Syria (ISIS). This was an important fight, but auxiliary to the main conflict between Syrian regime forces (supported by Iran and, after 2015, by Russian armed forces) and various Syrian armed opposition groups (supported by Saudi Arabia, Turkey, and the US). Following Russian intervention in 2015, Syrian civilian casualties had risen sharply, according to human rights organizations, intensifying a refugee crisis that now threatened the regional and European political orders.

After Haley's ultimatum to the Security Council, Trump spoke at a White House news conference, saying the chemical attack "crossed a lot of lines for me" and that his views of Syria and Assad had "changed very much." Trump said he was especially moved by "horrifying" images of children and "beautiful little babies" killed in the attack. Two days later, Trump ordered Tomahawk missile strikes against the Shayrat Airbase in Syria, controlled by the Assad government. It was the first direct US military action targeting Syrian government forces in the war. Trump said the response was "in the vital national security interest of the United States to prevent and deter the spread and use of deadly chemical weapons."[25] Yet within hours, presumably tipped off by Russia to mitigate damage, Syrian forces were able to resume use of the airbase to launch airstrikes against rebels. The US had given Russia advance notice of the operation, using an established deconfliction line.[26]

On April 10, Haley again seemed to be leading the administration's messaging when she told CNN's Jake Tapper that removing Assad from power was now a US priority. Haley said the administration did not believe that a political solution would be possible with Assad in power, though she stopped short of saying that regime change was official US policy. She elaborated:

> Regime change is something that we think is going to happen because all of the parties are going to see that Assad is not the leader that needs to be taking place for Syria. . . . Getting Assad out is not the only priority. So what we're trying to do is obviously defeat ISIS. Secondly, we don't see a peaceful Syria with Assad in there. Thirdly, get the Iranian influence out. And then finally move towards a political solution, because at the end of the day this is a complicated situation, there are no easy answers and a political solution is going to have to happen.

This basically aligned with Secretary Tillerson's more restrained talk in a CBS interview the same day, in which he said the threat from ISIS would first need to be reduced, and then "I think we can turn our attention directly to stabilizing the situation in Syria." But there was a key difference: Tillerson did not speak about Assad's removal as US policy, political imperative, or inevitability.

Unlike Trump or Tillerson, Haley repeatedly said human rights were a top priority at the United Nations. Just days before the chemical attack, she had started her month-long April presidency of the Security Council by calling for a special session devoted entirely to human rights issues, over skepticism from China and Russia. When the session went forward on April 18, Haley hailed it as "an unprecedented step" in a column she wrote for CNN.

As she explained, "Traditionally the United Nations Security Council has been considered the place where peace and security are debated, not human rights."[27] In fact, though, the Security Council often discussed human rights issues. Since the 1990s, it has debated humanitarian interventions in cases of human rights violations against civilians by sovereign governments. At the 2005 World Summit in New York, all UN member states endorsed the "Responsibility to Protect" (RtoP or R2P) doctrine for cases of genocide, war crimes, ethnic cleansing, and crimes against humanity. In practice, the veto power of any one of the five permanent Security Council members could prevent humanitarian intervention where the state's interests, or those of an ally, were involved. This structure made Security Council resolutions against Syria politically impossible, given Russian support for Assad.

Haley's push to make the Security Council the UN's new organizational center for human rights reflected an impulse to marginalize the UN Human Rights Council, which she had criticized in her confirmation hearing for its regular rebukes of Israel and openness to repressive states. But it was unclear if she really believed the Security Council would be less hamstrung by disagreements among UN states over human rights issues.

Just after Trump's missile strike on the Syrian airbase, Haley told CNN that he was prepared for further strikes. "He will not stop here," she said. "If he needs to do more, he will." In late June, the White House said it had identified "possible preparations for another chemical weapons attack by the Assad regime," and threatened that Assad would "pay a heavy price" for such action. In a separate statement, Haley said that Russia and Iran also would be held accountable for any further use of chemical weapons in Syria.

In April 2018, following months of smaller chlorine attacks and arguing over investigations in the Security Council, there was another major chemical attack in Syria. This time, the United States and allies accused Assad's forces of killing several dozen civilians in an attack involving chlorine and possibly sarin, based on media and eyewitness reports. (Chlorine traces, but not nerve agents, were later found by independent investigators.) Assad and Russian foreign minister Sergey Lavrov accused the US and allies of staging the attack.

Haley said, "Should the United States and our allies decide to act in Syria, it will be in defense of a principle on which we all agree." On April 13, Britain and France joined the US in launching airstrikes on three Syrian chemical weapons facilities. Trump said the action would "establish a strong deterrent against the production, spread, and use of chemical weapons." At the Security Council the next day, Haley turned up the volume on the message. "I spoke to the president this morning, and he said that if the Syrian regime uses this poisonous gas again, the United States is locked and loaded. When our president draws a red line, our president enforces the red line."

Trump, who reportedly watched hours of TV news every day, was surely seeing Haley's press. It was much better than Tillerson's press—or his own. The question was, did the president see that as an asset, or as a threat?

On April 24, Trump offered a clue suggesting the answer might be both. At a White House lunch with Security Council ambassadors and their spouses, Trump sat between Haley and National Security Advisor H. R. McMaster. Haley's husband, Michael, sat on her other side. A video of Trump's remarks was published by the *Washington Post*.

Trump began by welcoming the country ambassadors—"a very, very important and powerful group of people"—and joked that the White House event team "were going to leave out the spouses" in the original planning. He said, "You know, I heard there were a lot of angry spouses." Turning serious, Trump noted that the United States held the rotating monthly presidency of the Security Council, and said, "I want to thank Ambassador Nikki Haley for her outstanding leadership and for acting as my personal envoy on the Security Council. She's doing a good job."

Trump asked, "Now, does everybody like Nikki? Because if you don't, we can easily . . ." Trump trailed off, paused to smile, and said something inaudible. As guests realized he was apparently joking again, they began to laugh.

"Otherwise she can easily be replaced. Right, Nikki?" Trump turned to face Haley, who laughed along and nodded with a smile.

On the published video, one of the other ambassadors can be heard saying, "Don't do that," as others laugh.

"No, we won't do that, I promise," Trump said. "We won't do that. She's doing a fantastic job, and everyone, I see it—as we took pictures before, the friendship that you've developed, all of you together, that's really a fantastic thing."[28]

The scene played like a parody of Trump's former reality-TV show, *The Apprentice*, with the Nikki Haley ambassador contestant "staying on"—for now. Trump could have simply been playing the jester host and doing his tough boardroom character with a wink. Or he could have been sending a message about who was in charge. As with so many of Trump's performances, it was hard to tell.

★ ★ ★

Even more than Syria, North Korea would be Ambassador Haley's proving ground as President Trump's diplomatic enforcer. The North's nuclear threat was the issue that would lead Haley to some of her most Trumpian and over-the-top rhetoric—adding her voice to the president's war talk, which some feared could lead to actual war—but also to her most effective negotiation with UN Security Council members to achieve tough new sanctions against the regime.

Defying threats of international sanctions and Obama's warning that the United States could "destroy North Korea with our arsenals," North Korea had conducted twenty-four missile tests and two nuclear tests in the last year of Obama's presidency. When Obama and Trump met at the White House on November 10, 2016, the outgoing president warned the president-elect about the urgency of North Korea's nuclear threat.[29] Recalling this—their only meeting—Trump later told the press that Obama "essentially was ready to go to war with North Korea," and that he'd asked the president, "Have you spoken to [Kim]? Do you think it would be a good idea to speak with him maybe?"[30] Trump would talk to Kim Jong Un, the third-generation dictator who since taking power in 2011 reportedly had not met another head of state—even President Xi Jinping of China, his main trading partner and only ally. But first, Trump would talk *at* Kim, and loudly.

North Korea wasted little time in conducting its first missile test of the Trump presidency on February 12, 2017. Following military exercises between the US and South Korea, the North fired four more ballistic missiles on March 6. The severity of a growing crisis was made clear by the willingness of US officials to talk openly about preemptive military action against North Korea. Tillerson said this option was "on the table," and that the US would not negotiate with Kim on freezing its nuclear and missile programs. But he also said the US and China would "work together" to make North Korea take "a course correction and move away from nuclear weapons." Trump was, characteristically, more blunt in a tweet: "North Korea is behaving very badly. They have been 'playing' the United States for years. China has done little to help!"[31]

North Korea kept firing missiles of various ranges in May and June, including mid-range ballistic missiles, a short-range Scud ballistic missile, and surface-to-ship cruise weapons. Then on July 4, North Korea tested its first intercontinental ballistic missile, which it said could carry nuclear warheads to anywhere in the continental United States. On July 8, US bombers flew from Guam to conduct live-fire drills in South Korea. North Korea again tested an intercontinental missile on July 28.

In a weekend session on August 5, the Security Council voted unanimously (15–0) to impose new sanctions on North Korea. The US-sponsored resolution banned the country's largest export, coal, along with iron and iron ore, lead and lead ore, and seafood, together amounting to more than $1 billion in annual income and nearly one-third of its total export earnings. Securing China's vote was a particularly significant diplomatic victory. Haley said the vote showed how the world stood together behind pressuring North Korea to give up its nuclear and ballistic missile programs. But, she said, "We should not fool ourselves into thinking we have solved the problem. Not even close. The North Korean threat has not left us, it is rapidly growing more dangerous."[32]

Indeed, days later, US intelligence reported that North Korea had made a nuclear warhead small enough to fit its missiles. On August 8, from his golf club in Bedminster, New Jersey, Trump interrupted a press briefing on America's opioid crisis to tell reporters, "North Korea best not make any more threats to the United States. They will be met with fire and fury like the world has never seen." Referring to Kim, he said, "He has been very threatening beyond a normal state, and as I said, they will be met with fire and fury, and frankly power the likes of which this world has never seen before."

While editorialists, Democrats, and even some Republicans expressed worry that Trump might stumble into war, Republican hawks defended the harsh language. From South Carolina, Senator Lindsey Graham told CBS This Morning that Trump had drawn a "red line" signaling that the US would act if North Korea didn't pull back. "This is not a language problem," Graham said. "This is a North Korean regime trying to get the capability to strike America. We've failed for thirty years. It's time to try something new."

The day after a new North Korean nuclear test on September 3, its sixth and most powerful to date, Haley told the Security Council, "Kim Jong Un's action cannot be seen as defensive. He wants to be acknowledged as a nuclear power. But being a nuclear power is not about using those terrible weapons to threaten others," she said. "Nuclear powers understand their responsibilities. Kim Jong Un shows no such understanding. His abusive use of missiles and his nuclear threats show that he is begging for war."

"Begging for war" would be the sound bite, but Haley did not insinuate that unilateral US action might be coming, as she had over Syria. Her plea was for tougher multilateralism: "Enough is enough," she said. "The time for half measures in the Security Council is over. The time has come to exhaust all of our diplomatic means before it's too late."[33]

Haley's comments were widely reported, and drew some criticism. Daryl Kimball, executive director of the nonpartisan Arms Control Association, said, "Nikki Haley is very incorrect in saying that North

Korea is 'begging for war'—they are responding in a provocative way, yes, but there's a cold logic to what they are doing. They are pursuing a nuclear missile capability to deter what they fear, which is U.S. aggression and the possibility of an attempt to decapitate the regime in North Korea."[34]

In a speech at the United Nations on September 19, Trump said, "The United States has great strength and patience, but if it is forced to defend itself or its allies, we will have no choice but to totally destroy North Korea." He then called Kim a nickname he had given him on Twitter days earlier: "Rocket Man is on a suicide mission for himself."

The next day, Haley was asked by George Stephanopoulos on *Good Morning America* if she thought it was "appropriate to use a term like Rocket Man to talk about the leader of another country who has got nuclear weapons." The ambassador responded, "Well I tell you, George, it worked. I was talking to a president of an African country yesterday, and he actually cited Rocket Man back to me." Smiling, she added that Trump's nickname had the international community talking about Kim, implying that had been the point.[35]

More seriously, over the following months, Haley worked to cull a consensus in the Security Council for putting maximum economic pressure on North Korea. China held the most important cards, accounting for 90 percent of North Korea's limited external trade. Over the years, it had regularly violated various UN sanctions against its ally. So had dozens of other countries accounting for smaller trade with North Korea, including Russia, Iran, Syria, and Cuba—but also American friends Germany, Brazil, India, and France.[36]

There was important symbolism at stake: China, as a rising power, did not wish to be seen as giving in to US pressure. But more fundamentally, Beijing sought to prop up the Kim regime for fear of economic and humanitarian catastrophe were it to collapse, along with the prospect of South Korean and US forces at its border. Chinese interests were not necessarily advanced by North Korea's nuclear and missile programs, but if sanctions were to push Kim's government to the breaking point, China had the most to lose of any country.

In November, North Korea conducted yet another intercontinental ballistic missile test, firing higher and further than the last. On December 22, the Security Council voted unanimously to impose new sanctions, limiting by 90 percent North Korea's import of refined petroleum products and restricting its access to crude oil. The US-drafted resolution also committed the Security Council to further action if the North were to conduct another nuclear test or launch another intercontinental missile.

Strikingly, this diplomatic victory for the US came just one day after the UN General Assembly voted overwhelmingly on a resolution condemning Trump's decision to move the US embassy in Israel to Jerusalem from Tel Aviv (128 states for, 9 against, 35 abstaining), a rebuke that led Haley to warn, "The United States will remember this day in which it was singled out for attack in the General Assembly, for the very act of exercising our right as a sovereign nation. We will remember it when we are called upon to once again make the world's largest contribution to the United Nations. And we will remember it when so many countries come calling on us, as they so often do, to pay even more and to use our influence for their benefit." A week earlier, the Security Council had voted 14–1 to condemn the US decision on Jerusalem. Haley's veto, which she later called her "great honor," was her first for the United States.

The juxtaposition showed that while most UN member states were eager to stand against Trump's swaggering unilateralism, Security Council countries were still willing to follow America when it led, in the face of a threat to collective security, through multilateral institutions. This also exhibited Nikki Haley's split personality at the UN. Often pugnacious in public, especially on favorite subjects such as Israel and the UN's human rights "hypocrisy," Haley could be quietly effective behind the scenes, pushing hard for consensus involving powerful Security Council counterweights China and Russia. In all, the Security Council passed four resolutions on North Korea in 2017, three of which would put unprecedented economic pressure on the country. In a congratulatory response to Trump's August 5 tweet about the 15–0 vote, the former Obama administration ambassador to Russia, Michael McFaul, called it "a genuine foreign policy achievement."

Haley deserved much of the credit. The *Washington Post* reported, "Even Trump skeptics in the foreign policy community are hailing the work of the administration and, specifically, Ambassador to the United Nations Nikki Haley." Thomas Weiss, a UN scholar at the City University of New York, told the newspaper, "Had anyone asked me to lay a bet last week, I would have hoped at most for an abstention from Beijing. . . . The Chinese never want to appear to be responding to pressure. This suggests that even our ill-informed and inexperienced and incompetent president may come to appreciate the value of multilateralism."[37]

Those closest to the process hailed Haley's sustained focus on the sanctions effort. A US official directly involved in the negotiations told Fox News on background, "Ambassador Haley's diplomacy behind the scenes, in particular with the Chinese ambassador here, as well as the Russian ambassador, made it very, very clear that we were not kidding around. We were literally just one more provocation away from some kind of a military action that would bring great harm to the entire region, and that the threat we perceived from North Korea's development was no longer theoretical by any means." The official added, "I have been in government for maybe thirteen or fourteen years, and never seen anything like this so singularly focused on bringing down a country economically to get them to the negotiating table."[38]

Hugh Dugan, professor at Seton Hall University's School of Diplomacy and International Relations and a former UN official under eleven US ambassadors to the UN, told Fox News, "Compared to previous U.S. presidents, Trump's worldview has engendered much more second-guessing by others of U.S. action. In turn, this has dealt to Ambassador Haley a wider range of hands to play. But the poker face and the bluff were all hers."

Fox News asked French UN Ambassador Delattre about Haley's role. He responded, "Nikki Haley deserved much credit indeed for bringing the Security Council together on the three sets of sanctions" targeting North Korea's economy. On the other hand, Russia's UN Ambassador Vasily Nebenzya wasn't quite ready to give Haley the credit, saying, "Sanctions against North Korea is a collective effort of all Security Council members."[39]

★ ★ ★

Iran's nuclear program presented a different set of issues, and the administration's policy put Ambassador Haley in a very different situation diplomatically. President Trump's priority with Iran seemed to be to unravel an existing multilateral agreement on the country's nuclear program, which he had repeatedly called "the worst deal ever"; the president castigated "stupid" Obama administration officials and European allies for entering into the agreement with Iran. Haley did what she could to advance the administration's argument that Iran was violating—"in spirit," if not in letter—the Joint Comprehensive Plan of Action (the JCPOA), the interim agreement signed by Iran, the five permanent Security Council members, Germany, and the European Union in 2013.

Trump telegraphed US intentions to withdraw from the JCPOA and negotiate "a better deal." He reluctantly recertified Iran's compliance to Congress in January and July 2017, as required by US law, before refusing to do so a third time in October over objections from Secretary Tillerson and Defense Secretary James Mattis. Congressional Republican hawks argued for either scrapping the deal, which Congress "had never voted on" since it wasn't a treaty, or tacking on new conditions having to do with Iran's regional policies. Iran would never have agreed to these conditions—and this may have been the point. None of the European signatories favored ending the agreement, which placed limits on Iran's uranium enrichment capabilities and set up a compliance monitoring and a verification role for the International Atomic Energy Agency (IAEA). Like congressional Republicans, Haley would embrace the somewhat misleading claim that during the Obama administration, Congress was "never allowed" to debate or even discuss the agreement.[40]

Republicans offered several criticisms of the JCPOA, complaining about the deal's sunset provisions and echoing Israeli prime minister Benjamin Netanyahu's claim that it would allow Iran to remain on the verge of "nuclear breakout" in very short order after its expiration. But the criticisms went to issues, however serious, that the JCPOA did not purport to address: Iran's state sponsorship of terrorist proxies and militias including Hamas and Hezbollah, its missile exports, and its involvement in conflicts across the Middle East. This was the line of criticism that Haley's aggressive diplomacy pursued.

In August, Haley made a trip that, as she later wrote, "very few people supported, to investigate an issue no one wanted to talk about": she went to Vienna, Austria, to meet with officials for the IAEA in charge of verifying Iran's compliance with the agreement. She devotes a full chapter of her memoir *With All Due Respect* to the Iran nuclear-agreement issue, in which she argues, "The deal didn't end Iran's development of a nuclear bomb, it just paused it, at best" and offered insufficient assurances against future Iranian enrichment of uranium and development of advanced centrifuges—the key components of a nuclear weapons program.[41] She maintained that international inspectors under the agreement had access only to Iran's "declared" nuclear sites—those that it admitted to—and that the regime fundamentally could not be trusted, given its historical record and regional policies of supporting terrorist proxies.

In a September 5, 2017, speech at the American Enterprise Institute, Ambassador Haley offered a brief history lesson in which she pointed out that "the Islamic Republic" regime had been "born in an act of international lawbreaking"—referring to the November 4, 1979, takeover of the US Embassy in Tehran by Islamic revolutionaries, mostly students—and had always existed outside the community of responsible nations. Effectively, her position amounted to a declaration that Iran could only be trusted only if it changed its regime—anathema, obviously, to the country's leaders, even (relative) moderates. "Judging any international agreement," she said, "begins and ends with the nature of the government that signed it: does it respect international law? Can it be trusted to abide by its commitments? Is the agreement strong enough to withstand the regime's attempt to cheat?"[42]

(Ambassador Haley did not mention the CIA-backed coup in 1953 that overthrew Iran's democratically elected government and facilitated the authoritarian rule of the Shah, Mohammad Reza Pahlavi, against whom the Iranian Revolution was directed twenty-five years later; in their bitter non-diplomacy, both countries had their collective "chosen traumas" brought on by the other side's international lawbreaking.)[43]

That fall, Haley went all-in behind the Trump administration's efforts to make the case that Iran was violating an international agreement to limit its arms dealing. *Foreign Policy* reported that the administration was "pressing to declassify intelligence allegedly linking Iran to short-range ballistic missile attacks by Yemeni insurgents against Saudi Arabia, part of a public relations blitz aimed at persuading America's UN counterparts that Tehran is helping to fuel [Yemen's] conflict."[44]

Yemen's civil war had become a humanitarian catastrophe by 2017. Two years earlier, insurgents from the armed Houthi movement had forced the resignation (later rescinded) of the country's president Abdrabbuh Mansur Hadi. The conflict between the Houthis and regime forces had since evolved into a regional proxy war between Iran and Saudi Arabia, with the Saudis leading a coalition to restore the former government—and, using American-made weapons, sometimes killing Yemeni civilians in their homes and in hospitals. Saudi forces had bombed a funeral in Yemen's capital, Sanaa, in 2016, killing one hundred civilians (the Saudis cited faulty intelligence). Saudi Arabia now faced international condemnation for enforcing a blockade on Yemeni ports that threatened to trigger starvation.

Bruce Riedel, a career CIA officer and former Middle East advisor to Presidents Clinton and Obama, told *Foreign Policy*, "[Trump administration officials] desperately want to change the conversation away from starving children to Iranian bad guys. But I'm skeptical it's going to work. Because the imagery of kids that you see on the BBC or *60 Minutes* is a lot more powerful than the imagery of a declassified document."[45]

Ambassador Haley may not have been able to draw on such powerful "imagery of kids" as produced by Syria's awful war, but she did have some visuals to show in making the US case against Iran. In December 2017, speaking to reporters from Joint Base Anacostia-Bolling in Washington, DC, Haley accused Iran of arming Houthi rebels in Yemen. The *New York Times* reported, "Ms. Haley stood in front of pieces of what [US] defense officials said were Iranian-made Qiam missiles, including one that was fired by Houthi militants at an airport in Riyadh, Saudi Arabia." Saudi officials had called the attack an "act of war" by Iran. "When you look at this missile, this is terrifying, this is absolutely terrifying," Haley said. "Just imagine if this missile had been launched at Dulles Airport or JFK, or the airports in Paris, London or Berlin."

At Haley's urging, the Pentagon and US intelligence agencies had declassified the weapons, which apart from the short-range ballistic missile included a drone and an anti-tank weapon recovered in Yemen. "The fight against Iranian aggression is the world's fight," she said. "We do not often declassify this type of military equipment recovered from these attacks. But today we are taking an extraordinary step of presenting it here in an open setting." She added, "You will see us build a coalition to really push back against Iran and what they're doing," she said.[46]

But the ambassador did not specify just what she was seeking, and the case she presented was less than conclusive. Haley cited Security Council Resolution 2231, passed in 2015, which prohibited the sale, supply, or transfer of certain weapons outside of Iran unless approved by the council itself. The weapons she displayed—provided to the Pentagon by Saudi Arabia and the United Arab Emirates—were of unknown vintage, and in theory could have been transferred into Yemen before the 2015 resolution.[47] This was not a moment to stand with former US ambassador Adlai Stevenson's fabled performance at the Security Council in 1962, citing evidence of Soviet missiles in Cuba, or even with Haley's own heralded condemnation of Assad's chemical weapons use in Syria seven months earlier.

Iran's foreign minister, Mohammad Javad Zarif, invoked a less flattering comparison. He tweeted side-by-side photos of Haley and Colin Powell, then-US secretary of state, from his 2003 UN speech calling for the invasion of Iraq based on what turned out to be false assertions about weapons of mass destruction. "When I was based at the U.N., I saw this show and what it begat," the Iranian minister tweeted.[48]

Haley's show-and-tell was met with skepticism by friends, as well. A UN panel of experts reviewing the missile fragments noted in a confidential report, obtained by *Foreign Policy*, that while the missile contained a component bearing the logo of an Iranian company targeted by US and UN sanctions, it also contained an American-made component. The panel concluded it had "no evidence as to the identity of the broker or supplier." Sweden's UN ambassador, Olof Skoog, had access to the UN panel report as a representative on the Security Council. While he gave polite cover to Ambassador Haley by saying the United States "may be in possession of evidence I have not seen," he stopped short of saying he'd been persuaded Iran was responsible. "The information I have up to now is less clear," he said.[49]

Haley tried again in January 2018, inviting Security Council envoys to Washington to see the evidence for themselves. The British UN ambassador, Jonathan Allen, tweeted support for Haley's argument, saying there was "clear evidence" that the missiles came from Iran. French ambassador François Delattre told reporters his country was "strongly attached to the JCPOA" but also "committed to addressing" the "ballistic-missile issue, as well as regional issues."[50]

The UN panel report, submitted to the Security Council in mid-January, gave Ambassador Haley the headline she sought by concluding that Iran had violated an arms embargo imposed on Yemen in Resolution 2216, adopted in 2015. Iran, the report said, had failed to prevent Houthi rebels in Yemen from obtaining Iranian missiles. While the report did not charge specifically that Tehran had supplied the Houthis with the missiles, Haley nevertheless took it as support for the administration's effort to marginalize the Islamic Republic.

In February, Haley wrote an op-ed column for the *New York Times*, in which she said, "The new U.N. report makes it clear that the weapons were introduced into Yemen after the arms embargo was imposed, putting Iran in undisputed violation of the United Nations resolution." She sought to link the violation to the signing of the JCPOA: "Since the signing of the nuclear agreement, the Iranian regime's support of dangerous militias and terror groups has markedly increased. Its missiles and advanced weapons are turning up in war zones all across the Middle East. . . . The world can no longer claim ignorance or skepticism of Iran's role in fomenting instability in the Middle East."[51]

Ultimately, Iran's missile violations were not enough to sell the administration's argument that the JCPOA was fundamentally flawed. On May 8, Trump made the long-anticipated announcement that the United States was pulling out unilaterally. New statements expressing support for the agreement were offered by Australia, Canada, China, the EU, France, Germany, Ireland, Japan, the Netherlands, Norway, Russia, South Africa, Sweden, Turkey, and the United Kingdom, adding to earlier statements by these and dozens of other countries over the preceding weeks and months. Trump's America, not Iran, stood isolated over the nuclear agreement.

Ambassador Haley's tough diplomacy didn't forge a consensus this time. Having spent political capital on the effort, Haley the human rights champion risked appearing indifferent to the Saudi role in Yemen's increasingly ugly war. By spring 2018, the Trump administration owned American involvement in the inherited conflict—and the EU, human rights groups, and UN Secretary-General António Guterres were all calling Yemen "the world's worst humanitarian crisis."

★ ★ ★

Elsewhere in the Middle East, Haley's advocacy (or apology) for Israel was an axiom of her basic orientation to the United Nations, as she had made clear in her confirmation hearing. The December 2017 General Assembly vote by 128 countries to condemn Trump's moving the US embassy to Jerusalem—in defiance of Haley's threats to withhold dollars—showed that she could stand isolated in defending American sovereign prerogative on this issue, even as she stood at the center of multilateral efforts to address a gathering crisis like North Korea.

Haley appeared unfazed by the reluctance of US allies to speak out against the resolution. On the contrary, she pointed out that fully 64 countries did *not* vote to condemn the Jerusalem decision: 7 countries besides the US and Israel voted against it (Guatemala, Honduras, Marshall Islands, Micronesia, Nauru, Palau, and Togo), 35 abstained, and 21 were absent. On December 21, 2017, Haley sent "save the date" cards to the representatives of the 64 countries, inviting them to attend a formal reception she would host on January 3.[52] Twice as many countries may have condemned the US decision, but she would make up for that by doubling the gratitude toward "Friends of the U.S.," as the evening was titled.

One of America's friends in the Jerusalem embassy vote was Guatemala, led by President Jimmy Morales, the first foreign leader to support the embassy move. Reporting by *Foreign Policy*'s Colum Lynch raised questions about what consideration Morales may have received from Haley and others in the administration in exchange for his support. In January 2018, the UN's International Commission against Impunity in Guatemala (known by its Spanish acronym, CICIG) uncovered alleged illegal contributions to Morales's 2016 campaign, as well as alleged corruption by the president's son and brother.

Morales responded by announcing plans "to terminate the UN commission's mandate, giving its investigators 24 hours to shut their office." The US response was a mild statement of concern about corruption in Guatemala from the US Embassy, which didn't even mention the UN commission. Lynch reported that Morales, an evangelical Christian, had become friendly with key administration figures including Haley and Pence, along with Senator Marco Rubio, and conservative thought-leaders inclined to disregard the UN commission's report.[53]

In March, Haley traveled to Guatemala City on a Central American "friendship tour" to express thanks to Guatemala and Honduras for supporting the US in the Jerusalem embassy vote. She said the visit was also intended to promote efforts to fight corruption, drug trade, and human trafficking in the region. In public, she expressed US support for CICIG and told Morales in a meeting that it was "in his best interest" to cooperate. But three diplomats briefed on Haley's visit told Lynch that in private, Haley "dressed down" the US ambassador, Luis Arreaga, for his public support of the UN commission, and was "particularly irked" that he had appeared at a press conference with the Colombian head of CICIG, Iván Velásquez. In photos from the press conference, the two men each held bumper stickers reading "I love CICIG" in Spanish.

In the meeting, which included the Guatemalan attorney general, Haley requested that no more press conferences be held on high-impact cases, since the accused were innocent until proven guilty. She delivered a similar message to the commission in public, saying it should be "like the FBI" and "not in the paper every day." A Guatemalan political analyst who negotiated the terms of the commission with the UN told Lynch that Haley's appeal ran counter to the country's criminal procedure code, which requires public disclosure of prosecutorial and judicial actions.[54] If Haley's concern was to avoid the appearance of US interference, the effect was the opposite. Her advice that CICIG should keep a lower profile might have carried some resonance coming from any other US administration. But in Trump's America, where the FBI *was* in the paper nearly every day (for its tense relationship with the president) Haley's position appeared bereft of any real principle—and as the shielding of a favored ally from accountability.

Haley's intervention weakened CICIG and therefore the UN, at least for Guatemalans, even as it cast doubt on the depth of her commitment to addressing a serious crisis of governance in Central America. This crisis, of course, was a major contributor to the northward flow of migrants and asylum seekers from the region, which the Trump administration professed to take so seriously as a an economic and national security threat to the United States. This contradiction, inherent in the administration's incoherent policy, may have been lost on Haley, or perhaps she really was more interested in clipping the UN's influence and using the organization as a platform to express unilateral US prerogatives—for domestic as much as international audiences.

On May 14, 2018, the seventieth anniversary of the Declaration of the Establishment of the State of Israel, the United States marked the move of its embassy with a large ceremony in Jerusalem, amid Israel's tear-gassing of Palestinian protests in the West Bank and ongoing demonstrations along the Gaza border. The Hamas-run health ministry said at least fifty-two Palestinians were killed by Israeli fire and more than twenty-seven hundred were injured, half by gunfire.[55] Along the Gaza security barrier, demonstrations had begun on March 30 and continued toward the approach of Nakba (Catastrophe) Day on May 15, when Palestinians mark their displacement following Israel's independence. Initially nonviolent, the Gaza demonstrations had turned to property destruction in April. Israel accused Hamas of using peaceful protests as cover for attacks, thus justifying its own use of force.

Haley was not among the eight hundred attendees at the Jerusalem embassy opening. But she strongly defended Israel's force at Gaza, against calls by several Security Council members and UN Secretary-General Guterres for an investigation. "Who among us would accept this type of activity on your border? No one would." Haley said. "No country in this chamber would act with more restraint than Israel has." Haley said that Hamas, backed by Iran, was at fault in the violence, and pointed to Molotov cocktails flown into Israel via kites. She did not mention reported Israeli sniper fire or the Palestinian death toll.[56] Later, when Permanent Observer of Palestine to the United Nations Riyad Mansour began to speak, Haley got up and walked out of the meeting. International media carried the image of America's UN ambassador, back to the chamber, making her exit.

On June 1, Haley's veto was the sole "no" on a Security Council resolution to condemn the "excessive, disproportionate and indiscriminate force by the Israeli forces against Palestinian civilians" and demand a halt to such actions. The Kuwait-sponsored resolution made no mention of Hamas's role. Ten members voted in favor, and four abstained. In the same session, Haley was the sole "yes" vote on a US-drafted resolution to condemn Hamas for the violence. Three members voted against, and eleven abstained. Haley said in a statement, "Further proof was not needed, but it is now completely clear that the UN is hopelessly biased against Israel."[57]

★ ★ ★

Away from the Security Council, Haley was frequently asked to weigh in on the repeated controversies surrounding the Trump presidency. As a self-described "brown" person in the cabinet, and given her prior role as a southern state governor, she would be asked repeatedly to comment on Trump's anti-immigrant stances and his statements defending Confederate monuments and white supremacists. As a woman, she would be asked by the media about sexual assault and harassment allegations against the president, brought by at least nineteen women who accused him of past crimes and misconduct. Haley must have known that in accepting a post in the administration, she risked association with the very worst of a man who, as candidate, had disparaged Mexicans and Muslims, and who in 2005 had bragged on the set of *Access Hollywood* that he was a "star" who could "grab [women] by the p---y," as captured in a video made public through reporting by the *Washington Post* just a month before Election Day in 2016.[58]

In April 2017, as reported by the *Post and Courier*, "The very same day Haley gave her noted Syria speech at the UN, she was booed at the *New York Times*' 'Women of the World' summit for her association with the Trump administration." Haley was interviewed by Greta Van Susteren, a former Fox News host who had moved over to MSNBC. "At one point," reporter Emma Dumain noted, Haley "was interrupted mid-sentence by an audience member asking about Trump's ban on Syrian refugees" entering the United States. "Rather than responding," Dumain reported, "Haley stopped, smiled, ignored the question and the interview continued. That video has gone viral, too."[59]

That August, an event called Unite the Right brought thousands of neo-Confederates, neo-Nazis, anti-government militia members, self-identified "White nationalists," and "alt-right" demonstrators to Charlottesville, Virginia, along with thousands of counter-protestors and a number of black-clad "antifa" (anti-fascist) militants opposed to the event. The rally was organized by a thirty-four-year-old Charlottesville native and University of Virginia graduate who sought to unify the Far Right in opposition to city plans to remove a statue of Confederate general Robert E. Lee from the recently renamed Emancipation Park.

White men mostly in their twenties and thirties, wearing white polo shirts and carrying flaming store-bought tiki torches, staged a nighttime rally on August 11 on the university's grounds, shouting slogans such as "Jews will not replace us!," "You will not replace us!," and "White lives matter." The marchers surrounded a group of around thirty counter-protestors, including UVA students, who locked arms around a statute of the university's founder Thomas Jefferson. Police broke up sporadic fighting.

The next day, there were violent clashes at Emancipation Park following a peaceful counter-protest led by interfaith clergy. An organizer of that effort, Harvard University's Professor Cornel West, credited "over 300, 350 antifascists" from preventing the group of twenty counter-protestors from being "crushed like cockroaches" as they stood against the shouting throng of white supremacists.[60] According to news reports, both the far-right and antifa groups brought weapons and protective gear to the rally. (Virginia permits the open carry of firearms.) Police did not separate the groups. Fighting took place in the park and at other locations, with a group of six white men severely beating a twenty-one-year-old Black man, DeAndre Harris, in a parking garage next to police headquarters. One white supremacist, using his speeding car as a battering ram, drove into a crowd of counter-protestors on a downtown pedestrian mall, injuring nineteen and killing Heather Heyer, a thirty-two-year-old white woman. Two Virginia state troopers died in a helicopter crash while attempting to monitor events.

Trump, given an initial briefing about the developing situation, spoke briefly from his private golf club in New Jersey. "We condemn in the strongest possible terms this egregious display of hatred, bigotry, and violence on many sides, many sides," Trump said. "It has been going on for a long time in our country. . . . It has no place in America." Trump's tone was subdued. He did not condemn any groups by name, and his call for further "study" struck some as casting doubt on eyewitness and media reports saying that the worst violence was from the far-right groups. (Numerous independent phone-camera recordings, investigations, and legal proceedings would later confirm this.) There were widespread calls for President Trump to say more, and specifically to repudiate the white supremacists.

Returning to the White House the next day, the president read a prepared statement: "Racism is evil. And those who cause violence in its name are criminals and thugs, including the KKK, neo-Nazis, white supremacists, and other hate groups that are repugnant to everything we hold dear as Americans."

But at Trump Tower the next day, Trump reverted back to his more equivocal view. "I think there is blame on both sides," he said in a heated exchange with reporters. He defended those who had gathered to protest the removal of the Lee statue. "Not all of those people were neo-Nazis, believe me. Not all of those people were white supremacists, by any stretch. . . . You had some very bad people in that group. But you also had people that were very fine people on both sides."[61]

Though some in conservative media defended the president's remarks as justified (and far-right reactions were celebratory), Trump's words set off days of criticism. Democrats condemned the comments. Some Republicans, including House Speaker Paul Ryan and Senator Marco Rubio, made statements condemning white supremacy, though not repudiating the president's remarks directly.

Charlottesville held a particular resonance for Nikki Haley, coming just over two years after the racially motivated shooting that killed nine at Emanuel AME Church in Charleston. The decision to remove the Confederate flag from the South Carolina State House in Columbia had made Haley a target of hate messages on social media. The Southern Poverty Law Center documented 364 rallies defending the Confederate flag around the South just in the six months after the Charleston shooting, along with increasing membership in far-right organizations. It was the issue that had made Haley a national symbol: a courageous leader to many, a turncoat to an increasingly confrontational minority.

Haley's first response to Charlottesville was a tweet on August 12, approximately two hours after the car attack that killed Heyer. She wrote, "I know all to well [sic] the pain hate can cause. The American Spirit that binds us has no place for actions like this. #PrayersForCharlottesville."

Over the following days, the Charleston shooting would be invoked by many commentators as a marked contrast in reacting to a national tragedy, with many recalling Haley's leadership of the state's response. At the *Sacramento Bee*, contributor and former executive editor Gregory Favre had advice for Trump: "Words matter, Mr. President. They can hurt or heal, and hurt is way ahead in your collection. If you need lessons on what to say, ask UN Ambassador Nikki Haley."[62]

In an email Haley sent to her staff four days after the Charlottesville violence, the ambassador said the "horrible acts" took her back to the "sad days of dealing with the Charleston tragedy in 2015." She added, "We must denounce them at every turn, and make them feel like they are on an island and isolate them the same way they wish to isolate others."[63]

Haley told CNN and ABC News on August 22 that she had spoken to Trump about Charlottesville. On CNN, she said she had a "private conversation" with the president about Charlottesville and would "leave it at that." On *Good Morning America*, George Stephanopoulos recalled to Haley, "You took on the white supremacists, you took down the Confederate flag, and you spoke out when the president—when candidate Trump was very slow to disavow David Duke and the KKK." (Duke, former grand wizard of the Knights of the Ku Klux Klan and 1991 Louisiana gubernatorial candidate, had endorsed Trump's candidacy and had just attended the Charlottesville rally.) Stephanopoulos asked Haley, "What were you thinking last week when you saw the president blame 'both sides' for the violence in Charlottesville, when he said that 'many very fine people' were marching with the white supremacists?"

Haley answered, "Well, I picked up the phone and I had a private conversation with the president about Charlottesville, and it was taken very well. What I will tell you is, there is no room for bigotry and hate in this country. I know the pain that hate can cause, and we have to isolate them, the way they want to isolate others."

Stephanopoulos interjected, "Does the president understand he made a mistake?"

Haley responded, "I think the president clarified, so that no one can question that he's opposed to bigotry and hate in this country, and that when our soldiers go out and fight, they fight unified. We need to make sure that we're a country that's unified back home."

Stephanopoulos cited a Trump remark that it was "foolish" to take down Confederate statues. "You took down the Confederate flag from the State House in Charleston," he said (confusing the city where the church shooting took place with the capital, Columbia).

Ambassador Haley ignored the host's error and sought to make a different distinction, saying, "Well, you know it was the state that decided, but what our focus was, the Confederate flag was a living, breathing thing. It was representative of the here and now. And there was no place for that, especially after we saw nine people murdered with the killer raising up the Confederate flag."

Haley kept her own counsel on what she said to Trump after Charlottesville. If she was signaling disapproval of his handling of the issue, her remarks also affirmed her own close access to the president and her discipline in discretion. It was about as good a statement as she could have made for Nikki Haley brand maintenance. But Haley's statements after Charlottesville were also noteworthy for what they did *not* say that could have linked its events to her perspective as UN ambassador. She could have spoken to international audiences as well as Americans, knowing that images of Charlottesville were seen around the world. She could have acknowledged the resurgence of far-right parties and ideologies of racial and ethnic chauvinism not only in the United States, but in European countries such as Hungary, Poland, and Germany. She could have called for unity not just among Americans taking inspiration from US armed forces, but also for worldwide solidarity among supporters of democracy and the human rights principles that the United Nations, at least in its ideal, sought to advance. Instead, Haley's frames were entirely domestic. She was asked to speak as a former governor, and she did so with characteristic grace, but she failed to do so as an ambassador.

★ ★ ★

Haley was similarly calibrated when asked about sexual allegations against the president. Candidate Trump had defended the *Access Hollywood* tape as "locker room talk" in a presidential debate with Hillary Clinton, but outrage at his victory helped drive the Women's March on January 21, 2017, which drew hundreds of thousands to Washington the day after Trump's inauguration, with millions more joining marches in other American and world cities. It was reported to be the largest single-day protest in US history.

That October, investigative reports in the *New York Times* and the *New Yorker* detailed allegations of sexual assault by film producer Harvey Weinstein, who was forced out of his company and expelled from the Academy of Motion Picture Arts and Sciences. Weinstein's fall sparked an outpouring of allegations against powerful men across the entertainment industry and other fields, especially politics, in the movement that became known for the hashtag #MeToo. Senator Al Franken of Minnesota, a Democrat, was forced to resign after allegations by several women. In an Alabama special election to fill the Senate seat vacated by Attorney General Sessions, Republican candidate Roy Moore stood accused by three women of sexually assaulting them decades earlier, when two of the women were minors. Trump had tepidly endorsed Moore's opponent in the primary, but now vigorously supported Moore in the general election.

In December, Haley was interviewed by John Dickerson on the CBS program *Face the Nation*. After questions about Israel and South Korea, Dickerson said, "Let me ask you about a domestic issue here. There's a cultural shift going on in America right now. You saw it, three members of Congress kicked out of Congress because of sexual behavior, misdeeds. You were the first woman senator of South Carolina," Dickerson said (getting Haley's former position wrong). He asked, "What do you think of this cultural moment that's happening?"

Again ignoring an interviewer's misstatement about her South Carolina background, Haley responded, "You know, I am incredibly proud of the women who have come forward. I'm proud of their strength. I'm proud of their courage. And I think that the idea that this is happening, I think it will start to bring a conscience to the situation, not just in politics, but in, you know, we've seen in Hollywood and in every industry. And I think the time has come."

Dickerson corrected himself. "Of course I'm wrong, you were the governor, first [woman] governor of South Carolina. Given that consciousness, how do you think people should assess the accusers of the president?"

Haley answered, "Women who accuse anyone should be heard. They should be heard and they should be dealt with. And I think we heard from them prior to the election. And I think any woman who has felt violated or felt mistreated in any way, they have every right to speak up."

Dickerson asked, "And does the election mean that's a settled issue?"

Haley said, "You know, that's for the people to decide. I know that he was elected. But you know, women should always feel comfortable coming forward. And we should all be willing to listen to them."[64]

This was a remarkable enough thing for any cabinet member to say. Even so, as on issues of race and right-wing nationalism, an American representative to the United Nations might have taken the opportunity to point out that #MeToo and sexual crimes against women were global issues, and not just American concerns. November 2017 Twitter data showed that after the United States, users in Britain, India, France, and Canada were using the hashtag #MeToo most heavily.[65] Ambassador Haley simply accepted Dickerson's casting of it as "a domestic issue."

Haley's remark about Trump's accusers drew notice. In a December profile for *Vanity Fair*, Abigail Tracy reported, "Haley has become a rare success story in Trumpworld, using her distance from Washington to defend the president's policies without burning her own credibility. So for those familiar with how Haley operates, the decision to criticize Trump appeared calculated." Still, Tracy observed, "As one of the highest-ranking women in the Trump administration, Haley's comments were both refreshing and stunning."[66]

Administration sources told the Associated Press that Trump "fumed" over Haley's response to Dickerson.[67] Rejecting this version of events, a White House official told NBC's Andrea Mitchell that Trump was "not upset" with Haley, and that he called her after the interview to say "she'd done a good job." Rather, the president's complaint was "with the news reporting" of Haley's remark.[68]

★ ★ ★

The #MeToo cultural pivot could also turn against the president's critics. On January 5, 2018, author Michael Wolff published *Fire and Fury: Inside the Trump White House*, a lurid book describing dysfunction in the administration. Wolff had been given permission to wander the White House for months, observing and speaking with staff. The book had debuted at the top of the *New York Times'* bestseller list (propelled partly by Trump's last-minute attempt to block its publication) but charges of sloppy reporting and outright fabrications soon followed, and not only from Trump's defenders.

Wolff's purple prose included the following innuendo about Haley: "She had become a particular focus of Trump's attention, and he of hers. . . . The president had been spending a notable amount of private time with Haley on Air Force One, and was seen to be grooming her for a national political future." Wolff quoted a White House staffer (anonymously, of course) who called Haley "as ambitious as Lucifer" and claimed that allies of Steve Bannon, by now fired from his position as Trump's strategist, feared "Haley's hold on the president," and that she believed "that she, with requisite submission, could be [Trump's] heir apparent."

In a publicity appearance on HBO's *Real Time with Bill Maher*,

Wolff said that while he had lacked "the blue dress" proof to put it in the book—an allusion to President Bill Clinton's sexual misconduct with White House intern Monica Lewinsky—he had "incendiary" information and was "absolutely sure" that Trump was having an affair. He told Maher, "Now that I've told you, when you hit that paragraph, you're gonna say, 'Bingo.'" It was not clear whether Wolff was aware of the history of ugly, unsubstantiated allegations of affairs during Haley's first campaign for governor. But he seemed to have misjudged the cultural appetite for a casual smear against a prominent woman in public life.

Haley was asked on the *Politico* podcast *Women Rule* about Wolff's spreading of "rumor that she was romantically involved with the president of the United States." Haley said, "It is absolutely not true. I have literally been on Air Force One once and there were several people in the room when I was there," referring to a July 2017 flight from Washington to Long Island. "He says that I've been talking a lot with the president in the Oval about my political future. I've never talked once to the president about my future and I am never alone with him."

Ambassador Haley added, "So the idea that these things come out, that's a problem. But it goes to a bigger issue that we need to always be conscious of: at every point in my life, I've noticed that if you speak your mind and you're strong about it and you say what you believe, there is a small percentage of people that resent that and the way they deal with it is to try and throw arrows, lies or not."[69]

As a marker of *Fire and Fury*'s flash-in-the-pan notoriety, the CBS broadcast of the Sixtieth Annual Grammy Awards featured a skit in which music celebrities followed by Hillary Clinton jokingly "auditioned" to read the audio version of Wolff's book. Haley tweeted, "I have always loved the Grammys but to have artists read the *Fire and Fury* book killed it. Don't ruin great music with trash. Some of us love music without the politics thrown in it."[70]

Wolff's slander against Haley turned some media commentators, already ambivalent about the book, against him. The attention-seeking author seemed intent on proving right the president's endless charges of "fake news," and journalists warned that the book could undermine more serious reporting efforts to expose Trump's malfeasance. On January 29, a *New York Times* op-ed by Bari Weiss condemned "The Slut-Shaming of Nikki Haley" and called out media outlets for not moving earlier to reject "this gutter journalism as thinly veiled sexism."[71]

★ ★ ★

After months of speculation, on March 13, 2018, Trump finally fired Tillerson, by tweet. The new secretary of state would be Mike Pompeo, the CIA director and a former US Representative from Kansas. Pompeo was reported to have emerged as Trump's "most trusted foreign policy advisor." The president told reporters, "I'm really at a point where we're getting very close to having the cabinet, and other things, that I want."[72]

Three days later, Trump confirmed further speculation when he fired McMaster and named John Bolton as his third national security advisor in thirteen months. Bolton was a leading proponent of preventive war with North Korea and a critic of the Iran nuclear agreement, as a foreign policy commentator on Fox News. From 2005 to 2006, he had served as George W. Bush's hawkish UN ambassador, appointed during a congressional recess and pulled from the post when it became clear that he could not be confirmed over concerns about his treatment of staff—and possibly over his assertion in a 1994 speech that if the UN headquarters "lost ten stories, it wouldn't make a bit of difference."

Amid all these personnel changes, Haley's place in the administration's inner circle was called into question in a very public row involving yet another newcomer. Larry Kudlow was Trump's new senior economic advisor. He had been another TV commentator who praised Trump's policies, and he spoke to the media regularly. On April 16, just two weeks into the job, Kudlow told reporters at Mar-a-Lago, Trump's Florida residence, that Haley "got ahead of the curve" in announcing a new round of US sanctions against Russia the day before, for its role in supporting Assad's chemical weapons in Syria. The president apparently had changed his mind since Haley's announcement, which had been unambiguous.

Kudlow's remark cast Haley as out of the loop. "She's done a great job, she's a very effective ambassador," he said. "There might have been some momentary confusion about that." He added that new sanctions were "under consideration," but presently they were not being implemented.

Kudlow was not the only administration official who seemed to want to isolate Haley over her firm announcement of new Russia sanctions. White House Press Secretary Sarah Huckabee Sanders told reporters the administration was "considering additional sanctions on Russia" but that a decision had not been made. Separately, "two senior administration officials" told CNN that "the President had not signed off on the new sanctions by the time Haley made her comments on two news programs Sunday, and said Haley must have walked away from a Friday White House meeting about the sanctions having misunderstood how firm the plans were."[73] One anonymous official told the *Washington Post* that Haley had made "an error that needs to be mopped up."[74]

Who knew what the policy was? Did Pompeo and Bolton know? Did the president? The debacle certainly called into question whether Haley still spoke for the president. But it was a mark of this White House's chaotic policy process and Haley's own reputation, by now firmly established, that she managed to hold her ground even as she delivered one of the defining one-liners of her UN tenure.

Responding to Kudlow's "momentary confusion" comment, which had received wider attention than the more cutting, anonymous criticism, Haley send a statement to Fox News's Dana Perino, to be read on-air:

"With all due respect," Haley's message said, "I don't get confused."

Haley's remark was widely reported, and drew plaudits from different quarters. At the conservative *RedState* blog (which had often criticized Trump as a candidate) Grant Gambling wrote, "If this nonsense blows up into a media scandal President Trump could lose his most vital foreign policy asset at a crucial time. Haley is utterly critical and superbly effective. Is it worth blowing her up to preserve one man's pride?" Gambling urged readers to "just go watch the videos" of Haley at the UN Security Council, "where she's been sticking it to the Russians with poise, grace, and refinement." He concluded, "Haley is in possession of qualities this White House cannot afford to lose. Not least the unique in this administration ability to deliver crushing blows to Russia with little to no blowback from the Trump base."[75]

At the *Washington Post*, Aaron Blake called Haley's statement "an extraordinary rebuke of the White House," and saw the episode as emblematic of the administration's dysfunction. "Nikki Haley might as well have called the White House a bunch of liars," Blake said.[76]

Kudlow called Haley to apologize after her statement. He told the *New York Times*, "She was certainly not confused. I was wrong to say that—totally wrong. As it turns out, she was basically following what she thought was policy. The policy was changed and she wasn't told about it, so she was in a box."[77]

Haley may have weathered this storm well enough to maintain her independence, and she certainly got points for her mettle. But Kudlow's explanation ended the episode on an unsettled note, suggesting she might need to reassess her position in Trumpworld. If Haley was going to stand outside the inner circle, it would be on her terms.

5 ⋆ Hedging Bets

IN HALEY'S SOPHOMORE YEAR AS AMBASSADOR, HER POLICY influence may have been curtailed, but she remained adept, as ever, in showing her independence. In part, Haley's somewhat diminished profile in Trumpworld reflected a relatively more orderly foreign policy process within the administration after Rex Tillerson's departure. Even before his firing, Tillerson had been eclipsed by his eventual successor, CIA director Mike Pompeo. As Pompeo held Trump's confidence and sought to restore order and "swagger" to the State Department, Ambassador Haley faced a new need to coordinate with the secretary of state as much as with the White House.

Haley's hawkish and sometimes hectoring side was drawn out by the new foreign policy team, which also included John Bolton (who had once held her job) as the new national security advisor. Pompeo and Bolton were both well-versed in Washington ways and, seemingly, willing to tote whatever Trump baggage was necessary to advance a neoconservative agenda. Trump now had a foreign policy team that would have fit rather comfortably into the George W. Bush administration a dozen years earlier (indeed, one of them had). Haley seemed at home in it.

This was still an administration to be graded on a curve. The personal relationships may have improved, and the new personnel may have shared a more consistently hawkish ideology, especially regarding Iran. But President Trump himself seemed no more inclined to respect American foreign policy traditions or past presidential norms. Trump continued to jab at allies and trading partners, while reserving respect— even deference—for foreign autocrats. If anything, Trump's tendencies only intensified, reaching an apogee during a summer trip to Europe. As *The Economist* noted, "In Brussels he chided Germany for a gas deal that left it 'totally controlled by Russia.' In England he humiliated his host,

[British prime minister] Theresa May, blasting her Brexit plan before holding her hand and hailing 'the highest level of special' relationship. From his Scottish golf resort he called the European Union a 'foe' on trade. And in Helsinki, asked whether Russia had attacked America's democracy, he treated President Vladimir Putin as someone he trusts more than his own intelligence agencies." The British newspaper added, tartly, "It was a rotten result for America and the world."[1] But no matter how much the president's behavior alarmed and offended observers, no matter how many editorials in august newspapers decried his assault on American institutions and basic decency, Trump retained solid majority support among Republican voters and remained very popular with his base.

Around Ambassador Haley's one-year mark at the United Nations, observers who had earlier hailed her independence began to ascribe a different political calculus to her conduct. Above a January 2018 article by Abigail Tracy (who had twice previously written mostly flattering pieces about the ambassador), *Vanity Fair* put it this way: "After a successful start at the U.N., Haley appears to be trading diplomacy for a more valuable political prize: Donald Trump's base." Tracy said Haley had largely defied expectations to emerge as "an unlikely success story" throughout much of her first year in the job.

Richard Gowan, a UN scholar at Columbia University's School of International and Public Affairs, told Tracy, "When Haley came here, there was all this talk about how she was inexperienced, was going to be a gauche diplomat, she wouldn't be able to manage the Russians. Most of that turned out to be nonsense." But in describing Haley's more recent performance, Gowan said, "Weirdly, what we've seen—the hectoring, the public diplomacy, the lack of calculation—is actually more like what her critics were predicting a year ago. And it's not a good look."

As Tracy saw it, "After attaining a certain level of respectability, Haley rapidly migrated to Trump island—threatening to destroy North Korea, cutting off funds to countries that voted against the U.S. on Israel, and routinely condemning the Iran nuclear deal—a potentially dangerous place for those with future political ambitions." On the other hand, Tracy added, "If Trump, for whatever reason, doesn't run in 2020, his base will be the most valuable prize in Republican politics. . . . Going rogue may take you completely off the board—and moving toward Trump may be the only way to stay in the post-Trump game."

Republican strategist Jeff Roe, Senator Ted Cruz's 2016 campaign manager, put it this way: "She is becoming a rock star in national GOP circles. Agree with her policies or disagree, her optics, tone, and fortitude on the world stage [are] making her a hero to many."[2]

For her part, Haley insisted that she remained entirely focused on the job in front of her. And though she didn't say so in so many words, this meant she would have to retain a mercurial president's confidence. It just so happened that this meant endearing herself to Trump's supporters, which might serve her well politically in the future. There is no evidence that Haley at this point was plotting any immediate moves, but this didn't stop the media rumors. In April, a story circulated that Haley would join Vice President Mike Pence in a primary challenge to Trump in 2020, presumably not as a sitting cabinet member. Since 2017, *Politico* reported, the Democratic National Committee had been doing opposition research on Haley (along with Pence, Ohio governor John Kasich, and others supposedly planning 2020 presidential runs).[3] But this reported joining of forces with Pence was a new angle.

The story emerged in the long news cycle that followed Haley's "I don't get confused" response to Kudlow, with even the *New York Times* reporting, "Mr. Trump has grown suspicious of [Haley's] ambition, convinced that she had been angling for Mr. Tillerson's position and increasingly wondering whether she wants his own job. Republicans close to the White House whisper about the prospect of an alliance between Ms. Haley and Vice President Mike Pence, possibly to run as a ticket in 2020." Plunging deeper into speculation, the *Times* article continued, "Aides to both scoff at such suggestions, but the slightest hint of such a pairing would be likely to enrage Mr. Trump, who has made it clear that he plans to run for re-election."[4]

Adding to the intrigue was Pence's attempted hiring of Haley's top Washington deputy, Jon Lerner, as his national security advisor. Somehow, Lerner was going to continue to work with Haley while advising Pence "full time," according to the vice president's spokesperson.[5] Lerner, a former Republican pollster who managed Haley's 2010 gubernatorial campaign, had not previously specialized in foreign policy issues before following Haley's move to the United Nations. Trump was reportedly "furious" when he learned that Pence planned to hire Haley's deputy, White House sources told *Axios*, especially since the president considered Lerner disloyal for having crafted an anti-Trump ad during the 2016 primaries.[6] After Trump's anger was reported, Lerner withdrew from his advisory role to Pence and remained with Haley.

When a Reuters news agency reporter asked Ambassador Haley if the president should be worried about a Pence-Haley campaign, she said no. Asked about her relationship with Trump, Haley said, "It's perfect."[7]

★ ★ ★

Pompeo's own proximity to Trump became even clearer in April, when it was revealed that while still serving as CIA director, he had secretly traveled to North Korea to meet with Kim Jong Un. This meeting was to lay groundwork for a summit between Kim and Trump, who even had commemorative coins minted for the White House gift shop. After weeks of on-, off-, on-again buildup, the two leaders met in Singapore on June 12. Trump and Kim signed a joint statement committing to work toward "complete denuclearization of the Korean peninsula," along with fuzzier language about shared desires for "peace and prosperity" and building "a lasting and stable peace regime." The one concrete step called for by the communiqué was North Korea's return of US soldiers' remains from the Korean War, a welcome but modest confidence-building measure. Before the summit, North Korea had agreed to a moratorium on nuclear and missile testing (and blew up one nuclear test site, for show). The joint statement did nothing to formally buttress this restraint. Other notions, such as a US halt to joint military exercises with South Korea were discussed, with Trump reportedly accepting the North Korean formulation that these activities were "provocative." According to press reports, Trump even told Kim he would sign a declaration to end the Korean War soon after their meeting.[8] But nothing so dramatic was included in the Singapore joint statement.

In the history of failed nuclear diplomacy between North Korea and the United States, there had been much more robust agreements than this. But Trump said they had been negotiated by "very stupid" American leaders. He had established a "special bond" with Kim, "a very talented" and "very smart" leader who "loves his country very much." Trump told the American people that North Korea was "no longer a nuclear threat."

It was far from clear that the two sides had the same understanding of the term *denuclearization*. For more than two decades, US officials have used the term to mean a complete and verifiable dismantling of the North Korean capability to produce and deliver nuclear weapons, whereas North Korean officials have said it must mean something like global disarmament—which would include the withdrawal of America's nuclear umbrella over South Korea. The agreement did nothing to narrow this divide. Still, the summit was a dramatic shift from "fire and fury" and the rumors of war only months earlier.

These developments called for reappraising the sanctions regime that had been Ambassador Haley's biggest Security Council victory in 2017. Some analysts contended that the "maximum pressure" campaign worked, by giving Kim strong economic incentives to negotiate. In the lead-up to the summit, University of California, San Diego, political scientist Stephan Haggard suggested that after years of less-than-decisive multilateral sanctions against North Korea, China's willingness to significantly step up pressure on its trading partner might be making a real difference inside the opaque country. "The recent rounds of sanctions may work not through a slow squeeze," Haggard wrote, "but instead create a balance-of-payments crisis—and a loss of confidence in the informal markets that are keeping the [North Korean] economy afloat."[9]

On the other hand, for its propaganda value to the regime, the carrot of meeting with a US president may have been an even greater motivator than the stick of sanctions. For all of Trump's hot talk, his asking price for Singapore's symbolism was surprisingly low. And despite the UN sanctions and Haggard's prediction, a clear pattern of violations kept the North Korean economy afloat and preserved the regime's access to foreign goods.

In July, Pompeo abruptly canceled a planned visit to India to travel back to North Korea for a follow-up to the Singapore summit. As CNN reported, Trump sent Pompeo with a bag of gifts for Kim, including an Elton John CD (featuring "Rocket Man," of course). The joke was on Pompeo. The meeting was a failure, with North Korea issuing a statement rejecting the administration's "gangster-like demands" for denuclearization. Adam Mount of the Federation of American Scientists, whose mission is to reduce nuclear dangers, told CNN, "By now it's abundantly clear that this approach is a dead end. The White House has essentially tried to shoot for the moon and total disarmament, and it's clear that North Korea is not only not willing to do that, but sees very little reason to take steps in that direction."[10] Within weeks of the Singapore summit, the United States was complaining about illegal ship-to-ship oil transfers to North Korean vessels in international waters.

Ambassador Haley submitted a report to the Security Council of at least eighty-nine transfers already in 2018 (January through May), indicating that throughout the six months leading up to the summit,

China and Russia helped North Korea blow through its annual cap of five hundred thousand barrels as set in the December 2017 resolution. The analysis by Haley's team suggested that if North Korean vessels were filled to 90 percent capacity, they may have already delivered nearly three times the annual quota. Haley said the Security Council must "order an immediate halt to all transfers of refined petroleum products" to North Korea and must "call on all member states" to increase efforts to prevent smuggling.[11]

But China and Russia refused to support Haley's demand, made formally at the Security Council on July 19, citing insufficient evidence. The additional diplomatic weight of a visit by Pompeo to UN headquarters on July 20 did nothing to change this, but the optics of Pompeo's visit did signal the changed relationship between the State Department and Haley's New York office since Tillerson's departure.

Speaking to the media together, Pompeo and Haley offered a mix of accusations, exhortations, tough talk, and dogged optimism about denuclearization. The secretary spoke first. He thanked "Ambassador Haley and her excellent team" for "her leadership in advancing U.S. interests on North Korea and many other issues." Pompeo turned to face Haley, who stood at his side. "So thank you, Nikki," the secretary said, as the ambassador placed her hand on her heart. "Countries of the Security Council are united on the need for final, fully verified denuclearization of North Korea, as agreed to by Chairman Kim," Pompeo said. "Strict enforcement of sanctions is critical to our achieving this goal." He added, "President Trump remains upbeat about the prospects of denuclearization of North Korea. So do I, as progress is happening." He offered no specifics.

Haley then commended the Security Council (and by implication, her own team) for "the Herculean task" of putting the sanctions in place and asserted that the pressure campaign, along with Trump's outreach, had brought North Korea "to the table." Against the evidence that her own work had put forward, and in spite of the Chinese and Russian intransigence, she hailed a "very successful day, again promising that the Security Council has remained united" behind denuclearization.[12]

It was hard not to see that the US had been outmaneuvered. Besides the illicit oil transfers, there were reports that China was breaching UN sanctions by allowing entry to North Korean workers, under the guise of educational exchanges, and that Russia, too, was taking in North Korean laborers despite the ban.[13] The *Los Angeles Times* reported, "Those workers send home hard-cash wages that, combined with large slush funds likely from prior years of coal sales and clandestine trading networks built up across China and southeast Asia, allow Pyongyang to pursue its nuclear ambitions while keeping its political elite happy with fine liquor, designer watches and the latest electronics normally unobtainable at home."[14]

Haley issued a statement on August 3 complaining about Russia's actions. "Credible reports of Russia violating UN Security Council resolutions on North Korean laborers working abroad are deeply troubling," she said. "Talk is cheap—Russia cannot support sanctions with their words in the Security Council only to violate them with their actions." But with Russia and China signaling no intention to end the violations, it was Haley and Pompeo who risked looking like cheap talkers.

On August 24, Trump abruptly canceled a planned visit by Pompeo to Pyongyang, tweeting that he had made the decision "because I feel we are not making sufficient progress with respect to the denuclearization of the Korean Peninsula." The *Washington Post* later reported that the White House had received a "sufficiently belligerent" letter from a key North Korean official to warrant canceling the trip.[15] If Trump's tweet was a rare acknowledgement that his North Korea policy was not working, he also blamed China for North Korea's lack of cooperation—unfolding against the backdrop of his escalating tariff war with Beijing.

In an August 28 speech at the Foundation for Defense of Democracies in Washington, DC, where she received the organization's Jeane J. Kirkpatrick Award, Ambassador Haley still sought to put the leaky UN sanctions regime in a positive light. "The positive is that we have sanctions that basically cut off 90 percent of their trade, 30 percent of their oil, and we're holding tight on those sanctions," she said. "I mean, if you look at cutting off 90 percent of trade, 30 percent of oil, stopping their foreign laborers from working, stopping all foreign investment, literally all the money they use to build their intercontinental ballistic missiles is gone."[16]

Not only did Haley's statement seem untethered from reality, it was at odds with the administration's own assessments. A month earlier, a Defense Department official had told the *New York Times* that new intercontinental ballistic missiles were still being built at a facility near Pyongyang.[17] In congressional testimony, Pompeo had told US senators that North Korea continued to produce nuclear fuel.

Even so, Haley said that the current impasse was an improvement over the previous year's brinkmanship. "The good thing I can tell you is we haven't had to deal with ballistic missile testing in months," she said in her August 28 remarks. "So the positive is we're now talking. The positive is we're not dealing with ballistic missile tests."[18] The ambassador might have recalled her own earlier rhetoric and added that North Korea was no longer "begging for war."

But had it ever been begging for war? Kim's gamble—that the United States would rather negotiate than go to war—seemed to have paid off, elevating his own standing substantially while ceding little ground over its nuclear and missile programs. Kim had secured a historic summit with an American president, Trumpian praise for his "wise" leadership, and an apparent US willingness to negotiate on key pillars of its alliance with South Korea.

Back in 2017, Haley had spoken of the "Herculean task" of enacting successive sanctions rounds against North Korea. But was the better analogy to Hercules or to Sisyphus? Either way, it was President Trump's show, and Ambassador Haley had played her part.

★ ★ ★

On June 19, 2018, Ambassador Haley stood beside Secretary Pompeo, on his turf at the State Department, to announce the US withdrawal from the UN Human Rights Council. The forty-seven-nation body had been warned: a year earlier, Haley had called it a "forum for politics, hypocrisy, and evasion," and threatened US exit if the council did not expel human rights abusers and end its standing "Item 7" denunciations of Israel's treatment of Palestinians. Haley was particularly piqued over the January 2018 admission of the Democratic Republic of Congo, even as mass graves were being discovered there, and the council's inability or unwillingness to address human rights violations in Iran and Venezuela. She had repeated her reform demands and ultimatum in mid-June.

In making good on the US threat to leave, she called the council "a protector of human rights abusers and a cesspool of political bias." She sought to clarify that the decision did not signify a diminishment of human rights protection as a US policy goal, saying, "I want to make it crystal clear that this step is not a retreat from our human rights commitments. On the contrary. We take this step because our commitment does not allow us to remain a part of a hypocritical and self-serving organization that makes a mockery of human rights."[19]

There can be little argument that the UN Human Rights Council is a deeply flawed institution. The council (and its pre-2006 predecessor body the Human Rights Commission) long has been a bête noire of American conservatives, and the previous Republican administration of George W.

Bush refused to seek US membership. The Heritage Foundation's Bret Schaefer praised the announcement by Haley and Pompeo, calling the US withdrawal a "measured" response and asserting to the *Washington Post*, "The Trump administration seems to be the only government that seriously wanted the Human Rights Council to promote universal respect and protection of human rights and fundamental freedoms in a fair and equal manner."[20]

But others contend that the council is less flawed, at least, with the United States in it. The Obama administration had secured the three-year US term that Trump's team was cutting off midway, believing the council would be less hostile to Israel and more genuinely committed to safeguarding human rights if the US were at the table. On Israel, the results were measurable: the *Post* reported, "Before the United States joined, half the country-specific votes condemned Israel. During the first six years the United States was a member, resolutions critical of Israel dropped to one-fifth. U.S. membership also led to a sharp decrease in the number of special sessions that focused exclusively on Israel's treatment of the Palestinians." Even so, since 2006 the council has passed more than seventy resolutions criticizing Israel—ten times as many as for Iran—including five in one day in March 2018. Peter Yeo, a United Nations Foundation liaison to NGOs and private foundations, told the *Post*, "It's true, the Human Rights Council continues to disproportionately focus on Israel. But with U.S. leadership, the attention Israel brought has dropped significantly. U.S. leadership matters. We're still the only ones with credibility on human rights on the world stage."[21]

But the timing of Haley and Pompeo's announcement made it all too easy to accuse the US of hypocrisy. Only the day before, UN High Commissioner for Human Rights Zeid Ra'ad al Hussein had criticized the Trump policy of detentions and family separations at the US-Mexico border, saying, "The thought that any state would seek to deter parents by inflicting such abuse on children is unconscionable."[22] The UN Secretary-General, António Guterres, had also issued a statement that implicitly criticized the US policy by saying that "refugees and migrants should always be treated with respect and dignity, and in accordance with existing international law. Children must not be traumatized by being separated from their parents."[23]

After Haley and Pompeo announced the withdrawal from the Human Rights Council, other UN voices came out strongly against the US detentions policy. A group of eleven Special Rapporteurs and other experts appointed by the Human Rights Council itself said that the detention of migrant children, largely asylum-seekers from Guatemala, Honduras, and El Salvador, "severely hampers their development and in some cases, may amount to torture."[24]

The US withdrawal also revealed a wide gulf between Ambassador Haley the would-be human rights champion and leading human rights NGOs. In what the *New York Times* called "a scathing letter," the ambassador had criticized Amnesty International, Human Rights Watch and sixteen other organizations for, in her view, thwarting US efforts at reforming the council by refusing to support an American proposal to reopen its institutional framework in the UN General Assembly. Haley charged that the NGOs were, at least in part, responsible for the US exit. "You put yourself on the side of Russia and China, and opposite the United States, on a key human rights issue," she wrote. "You should know that your efforts to block negotiations and thwart reform were a contributing factor in the U.S. decision to withdraw from the council."[25]

State Department officials told the *Times* that Haley's rebuke of the NGOs had grown out of her "intense frustration that the groups banded together to oppose her efforts without talking to her first." But leading NGOs maintained that they had real concerns that an American charge to upend the council's structure could backfire in the General Assembly—essentially calling Haley naive. Human Rights Watch's UN director, Louis Charbonneau, told the *Times*, "The risk was that it would have opened a Pandora's box of even worse problems." In other words, Haley's proposed changes could have led to a raft of follow-on amendments from China, Russia, and others that would weaken the council.

The eighteen organizations responded to Haley's letter with one of their own, saying, "The decision to resign from the Council was that of the US administration alone. We had legitimate concerns that the US's proposal to reopen the Council's institutional framework at the General Assembly would do more harm than good." While acknowledging that the council was "not perfect," the organizations defended it, saying, "The Council and its mechanisms have played a key role in securing the freedom of detained human rights defenders. . . . It continues to address thematic issues of global concern including nondiscrimination, freedom of expression online and offline, freedom of assembly, housing, migration, counterterrorism, and the protection of the rights of women, rights of LGBTI people, and rights of people with disabilities."[26]

In a letter to the editor published by the *Chicago Tribune*, Brian

Houser of Crestwood, Illinois, offered an incisively plainspoken take on the US decision:

> Nikki Haley, the U.S. ambassador to the United Nations, has indicated that the reason for the withdrawal from the Human Rights Council was due to the inclusion among its membership of nations with known human rights abuses. I find the point is a solid framework for debate—should the U.N. Human Rights Council be totally inclusive to all nations or should it be vetted and only "qualified" nations granted a voice on the panel?
>
> However, I still find the decision to leave baffling. Please explain how the United States choosing to remove its own voice in the council's proceedings furthers this administration's goals of getting the offending parties out of it? It seems as if we simply eliminated ourselves from the conversation rather than effected the change we were seeking.
>
> This change, by the way, is one that Haley has had only a little over a year to work toward and [she] should never have expected an expeditious resolution. The pending result seems clear: Either the council will fold without U.S. support, leaving even more abusive regimes to freely practice their inhumanity, or the council will now feel much more free to examine our own country— and I have a bad feeling we are going to see some thing(s) in our reflection we don't like.[27]

The ink was not dry on this prediction when media attention turned to a UN report on extreme poverty in the United States, first published weeks earlier but now presented to the Human Rights Council in the same week that the American withdrawal was announced. Philip G. Alston, an Australian scholar at the New York University School of Law and UN Special Rapporteur on extreme poverty and human rights, had traveled across the US in late 2017—going to California, Alabama, Georgia, Puerto Rico, West Virginia, and Washington, DC—where he spoke with "many people who are homeless or living in deep poverty."

He previewed his analysis in a statement to the UN High Commissioner for Human Rights: "My visit coincides with a dramatic change of direction in U.S. policies relating to inequality and extreme poverty." Noting Republican-proposed tax cuts and threats to a social safety "already full of holes," he said, "The United States is one of the world's richest and most powerful and technologically innovative countries; but neither its wealth nor its power nor its technology is being harnessed to address the situation in which 40 million people continue to live in poverty."[28]

Alston's full twenty-page report did not mince words. He wrote, "The United States is a land of stark contrasts. . . . Its immense wealth and expertise stand in shocking contrast with the conditions in which vast numbers of its citizens live." Citing statistics on poverty and inequality in America, Alston continued, "Its citizens live shorter and sicker lives compared to those living in all other rich democracies, eradicable tropical diseases are increasingly prevalent, and it has the world's highest incarceration rate, one of the lowest levels of voter registrations among OECD countries and the highest obesity levels in the developed world."

Alston's criticism for Trump-era Republican economic policies was damning. "The new policies," the report said, "provide unprecedentedly high tax breaks and financial windfalls to the very wealthy and the largest corporations" and "pay for these partly by reducing welfare benefits for the poor," while making "no effort to tackle the structural racism that keeps a large percentage of non-Whites in poverty and near-poverty." Alston continued, "This situation bodes ill not only for the poor and middle class in America, but for society as a whole. . . . Defenders of the status quo point to the United States as the land of opportunity and the place where the American dream can come true because the poorest can aspire to the ranks of the richest. But today's reality is very different. The United States now has one of the lowest rates of intergenerational social mobility of any of the rich countries."[29] Alston cited extensive literature and statistics to support these claims. His report was more than an indictment of the Republican agenda under Trump: it lacerated the "land of opportunity" mythology that politicians of both parties routinely invoke and that Governor Nikki Haley had often invoked in South Carolina.

Vermont's US senator Bernie Sanders (Independent), the former and future presidential candidate, formally requested Ambassador Haley's comment on the UN's American poverty report. In her June 21 response, Haley said, "It is patently ridiculous for the United Nations to examine poverty in America. In our country, the President, Members of Congress, Governors, Mayors, and City Council members actively engage on poverty issues every day. Compare that to the many countries around the world, whose governments knowingly abuse human rights and cause pain and suffering." Haley said Alston had "categorically misstated" America's progress in reducing poverty, but she offered no data to rebut his analysis.

She said she was "deeply disappointed" that Alston had "used his platform to make misleading and politically motivated statements about American domestic policy issues," and that his report was "an all too common example of the misplaced priorities" of the UN.[30]

Haley elaborated on her criticisms in a July 9 essay for *National Review*. After opening with a sweeping dismissal of the "farcical notions" of a "single researcher," Haley turned briefly conciliatory: "Everyone knows there is poverty in America. Thousands of public officials at the federal, state, and local levels of government attempt to address poverty, as they should. Thousands more nonprofit, charitable, and religious organizations honorably dedicate themselves to fighting poverty in our country." As governor, she said, she "saw firsthand the struggles of poor communities that often lack the economic and educational opportunities enjoyed elsewhere in America," and she defended her gubernatorial record as one of bringing "a record-breaking number of new jobs to South Carolina, spanning each one of our state's 46 counties."

Haley ultimately returned to her role as UN ambassador, and to her uncompromising tone. "But as the United States ambassador my job is to help protect American interests and tax dollars at the U.N.," she said. "It is patently ridiculous for the U.N. to spend its scarce resources—more of which come from the United States than from any other country—studying poverty in the wealthiest country in the world, a country where the vast majority is not in poverty, and where public and private-sector social safety nets are firmly in place to help those who are." She went on to suggest that the UN might have chosen to study poverty in the Congo, Burundi, or Venezuela—citing dismal statistics for each—and asked, "When there are many dozens of countries where poverty consumes most of the population, and where corrupt governments deliberately make the problem much worse, why would the U.N. study poverty in America? The answer is politics." Haley concluded, "When the U.N. wastes American tax dollars, like it did on this unnecessary, politically biased, and factually wrong report, we're going to call it out for the foolishness that it is."[31]

Haley's polemic hadn't offered statistics to rebut Alston's report, but another official response did, by the Permanent Mission of the United States to the United Nations and Other International Organizations in Geneva, Switzerland. As the Human Rights Council is based in Geneva, the American mission there is the first point of contact for the US government. President Trump had not posted an ambassador to Geneva since the resignation of President Obama's envoy Keith Harper in January 2017, leaving the mission without leadership.[32] The *Washington Post*'s Jeff Stein mistakenly attributed a statistic in the Geneva statement, regarding the number of Americans living in "extreme poverty," to Haley. Alston's report cited 18.5 million Americans living in "extreme poverty," of which he said 5.3 million live in "Third World conditions of absolute poverty." The real figure of extremely poor, the Geneva office's statement argued (using an alternative consumption-based measurement) was "only approximately 250,000 persons."

Stein reported for the *Post* on June 25 that the figures cited in the Geneva Mission's response were produced by the Heritage Foundation, a conservative think tank. Independent poverty scholars contacted by the newspaper said that Alston's use of official US Census poverty definitions, which count income but not government spending on social assistance, may have led him to somewhat overstate the number of extremely poor. But scholars were far more critical of the grossly inaccurate Heritage figure, calling it "much too low" and "a total joke."[33]

Stein and colleague Tracy Jan penned a follow-up for the *Post* on July 14, in which Haley's June 21 denouncement of Alston's report as "misleading and politically motivated" was discussed in the same paragraph as the Geneva Mission's June 22 use of the 250,000 figure for the number of "extremely poor" Americans.[34] In a tweet about their story, Stein apparently conflated the two things, saying, "Last month, Nikki Haley said only 250K in US are in poverty" and "The White House is now declaring the War on Poverty 'over and largely a success,'" the latter as reported in the new article.

Ambassador Haley took to Twitter to say that her staff had demanded a retraction from Stein, and that he take down his tweet attributing the figure to her. She implied that Stein had agreed but then failed to do so. She personally reiterated the demand: "Unfortunate when a reporter doesn't follow through and I have to do this: @JStein_WaPo I never said this. My team has asked you to retract this and take down your tweets. I am now respectfully asking that you follow through with what you told my team you would do. Thank you."

Haley neither denied nor corrected the Geneva Mission's lowball poverty statistic; she simply went after a reporter for connecting her to it.

After Haley's pushback, Stein took down the offending tweet, saying, "I've deleted earlier tweets indicating that Nikki Haley, U.S. Ambassador to the U.N., had said only 250,000 Americans are in 'extreme poverty.'

The U.S. Permanent Mission to the United Nations and International Organizations in Geneva had said this."[35]

In conflating the Geneva mission statement with a similar statement by Haley, Stein may have simply made an honest mistake. Even so, many of Haley's Twitter followers saw a clear message in the exchange: the *Washington Post* was "fake news."

Haley herself had not used Trump's signature phrase. She didn't have to; her followers did it for her. Intentionally or not, Haley seemed to have "won" this minor dustup with a reporter. Not only was she able to claim that she "never said" something that was in the disorganized Geneva team's official statement, which Stein had reported to be a Heritage Foundation data point of dubious merit, but by forcing his correction, she helped further discredit establishment media for Trump supporters and right-wing outlets like the *Daily Caller*, which said she "shamed" the *Post* into correcting its "false reporting" about her.[36] Stein's tweeted error had never been in the newspaper, so in fact there was no "correction." As message coordination between Geneva and Haley's team in New York, it may have been slipshod, like so many policy processes in Trump administration. But as an exercise in Trumpian public relations, it worked perfectly.

While Haley took aim at the Alston poverty report in the wake of the US withdrawal from the Human Rights Council, the Trump administration's "zero tolerance" policy toward undocumented immigrants intensified. Haley could have avoided commenting on the detentions and family separations drama that dominated headlines, as the administration's policy did not directly engage her in any official capacity. But on June 5, 2018, a spokesperson for the Office of the United Nations High Commissioner for Human Rights, Ravina Shamdasani, said, "The use of immigration detention and family separation as a deterrent runs counter to human rights standards and principles. The child's best interest should always come first, including over migration management objectives or other administrative concerns."

Haley immediately hit back at this (fairly clinical) criticism with an impassioned press release, fully embracing Trump's border policy. "Once again, the United Nations shows its hypocrisy by calling out the United States while it ignores the reprehensible human rights records of several members of its own Human Rights Council," she said. "While the High Commissioner's office ignorantly attacks the United States with words, the United States leads the world with its actions, like providing more humanitarian assistance to global conflicts than any other nation. We will remain a generous country, but we are also a sovereign country, with laws that decide how best to control our borders and protect our people. Neither the United Nations nor anyone else will dictate how the United States upholds its borders."

Haley's human rights moralism in the face of the administration's detentions debacle drew charges of hypocrisy. Former Mexican president Vicente Fox tweeted, "Really? The U.S. is out of the UN Human Rights Council, in the middle of a humanitarian crisis at the border?"[37] Bethany Albertson, an associate professor of political science at the University of Texas at Austin, tweeted, "I remember saying that Nikki Haley might be the only one to make it out of this administration unscathed. I take that back." (Anjali Dayal of Fordham University replied, "I actually still think she might. . . . Haley projects the confidence of a GWB-era conservative and she is notably not white. It will be up to the press to get her on the hook for family separation, as she should be").[38]

To Stephen Schlesinger, an American scholar and former UN official, Haley seemed to be "going through one of the roughest patches in her public career"—and for more than her defense of Trump's immigration policy. "Her star, which was burning so brightly in the first year of the Trump administration, is beginning to dim significantly in the second year," Schlesinger wrote for CNN. All in all, he surmised, "upheavals in Washington have now left her as the odd woman out in Trump's foreign policy team." Referring to Pompeo and Bolton, Schlesinger predicted, "Neither man is likely to give Haley any further free rein at the United Nations."[39]

Conservative Clifford May offered a different perspective in the *Washington Times*, calling Haley "a woman for our times" and comparing her favorably to Reagan appointee Jeane Kirkpatrick, the first woman to hold Haley's post and the only other woman to serve in the position with cabinet rank in a Republican administration. "Mrs. Haley is, like Mrs. Kirkpatrick was, combative, authoritative, eloquent and elegant—a potent cocktail, one not often or easily mixed," May said. Like Kirkpatrick, Haley was showing herself to be "the nemesis of totalitarians" in standing up to North Korea, Iran, and Russia, and a friend of Israel in "confronting the relentless UN bias against the Jewish state." Haley, May said, was proving a similarly "staunch defender of human rights—which is why it was necessary to exit the UNHRC; to end America's participation in this Orwellian fiction; to stop facilitating the lie that the commission does good, or is even headed in that direction." May credited Trump with recognizing Haley's talent as "an individual with a distinctly American voice and a precise moral compass."[40]

What this comparison failed to recognize was that Kirkpatrick eventually came to believe that "relative isolation in a body like the United Nations *is* a sign of impotence," and that the United States risked isolation in ignoring the power of the UN to shape norms for the world about "what is legitimate and what is illegitimate."[41] For Haley, serving Trump, "standing alone" risked becoming an end in itself.

☆ ☆ ☆

The US detentions included persons of Indian and South Asian origin, some far from the Mexico border. In mid-June, *The Oregonian* reported that 52 of 123 "would-be asylum seekers" detained in a federal facility in the town of Sheridan were from India, including a number of Christians and Sikhs claiming persecution by the country's Hindu majority. The Hindi- and Punjabi-speaking Indians were the largest contingent in the Oregon facility, ahead of Central Americans and Mexicans, and they claimed to have been held incommunicado for weeks—until four Democrats from Oregon's congressional delegation arrived with translators. "This is a shameful hour in U.S. history," said US Rep. Earl Blumenauer. "I don't care what your stance on immigration is, no one should favor ripping children out of their parents' arms."[42]

A Sikh dimension to the detentions issue was not new. During the Obama presidency in 2014, more than forty Sikh men had waged a weeklong hunger strike at the El Paso Processing Center run by US Immigrations and Customs Enforcement (ICE). One of the men, twenty-six-year-old Gurbinder Singh, later told *Texas Monthly* that he'd been trafficked from Delhi through Amsterdam and Suriname before making his way through Central America and Mexico to Texas: "I barely even knew this was America when I crossed."[43] The episode joined a history of sporadic strikes by Sikhs and other South Asians in US detention facilities, in Texas and elsewhere, at least since the 1990s.[44] But there had never been an Indian American, let alone one of Sikh heritage, serving as UN ambassador—and it was a fair bet that Nikki Haley would be asked about the issue.

☆ ☆ ☆

In July, Haley embarked on a three-day trip to India—her first as UN ambassador. (She had visited India as governor in late 2014.) The visit was a somewhat unusual one for a UN ambassador, pitched almost as if Haley were surrogate secretary of state or US ambassador to India, not the UN. Haley's India visit took on additional interest when, while she was there, Pompeo suddenly canceled his own visit, scheduled for just over a week later.

This was the second time ministerial-level talks in a planned "2 + 2 dialogue" between the United States and India had been called off by one side. The novel format was intended to bring together the two countries' foreign ministers and defense ministers, but the protocol-sensitive Indian government had backed away from a planned April meeting after Tillerson's departure from the State Department, not wanting to diminish the status of the meeting by hosting Pompeo before his Senate confirmation.[45] Now Pompeo's cancellation set off hand-wringing in the Indian press about the state of the Indo-American partnership, and speculation over whether the Trump administration was taking the relationship for granted. It soon emerged that Pompeo was skipping India for another round of nuclear diplomacy in North Korea (the one that ended with its negotiators denouncing the US for its "gangster-like" demands).[46]

The most significant meetings on Haley's India itinerary were with Sushma Swaraj, the foreign minister, and with Prime Minister Narendra Modi, nearly four years after their first meeting in New York in 2014 (just moments before the Indian leader gave a triumphal post-election speech to a largely Indian American audience at a packed Madison Square Garden). Haley and Modi met at the prime minister's New Delhi residence to discuss a range of subjects in US-India relations and on the Trump administration's foreign policy agenda. Prime ministers ordinarily do not meet with UN ambassadors, and the meeting underscored both Haley's unusually high profile and the surrogacy of her visit for Pompeo. The Trump administration may have reasoned that Haley's star power would charm her Indian hosts, even in the absence of any major advance in US-India relations. As one of the most high-profile Indian Americans globally, Haley was covered like a film star in the Indian press.

Indian leaders were more circumspect on a key policy issue in their country's relations with Iran. While emphasizing much common ground on counterterrorism, military cooperation, trade, and other issues, Ambassador Haley also called for India to cut all imports of Iranian oil. The push followed the Trump administration's May withdrawal from the Joint Comprehensive Plan of Action, the 2015 agreement between Iran and six world powers (including China but not India), aimed at checking

Iran's nuclear capabilities in exchange for the lifting of some sanctions against the country. The issue had been a sore point between the United States and India ahead of Haley's visit; just a month earlier, Swaraj had come out of a meeting with her Iranian counterpart pledging to maintain trade despite American threats, and saying that India would comply only with UN sanctions on Iran, not unilateral US ones.[47] The US was insisting that it would make no exceptions to financial penalties for countries doing business with Iran, even for friends like India.

Haley was firm. "Sanctions are coming [on Iran] and we're going forward on that, and with India and the U.S. building strong relationships we hoped that they would lessen their dependence on Iran," she told reporters after her meeting with Modi. "There's a will, a political will, from both sides to figure out how to make this work. Prime Minister Modi very much understands where we are with Iran, he didn't question it, he didn't criticize it, he understood it and he also understands that [India's] relationship with the U.S. is strong and important and needs to stay that way."[48] In an interview with an Indian TV channel, Haley said, "I think for the future of India, future of resources, we would encourage them to rethink their relationship with Iran. All of us have to rethink who we do business with. . . . I had that conversation with PM Modi. It was a constructive conversation."[49]

What Haley didn't say was if Modi had actually accepted the US request. He hadn't.

Indian oil minister Dharmendra Pradhan told reporters in Mumbai that India would "go by its interests" in deciding on its oil import policy.[50] Trump would have understood, no doubt.

Ambassador Haley also spent time in India meeting with human rights activists and religious leaders from Christian, Hindu, Jain, Muslim, and Sikh communities, including an "interfaith tour" in bustling Old Delhi. She visited historical and religious sites, posing for photographs wearing a *salwar kameez*, head covered, and posting selfies with Indian students on Twitter.

In one strange and rather sad sign of the times, Reuters posted and quickly deleted a picture of Ambassador Haley at a Hindu temple showing a swastika in the background. The news agency explained on Twitter, "Reuters has removed an earlier photo of U.N. Ambassador Nikki Haley with a swastika seen behind her at a Hindu temple in Delhi. The swastika is an ancient religious symbol for Hindus and Buddhists. It was also used as a symbol by Nazi Germany."

It was unclear why the photo was taken down—whether by editorial decision, reader complaint, or request from Haley's people—but the move disappointed some Indian commentators. A blogger for *Samudra* (Sanskrit for "gathering together of waters") wrote that Reuters had "failed as journalists" to educate their readers as to the meaning behind the dharmic symbol and "to its use in India and South Asia as a symbol of auspiciousness, blessing, and hope dating back to the earliest recorded settlements there."[51] Another commentator said that Reuters had been more concerned with "the sensibilities of its Western readers" than in using the lens of local cultural context.[52] If the Reuters decision was taken so as not to encourage white supremacist associations with a member of the Trump administration, these reactions suggested that it also erased an ancient Indian symbol and thus inadvertently reinforced the Nazi appropriation and inversion of it. The small episode seemed to encapsulate something about great expectations that Nikki Haley could somehow bridge cultural divisions—and disappointment that she did not fully do so.

Ambassador Haley was pressed in India about the fifty-two Indians, mostly Sikhs, in federal detention in Oregon. Manjinder Singh Sirsa, a member of the Delhi Legislative Assembly from the Bharatiya Janata Party and general secretary of the Delhi Sikh Gurdwara Management Committee, interacted with Haley and US Ambassador to India Kenneth Juster during their visit to the Gurdwara Sis Ganj Sahib in Old Delhi. Using the honorific "Ji" after her Twitter handle and name, Sirsa tweeted his hope vested in Ambassador Haley: "We are humbled to have @nikki haley Ji and @USAmbIndia paying obeisance at Gurdwara Sis Ganj Sahab. We requested Nikki Ji to address the problem of 52 Indians detained in Oregon Jail. @nikkihaley Ji immediately took note and discussed it with @USAmbIndia to resolve the issue."[53] In December 2018, the Sheridan detainees indeed were released, but only after a lawsuit was filed by the American Civil Liberties Union.[54]

Haley capped off her visit to India with an invitation-only special address at the Observer Research Foundation (ORF), a leading policy and international affairs think tank, cosponsored by the US Embassy in New Delhi. She themed her talk "Advancing India-U.S. Partnership" and assured the well-heeled audience that the bilateral relationship remained strong, Pompeo's canceled visit notwithstanding. She promised that the "2 + 2" format would move forward "soon" to address military cooperation and American support for India "as a provider of regional security, especially in and around the Indian Ocean." She also underscored the tough US line on Iran.

Some of Ambassador Haley's remarks were ritual diplomacy that could have been offered by almost any US official on a visit to India since the early 2000s, when the two countries embarked on the strategic partnership (not quite an alliance) that has defined their post–Cold War relations. But Haley also struck deeply personal notes that underscored her unique position in American diplomacy. "My parents met at a hill station near Dharamsala," she told the audience. "Fifty years ago, they came to America with eight dollars in their pockets. They came to a southern town in America. It wasn't always easy for them."

Echoing themes from her 2012 memoir and from interviews over the years, she continued,

> They stood out in rural South Carolina in the early 1970s. My father wore a turban—he still does. My mother wore a sari. I was born in the small town of Bamberg. We were the only Indian family in town, which put us in a kind of no-man's land. No one quite knew what to make of us. We were different.
>
> Over time, that small community came to accept—and then embrace—us. Our differences didn't disappear. But as our neighbours got to know us, the focus was no longer on differences but on our similarities. But my story is not unusual. Everywhere I go I meet Indian Americans who are amazing people. They have given so much of themselves to their new country. And they have brought so much of the customs and teachings of India with them. And that has served them well.
>
> Indian Americans are the most highly educated and the most philanthropic of any minority group in the United States. And it's no mystery why we've been so successful in America. There's a kind of magic in America. Generations of immigrants, from every corner of the world, have found opportunity and success in America, since before the United States was even a country. But Indians seem to be particularly receptive to the idea of America.

The ambassador then recalled her last visit to India, as governor, in 2014:

> I had the honor of visiting the Golden Temple in Amritsar. It was a very special experience for me. My mother was born in

the shadow of the Golden Temple. She gave up family, friends, and a life of privilege to come to America. When I was a little girl, I could never have dreamed that I would be a governor and an ambassador. But my mom did. And so did my dad. They gave me the blessings of my Indian heritage and my life in America. I've worked to make the most of these gifts—and to pass them along to others.[55]

It was powerful stuff, and vintage Nikki Haley. But her hosts were not about to let her off so easily. After her speech, ORF president Samir Saran pressed the ambassador on the Trump administration's policies on trade, the Iran nuclear agreement, human rights, and other issues. He said that some in India had begun to openly question the direction of US-India relations, amid much uncertainty about American intentions. He asked Haley about the administration's commitment to human rights, noting the ambassador's personal passion in visiting refugee camps in Jordan and Turkey and her engagement on human rights issues during her stint as president of the Security Council.

Noting the US withdrawal from the Human Rights Council and the Trump administration's immigration and family separation policies, Saran said that for Indians following the news out of America, "There is a general assessment that something is going on vis-a-vis the immigration issue in the United States, parents and children being separated, and there is an impression that perhaps the U.S. is not staying the course on key questions around rights and other liberties that you have defended in the past."[56]

Haley affirmed the US commitment to human rights, and reasserted that the Human Rights Council was "a farce." She avoided the family separations issue, even as she argued the position she had taken as governor: "The one thing about America, and what I have always loved, is [that] America is a country of immigrants. It's the fabric of America, to have multiple cultures, multiple populations, multiple heritages that do come into America that make it what it is. But we believe in the rule of law. And we believe in legal immigration. My parents came to America. They put in the time. They put in the price. They went there legally. We can't start to have illegal immigration come in at harsh levels, especially now, during this time, when terrorism is starting to be more—we're starting to see it more predominantly around."

Haley seemed to stumble lexically in front of the Indian audience in her move from immigration to terrorism. She quickly concluded, "So all you're seeing the United States do at this point is find a way to make sure we know exactly who is coming into our country and that we are properly able to secure the people in the United States by knowing who is coming into the country."

Saran listened impassively during this response. But he brightened with his final question for Haley: "When are we going to see a woman of Indian origin, Republican, run for high office?"

Haley smiled. "So what I can tell you is, a woman, of Indian origin, is trying to survive this job that she has now," she said. "And that's enough for me."

☆ ☆ ☆

Haley spoke often to American audiences in 2018. The ambassador's reception at the University of Houston on May 22 was tense. In a video posted to YouTube, as Haley began to speak, a young man in the audience shouted, "Nikki Haley, the blood is on your hands! You continue to sign off on the genocide of a native people! You are an accomplice to terrorists and colonizers!" At this, a group of students chanted, "Nikki Nikki can't you see? You are on a killing spree!" and "Nikki Haley you can't hide, you signed off on genocide!" They held up Palestinian flags and chanted, "Nikki Nikki you will see, Palestine will be free!"[57] As Ambassador Haley waited at the podium, police removed the protestors, later identified by the *Daily Cougar* as UH students.

Resuming, Haley said Americans were "digging in" on polarized viewpoints. "We increasingly view those who disagree with us not just as wrong, but as evil," she said. "I have seen true evil. And it's not in the American political system."

Ambassador Haley's campus appearances were promoted as major events. At UH, president Renu Khator called Haley "one of the most remarkable figures in American politics today" in the announcement for Haley's speech (which the university live-streamed, disruption and all). At Duke University in April, political scientist Peter Feaver called Haley "a forthright and compelling articulator of America's role." Tickets for the public lecture at Duke, "Confronting Today's Global Governance Challenges," were free but limited, and all were claimed within hours of release. Posters for Haley's Duke appearance clung to lampposts nearby in Durham and even in Chapel Hill, at the University of North Carolina.

Next to flyers for shows at local music venues, there was Nikki Haley: the ambassador as rock star.

At the Christians United for Israel annual summit in Washington, DC, in July, Haley was introduced by Texan megachurch pastor John Hagee, who said, "Few people in the history of American public diplomacy can be compared to the woman whose last 18 months have been spent fearlessly confronting the unreasonable and immoral anti-Israel bias at the United Nations." The pastor presented Haley with an extravagant golden bowl, roughly the size of a satellite TV dish, bearing an inscription of a torch set against the text of Isaiah 62:1, "For Zion's sake, I will not keep silent, and for Jerusalem's sake, I will not remain quiet, till her righteousness shines down like the dawn, and her salvation like a blazing torch."

In her remarks to the group, Ambassador Haley said, "Israel needs friends. We live in a world in which anti-Semitism is on the rise. In some parts of the world, Jewish communities are enduring hate speech, harassment, vandalism and physical violence." She added, "Even here at home, there are some troubling signs." But Haley did not mention Charlottesville, where young white men had shouted, "Jews will not replace us!" She did not note the recent desecration of Jewish cemeteries in upstate New York and western Illinois with Nazi-inspired graffiti. Rather, Haley's example of anti-Semitism in America was the Boycott, Disinvestment and Sanctions movement targeting Israel, "a trendy cause for students and professors who should know better," and which she had opposed since her days as governor.

After recounting her pro-Israel stands at the United Nations, Haley turned to her personal motivations for supporting the Jewish state:

> I often get asked how I came to this place and to this worldview. I just believe what I believe. I have always been a person of deep faith.
>
> No, I am not Jewish—even though that surprises some people. I was not raised as a Christian either. Twenty years ago, my faith journey brought me to Christianity, where I have found strength in my faith and trust in my heart.
>
> But I'm also a person who is humble in her faith. I don't claim to have the wisdom to know what God has in store for me or for other people. What I do know is that God has blessed America with greatness and with goodness. And I know that in the dan-

gerous world we live in, it is absolutely critical for America to stand up and have the backs of our friends, and to stand strong against those who would do us harm.

If the United Nations spent its time relentlessly and unfairly attacking Japan, or Australia, or the United Kingdom, I would stand up for them too. I would do that because they are America's friends and it's the right thing to do.[58]

Nikki Haley could still surprise. The day after the Christians United for Israel meeting, she addressed the High School Leadership Summit, organized by the conservative group Turning Point USA and held at George Washington University. On the group's website, Haley received top billing among the speakers for the 2018 conference, in a roster that included Attorney General Jeff Sessions, Secretary of Education Betsy DeVos, Senator Orrin Hatch of Utah, and the president's son, Donald Trump Jr.

Ambassador Haley asked the approximately seven hundred conservative high schoolers, "Raise your hand if you've ever posted anything online to quote-unquote 'own the libs'" (to mock or provoke liberals). According to *The Hill*, "The vast majority raised their hands in response, and then erupted into spontaneous applause."

Haley continued, "I know that it's fun and that it can feel good, but step back and think about what you're accomplishing when you do this—are you persuading anyone? Who are you persuading? We've all been guilty of it at some point or another, but this kind of speech isn't leadership—it's the exact opposite. Real leadership is about persuasion, it's about movement, it's bringing people around to your point of view. Not by shouting them down, but by showing them how it is in their best interest to see things the way you do."[59]

Right-wing *Breitbart* said Haley had "scolded" the students with a "mixed message," since she also offered remarks that "confirmed the hypocritical double standards that lead to discrimination against young conservatives."[60] By contrast, the *Washington Post*'s Aaron Blake observed, "Haley, if she *is* interested in climbing the ranks, seems to be betting on a more genteel and pragmatic version of conservatism while the [Republican] party in recent years has demonstrated it desires anything but. Trump's entire election was basically a middle finger to political moderation—both in policy and rhetoric."

Blake added, "It does seem to be working for Haley, though—at least for now."[61]

★ ★ ★

In September, the *New York Times* published an unusual op-ed by an unnamed "senior official in the Trump administration" under the headline, "I Am Part of the Resistance inside the Trump Administration." The author said they supported parts of Trump's agenda, citing "effective deregulation, historic tax reform, a more robust military and more." But the author said they and many other senior officials in Trump's administration were "working diligently from within to frustrate parts of his agenda and his worst inclinations"—and that Trump did not "fully grasp" this internal resistance. "It may be cold comfort in this chaotic era, but Americans should know that there are adults in the room. We fully recognize what is happening," the mystery mandarin said. "And we are trying to do what's right even when Donald Trump won't."

One example of policy steering by senior administration officials, against Trump's impulses, stood out for its seeming specificity: "On Russia, for instance, the president was reluctant to expel so many of Mr. Putin's spies as punishment for the poisoning of a former Russian spy in Britain [in March 2018]. He complained for weeks about senior staff members letting him get boxed into further confrontation with Russia, and he expressed frustration that the United States continued to impose sanctions on the country for its malign behavior. But his national security team knew better—such actions had to be taken, to hold Moscow accountable."[62]

This certainly sounded like the confused policy process that led to Haley's public disagreement with Kudlow in April. Was the author someone who had been directly involved in that policy? As speculation commenced regarding the identity of the writer, it was perhaps inevitable that Nikki Haley would be brought up as a possibility. CNN's Chris Cillizza included the ambassador on a list of thirteen possible authors, which also included figures as senior as Vice President Mike Pence and White House Chief of Staff John Kelly.[63] John McCormack of the *Weekly Standard* hosted an "unscientific" Twitter poll asking who the official was, and with 233 votes cast, Haley was the winner of his four-candidate field at 32 percent, edging out Kelly (28 percent), Ivanka Trump (24 percent), and defense secretary James Mattis (16 percent).

Senior Trump administration officials lined up to deny authorship in the soberest of tones. They also sought to mollify the furious president, who called the writer "gutless" and demanded an investigation. Haley's initial denial was a simple "no," when a CNN reporter called out to ask if she was the author.

But as speculation continued, she went further than others to distance herself from the anonymous op-ed, penning a signed op-ed in the *Washington Post* with the headline, "When I Challenge the President, I Do It Directly. My Anonymous Colleague Should Have, Too." Haley began, "We have enough issues to deal with in the world, so it's unfortunate to have to take time to write this." She then offered a sharp rebuke of the *Times* piece. "The author might think he or she is doing a service to the country. I strongly disagree." The author, she said, had done a "serious disservice" to Trump and the country.

"I, too, am a senior Trump administration official," Haley continued. "I proudly serve in this administration, and I enthusiastically support most of its decisions and the direction it is taking the country. But I don't agree with the president on everything. When there is disagreement, there is a right way and a wrong way to address it. I pick up the phone and call him or meet with him in person."

Noting her cabinet and National Security Council positions, Haley said she had "very open access to the president" and could "talk to him most any time." He listens, she said, and "does not demand that everyone agrees with him." When she felt strongly enough about a disagreement, she said, she could raise it with the president. "Sometimes he changes course, sometimes he doesn't," she said. Haley contrasted this approach—"the way the system should work"—with the anonymous author's "very dangerous" and "extra-constitutional" handling of internal policy disagreements.

The ambassador concluded with advice for the anonymous author: "Step up and help the administration do great things for the country. If you disagree with some policies, make your case directly to the president. If that doesn't work, and you are truly bothered by the direction of the administration, then resign on principle. There is no shame in that. But do not stay in your position and secretly undermine the president and the rest of our team. It is cowardly, it is anti-democratic, and it is a disservice to our country."[64] (The author, who later expanded his criticism into a 2019 book, *A Warning*, revealed himself in 2020 as Miles Taylor, a former official in the Department of Homeland Security.)

Was Haley's op-ed a principled defense of transparency and

presidential authority, or a transparent exercise in self-promotion? Writing for *New York* magazine, Democratic strategist Ed Kilgore said Haley's counter-column had shown "how to exploit a crisis." Quoting the ambassador's "step up or resign" advice, Kilgore said, "This was a pitch-perfect and well-timed gambit by Haley. She managed to suck up to Trump even in the act of declaring her independence from him. She positioned herself as both unshakably faithful to the boss, and as having enough clout to tell the president to his face when he is wrong, showing loyalty but earning respect. And most of all, she offered a repudiation of the impression of an administration in chaos that Anonymous asserted and Trump reinforced by his over-the-top—even for him—reaction." Kilgore concluded, "She is an opportunist of the highest order, and I mean that as a compliment. If there is a betting pool on her prospects for the 2024 national ticket, count me in."[65]

At the conservative *American Spectator*, Joseph Duggan was blisteringly critical of Haley's op-ed. Duggan, who served as public affairs officer to President Ronald Reagan's arms control advisor General Edward Rowny, in a self-described "lowlier position" on the staff of ambassador to the UN Jeane Kirkpatrick, and later as a speechwriter to President George H. W. Bush, said that during the Reagan administration, "if a cabinet member wanted the prestige of an op-ed publication in the *Washington Post*, *New York Times*, or other major newspaper, he [*sic*] needed explicit approval from the White House for the text and the placement." The same principle applied to national television interviews, Duggan said (which only underscored how much had changed, given Haley's copious TV appearances).

Duggan expressed skepticism that Haley had consulted the White House. "Did [Press Secretary] Sarah Sanders, John Kelly, Mike Pompeo, and President Trump agree to the drafting and placement of the Haley article?" he wondered. "Did they really decide to give Nikki Haley the unique privilege of publication of a self-serving article in the *Post*, a privilege denied to all other administration officials? Or were the president and his top advisors blindsided by Haley?"

"Jeane Kirkpatrick would not have been allowed to publish a piece as sensitive as Haley's without personal approval from President Reagan and Secretary of State Shultz. Going rogue in such a fashion very well could have made her lose her job," Duggan said. But he wasn't just critical of Ambassador Haley's moxie. Turning to the content of the op-ed, he said, "It's an unpalatable chore to have to re-read Haley's 'Song of Myself.' But

I urge everyone to re-read it closely. It is a textbook example of how an extravagantly ambitious, insubordinate presidential appointee navigates The Swamp."

Given his pedigree from past Republican presidencies, readers who assumed Duggan was just another "never Trump" holdover might have been surprised at where he went next. "Many of us who voted for Trump did so in large part because of his promises to change American foreign policy from the sad state it had slumped into under Obama and the younger Bush," he said. "We have much to regret about Nikki Haley, with her abundance of ambition and utter lack of foreign affairs knowledge and experience, having a seat in the Cabinet and the National Security Council. Everyone with the president's best interests at heart should wish she had never been appointed."

Duggan offered an anecdote about Kirkpatrick, from a biography by Peter Collier. At the annual Gridiron Dinner in 1983, the ambassador sat at the head table with Reagan's deputy chief of staff Mike Deaver, who told her the president "always listens when you speak. He looks at you and his eyes light up. Maybe it's because you're a woman."

Kirkpatrick responded, "Maybe it's because he's interested in foreign policy."

Duggan said he never expected to meet Nikki Haley, but if he did, "I would give her this deflating information: 'Ambassador, I knew Jeane Kirkpatrick. And you're no Jeane Kirkpatrick.'"[66] He might have taken the opportunity to also question President Trump's commitment to truly transforming American foreign policy, or his competence to do so.

★ ★ ★

On September 25, 2018, Trump spoke at the UN General Assembly during the kickoff for its seventy-third session. His tone was notably less combative than in his "Rocket Man" speech a year earlier. But about a minute into his speech, Trump boasted about his accomplishments, saying his administration had achieved in less than two years more than "almost any administration" in American history. In live video feeds of Trump's remarks, a general reaction can be heard to spread across the previously silent room, described by the *Washington Post*'s David Nakamura as "audible guffaws in the cavernous chamber hall" and as laughter— seemingly at Trump's expense.[67] Trump waited while the laughter dissipated. "Didn't expect that reaction," he said, "but that's okay."

At a press conference the next evening, Trump said that reports that he had been mocked by foreign dignitaries were "Fake News." He said, "They weren't laughing at me; they were laughing with me. We had fun."

Ambassador Haley carried the same message in a morning appearance on *Fox & Friends.* "When he said that, they love how honest he is," she said. "It's not diplomatic, and they find it funny. I mean, when he goes and he is very truthful, they kind of were taken aback by it. Whether he said good things about him or not, they love that he's honest with them," she added. "And they've never seen anything like it, so there's a respect there. I saw that the media was trying to make it something disrespectful; that's not what it was. They love to be with him."

Two weeks later, the ambassador was with the president for an Oval Office press conference. Together, they announced her resignation.

6 ⋆ Citizen Haley

IT ENDED AS IT HAD BEGUN—ON NIKKI HALEY'S TERMS. THE ambassador sat side-by-side with the president in the Oval Office on October 9, 2018, to announce she was stepping down at the end of the year. "It was a blessing to go into the UN with body armor every day and defend America," Ambassador Haley told reporters. "I'll never truly step aside from fighting for our country. But I will tell you that I think it's time."

White House staff were "caught off guard by the announcement," the *New York Times* reported. According to the newspaper, President Trump said Haley "had informed him roughly six months ago that she wanted to take a break by the time his administration reached its second anniversary." The president said he hoped Ms. Haley would return in a different role.[1] "She's done a fantastic job, and we've done a fantastic job together," Trump said, standing with the ambassador. "We're all happy for you in one way, but we hate to lose you," he told Haley.

Haley made a point of signaling that she was leaving on good terms with others in the administration, particularly Trump family members. Ivanka Trump and Jared Kushner, the president's daughter and son-in-law and multipurpose advisors, had just hosted Haley and husband Michael for dinner in New York to mark her coming departure. "Jared is such a hidden genius that no one understands," Ambassador Haley said. "And Ivanka has been just a great friend, and they do a lot of things behind the scenes that I wish more people knew about, because we're a better country because they're in this administration."

Then there was Haley's relationship with the president. Sources close to the ambassador told the *Times* she "wanted to make her decision known before the midterms to avoid the potential for an embarrassing departure if the vote were to go against the president." Responding to speculation that she might be considering a presidential run herself, Haley said she had no intention of running, and that she would be out campaigning for "this one"—pointing at Trump—in 2020. Haley said that it had been the "honor of a lifetime" and a "blessing" to serve in the United Nations and as governor of South Carolina. "You know, I said I am such a lucky girl to have been able to lead the state that raised me and to serve a country I love so much."

Haley did not have to be pressed into disavowing 2020 intentions. Her released letter of resignation, dated October 3, even told the president:

> I expect to continue to speak out from time to time on important public policy matters, but I will surely not be a candidate for any office in 2020. As a private citizen, I look forward to supporting your re-election as President, and supporting the policies that will continue to move our great country toward even greater heights.[2]

"People familiar with her thinking," the *Times* reported, expected that for the time being she was "likely to work in the private sector and make some money." Her latest financial disclosure, the newspaper reported, showed "at least $1.5 million in debts, including a mortgage of more than $1 million"[3]—though a spokeswoman said the family's debt was "well below $500,000."[4]

★ ★ ★

But I will tell you that I think it's time. Haley's official candor often followed a variation on this phrase: *I will tell you that . . . , What I can tell you is . . . ,* or *What I will tell you is . . .* In its suggestion of honesty, there was also a hint of some discretion deployed, of something held back. By now, the Trump administration had seen many cabinet and senior staff departures, but most had been rumored for weeks or even months beforehand. Given the suddenness of this announcement, there was naturally speculation as to the "real reason" for Haley's departure, even if her nearly two-year tenure was not much shorter than the average: less than two-and-a-half years for all UN ambassadors since 1946.[5]

There had to be something more, didn't there? Was she getting out before a negative news story could undermine her position? Just the day before, the watchdog group Citizens for Responsibility and Ethics in Washington had asked the State Department to investigate whether Ambassador Haley had broken regulations by accepting seven flights between New York and South Carolina on private jets, along with her husband Michael, paid for by three business executives from the state in the previous year.[6] Had Haley underreported their value? (As governor, Haley similarly had been accused by state Democrats of ethics violations in the use of state-owned vehicles and aircraft for campaign travel and non-official events.)

Did her resignation have anything to do with the October 2, 2018, disappearance of Jamal Khashoggi, a Saudi journalist and contributor to the *Washington Post*, from the Saudi consulate in Istanbul? It was suspected that Khashoggi, in self-imposed exile as a critic of Saudi policies, had been murdered. Through Jared Kushner, the Trump administration had forged close ties with Saudi Crown Prince Mohammed bin Salman, who, speculation had it, was behind Khashoggi's disappearance and presumed death. Was Haley's resignation "triggered over the administration's tepid response to the disappearance and possible murder" of Khashoggi? The *Washington Post*'s opinion writer Jennifer Rubin, a conservative and Trump critic, wondered.[7]

CNN's Stephen Collinson said, "A more relevant question, politically at least, is why not now"? Haley, he said, "may have timed her exit perfectly," noting her high public approval and widely assumed ambitions for future office. He suggested, "She could cash in on her chance to make some serious money. And as odd as it might seem for a top politician, her stated reason—that she just wants a rest from public service after years as South Carolina's governor before her UN service—could actually be true."[8]

★ ★ ★

At American outlets, foreign policy analysts (mostly white men) wasted no time weighing in on Haley's legacies at the United Nations and in the Trump presidency. Duke University's Peter Feaver, who had hosted Haley for her public talk the previous April, wrote in *Foreign Policy*, "She was by far President Donald Trump's most effective spokesperson on national security and foreign-policy issues. She seemed sure-footed where her bosses—the president, the vice president, and the secretary of state—all seemed less comfortable or even uninterested in fulfilling the basic executive function of explaining U.S. actions to a thoughtful public."

"It is true that her public profile is lower now than it was in the spring, let alone in 2017, when Trump took office," Feaver said. But this was primarily because Pompeo was "much more effective at public diplomacy" than Tillerson had been. He added, "Her role today is roughly akin to the role enjoyed by other higher-profile U.N. ambassadors," citing Obama's representatives Susan Rice and Samantha Power, Clinton's ambassador Madeleine Albright, and George W. Bush's recess-appointed John Bolton (the only recent Republican on the list) as having had similar visibility.[9]

The same day, *Vox* offered separate commentaries by Zack Beauchamp and Alex Ward.

To the former, "Haley played the White House game—and won." Beauchamp said, "Whatever one thinks of Haley's job performance substantively, there's no doubt that it was brilliant politically. She's significantly improving her chances to be president down the line. The reasons appear to stem from both her ability to manage Trump personally and the issues she chose to focus on, particularly the Middle East. Haley, perhaps more than any other person in politics today, acted like she understands the real ideological fault lines in modern America—and figured out how to manipulate them to her advantage."

What were those fault lines? Beauchamp didn't say, exactly, though he said Haley had clearly mastered the art of straddling current Republican Party divisions. Beauchamp said Haley, as former governor of South Carolina, "appears to have a deep understanding of conservative movement politics—and, as a result, knew exactly what buttons to push to make herself into a heroine for the right."[10]

To Ward, Haley was a "paradox" in her ability to serve essentially as a standard Republican foreign policy hawk in the highly unorthodox Trump presidency. Ward gathered assessments from UN scholars. David Bosco said, "I think she's been as close to a traditional Republican UN ambassador as you can have in a very untraditional Republican administration." Richard Gowan, who previously had been critical of Haley, said, "Haley has to go down as a pretty effective representative of the US at the UN. . . . I think she will be missed." An anonymous source "familiar with her private discussions" at the UN said Haley's more "Trumpian moments" were generally shrugged off, because diplomats "generally thought she treated them well off camera."[11]

Daniel Drezner, a Tufts University professor and contributor to the *Washington Post*, said Haley "had two traits that made her unusual within the Trump foreign policy team. The first was that she was a professional politician. This meant she was able to send messages to key constituencies, pleasing the Trump White House at times and other groups at other junctures." But, Drezner said, "Haley's true gift, however, was to pick the right fight at the right time within this administration"—recalling her

"With all due respect, I do not get confused" and Larry Kudlow's apology in the flap over Russia sanctions. "In the end, that is the primary takeaway from Haley's departure," Drezner said. "She was adequate at the United Nations post at a time when so few Trump national security officials demonstrated adequacy. . . . Nikki Haley served in the Trump administration and departed with most of her dignity intact. That, in and of itself, is what makes her extraordinary."[12]

The Nation's national affairs correspondent John Nichols would have none of this. The ambassador, he said, left a legacy of "providing cover for the president's most extreme and dangerous pronouncements and policies." He concluded, "There is very little evidence to suggest that Haley served Trump as an 'adult in the room.' She was an ally, an apologist, and an acolyte of a man she once recognized as irresponsible. That's not how able diplomats operate, and Nikki Haley will never be confused with an able diplomat. But that is how politicians operate, and Nikki Haley will always be understood as a self-serving and self-promoting politician."[13]

Zak Cheney-Rice, writing for *New York's* "Intelligencer" column, mainly ignored Haley's UN record to reflect on her significance as an Indian American and leading GOP voice. The former governor, he said, "has come to symbolize the Republican Party's doomed flirtation with racial inclusiveness" in favor of "full-throated white identity politics instead." He recalled the party's post-2012 *Growth and Opportunity Project* and suggested, "Haley's journey mirrors the path of a conservative movement that gave itself good advice but chose to ignore it." Cheney-Rice even suggested that Haley's call to remove the Confederate flag after Charleston had not aged well. "In retrospect, this moment granted the GOP a thin sheen of plausible deniability," he said.

"In the end," Cheney-Rice said, "the coming wave would swallow both Haley and her party whole. . . . She saw her party's fortunes changing and cast her lot accordingly."[14]

★ ★ ★

Haley was the featured speaker at the Seventy-Third Annual Alfred E. Smith Memorial Foundation Dinner in New York, ten days after her Oval Office announcement with Trump. The dinner, a white-tie fundraising event for Catholic charities supporting the neediest children in the city's archdiocese "regardless of race, creed, or color," dates to 1945, the same year the United Nations was founded in San Francisco.

The Al Smith dinner, traditionally the last stage shared by Democratic and Republican presidential candidates before the November election, is a ritual of corny jokes, PG-rated roasts, and occasional truth-telling. Hillary Clinton and Donald Trump exchanged uncharacteristically (for Trump) mild unpleasantries at the 2016 dinner. House Speaker Paul Ryan told jokes about Trump in 2017, six months before the former Romney running mate announced his retirement from Congress.

Now Ambassador Haley's own recent resignation announcement had cast the 2018 dinner in a new light. Comedian Jim Gaffigan, master of ceremonies, introduced Nikki Haley as "the next president of the United States."

Her remarks were gracious in an in-on-the-joke way, with a few sharp (but not too sharp) edges. She said Trump had given her some advice as she prepared for the event. "He said if I get stuck for laughs, just brag about his accomplishments," she said. "It really killed at the UN, I got to tell you." She used her heritage to poke fun at a leading Democrat. "When the president found out that I was Indian American, he asked if I was from the same tribe as Elizabeth Warren," she said, referring to the senator from Massachusetts (who Trump repeatedly called "Pocahontas" to mock the white future presidential candidate's past claim of an American Indian ancestor).

Turning serious for a moment, Haley said:

> In our toxic political life, I've heard some people in both parties describe their opponents as enemies or evil. In America, our political opponents are not evil. In South Sudan, where rape is routinely used as a weapon of war, that is evil. In Syria, where the dictator uses chemical weapons to murder innocent children, that is evil. In North Korea, where American student Otto Warmbier was tortured to death, that was evil. In the last two years, I've seen true evil. We have some serious political differences here at home. But our opponents are not evil, they're just our opponents.[15]

★ ★ ★

But evil visited an American house of worship again on October 27. Shouting angrily about Jews, a forty-six-year-old white man carried an assault rifle and several handguns into the Tree of Life Congregation synagogue in Pittsburgh. He killed eleven and injured seven in one of the deadliest attacks ever against American Jews. The massacre came at an especially charged political moment, just ahead of the 2018 midterm elections. The suspect, who did not have a prior criminal record, expressed anger at what he saw as Trump's weakness. But Trump critics said the president was partly to blame for the violence, given his seeming encouragement of white nationalists and other far-right elements. Some, including family members of victims, called for the president to stay away from Pittsburgh as the community mourned.

If Ambassador Haley's resignation announcement had given her any sense of being at liberty to criticize Trump, she showed no inclination to do so now—and seemed to believe that there were no reasonable grounds for it. She tweeted on October 29, "I have struggled w/ what happened in Pitts bc it's so similar to what happened in Chas. The country was very racially divided @ the time. We didn't once blame Pres. Obama. We focused solely on the lives lost & their families. Have some respect for these families & stop the blame."

Ambassador Haley's Pittsburgh tweet may have been meant to encourage respect for grieving families, just as she had sought to keep the focus on the Emanuel Nine after the Charleston tragedy. But *Esquire* politics editor Jack Holmes saw "bullshit false equivalence" in Ambassador Haley's message. He said, "Maybe no one linked President Obama to the Charleston attack, in which a white supremacist walked into a black church and shot nine black congregants to death, because Obama did not advocate white supremacy or violence"—suggesting Trump had done both. "In fact, the people who talk about the 'racial division' during Obama's tenure never actually point to things he said or actions he took that contributed to that division—except, of course, his decision to continue Presidenting While Black."[16]

For Republicans eager to unify the party under someone other than Donald Trump, Nikki Haley looked more eligible than ever. Bill Kristol, editor-in-chief of the *Weekly Standard*, sought to draft Haley into a 2020 primary challenge to Trump. The struggling neoconservative magazine's final print issue, on December 24, 2018, would feature a cartoon Ambassador Haley on the cover with the headline, "Not the Retiring Type." Other efforts to draft Haley into political service merely seemed like wishful thinking. *National Review*'s John Fund thought Haley would be a great US House speaker in the event of a post-midterm deadlock, noting an arcane provision that "the Constitution allows the body to select a non-member to serve as speaker and run the place."[17] There were even some calls for Trump to "dump Mike Pence" and bring Haley in as vice presidential running mate for 2020.[18]

★ ★ ★

The remaining two months of Haley's ambassadorship saw a few noteworthy developments on foreign policy issues she'd been involved in, though no grand moments of closure. The State Department announced six-month waivers for eight countries importing oil from Iran, exempting them from US sanctions and easing pressure on Tehran. North Korea threatened to restart its nuclear program unless the US lifted sanctions. It refrained from testing missiles. There was talk of a second Kim-Trump summit, possibly in Vietnam.

In late November, Russia seized three Ukrainian vessels off the coast of Crimea—the most significant escalation of tensions between Russia and Ukraine since Trump's presidency began—and Ambassador Haley condemned it at an emergency Security Council meeting, speaking in strong terms that recalled her most demonstrative performances of 2017. *The Atlantic*'s Krishnadev Calamur said Haley, once again, had been ahead of the State Department and White House in responding—and wondered who would stand up to Russia after she was gone.[19]

On Israel-Palestine, Haley tried for a General Assembly resolution condemning the Islamic militant group Hamas for violence against Israel. The *New York Times* said Haley "positioned the measure as a capstone of her tenure" at the UN. Kuwait led a group of Arab states in a procedural maneuver that required a two-thirds majority for the measure to pass. It received 87 votes in favor and 58 against, with 32 abstentions. The measure failed, and Hamas claimed "a great victory" in this "slap in the face" to the United States and Israel. Ambassador Haley was prepared for the outcome. The morning before the vote, she said, "Today could be a historic day at the United Nations or it could be just another ordinary day."[20]

Loose ends are in the nature of diplomacy. Nikki Haley left quite a few, and it may be some time before her legacy at the United Nations can be fully appraised. In years to come, historians of international relations may judge the Trump administration harshly (and more so than the flawed UN) for its own blithe hypocrisies, its disparagement of international institutions, and its plain ineptitude. Haley, who so faithfully and consistently represented her president's policies, may rise above the overall assessments in the particulars of her tenure, or she may not.

On Russia, at least, she truly distinguished herself ("with all due respect") as an acolyte of Kirkpatrick, Reagan, and Thatcher. Russia may be seen both as a bloody stain on Trump's presidency (especially given Putin's support for Assad in Syria, and his war in Ukraine) and as something of a red herring, despite the Mueller Report's conclusions that Russia interfered in the 2016 US election in "sweeping and systemic fashion" and that President Trump sought to cover up the investigation into that interference.[21]

Much to her credit, Ambassador Haley never gave ground on Russia's interference in the American electoral process or on its other frontal challenges to US interests in Europe and the Middle East. On Syria, Haley may be remembered as the administration's leading voice for an emphatic US response to chemical weapons use—upholding, in the moment, a wobbly international norm. But this exerted no larger or lasting effect on Assad's brutal war.

The North Korean and Iranian nuclear dilemmas may come to be seen as something like mirror images, in which the administration's unprecedented credulity and unyielding hostility were with the wrong countries. In the North Korean case, it seemed like Trump's personal quixotic impulse to give credence to Kim's vague commitments, whereas the wider administration and congressional Republicans all basically shared the president's hostility toward the Iranian regime and the Iran nuclear deal. On North Korea, Ambassador Haley was exceptionally effective in bringing together unanimous Security Council votes behind tough sanctions (even if these were quickly breached in practice).

A month after Haley's departure, US intelligence chiefs testified at the annual congressional hearing on global security threats. Director of National Intelligence Dan Coats said that North Korea was "unlikely to completely give up its nuclear weapons and productions capabilities," which he said its leaders consider "critical to the regime's survival." Iran, on the other hand, was in technical compliance with the Joint Comprehensive Plan of Action. But CIA director Gina Haspel said that Iran's leaders were considering walking away from the nuclear deal without the economic benefits they were supposed to reap after the lifting of international sanctions.

The Trump administration was obsessed with North Korea and Iran. It invested significant diplomatic efforts in defending Israel at the United Nations. Meanwhile the fundamental threats to national security, US intelligence officials said, concerned China and Russia—working separately and in parallel to challenge American global leadership, achieve certain technological and military advantages, and undermine democratic governments around the world.[22]

As she sat with President Trump in the Oval Office, Ambassador Haley defended the administration's foreign policy record. "Now the United States is respected," she said. "Countries may not like what we do, but they respect what we do. They know that if we say we're going to do something, we follow it through. I can tell you that the U.S. is strong again. And the U.S. is strong in a way that should make all Americans proud."

International polls measuring overall approval of the United States and confidence in its leaders—not exactly "respect," but surely related—belied the claim. A Gallup poll across 134 countries and areas found that median approval of US leadership plunged from 48 percent in 2016 to 30 percent in 2017—a record low.[23] The poll's previous low of 34 percent occurred in 2008, at the end of the George W. Bush presidency and amid the unfolding US-led global financial crisis. A Pew Research survey across twenty-five countries, released shortly before Ambassador Haley's resignation announcement, found that 27 percent of respondents said they had confidence in Trump, while 70 percent had no confidence. During the final years of the Obama administration, 64 percent expressed confidence in the president, and 23 percent, no confidence. Some of the steepest Trump-era declines were among US allies and trading partners.

In late December 2018, Haley met with a group of mostly American journalists. According to *Bloomberg*, she told reporters she wasn't sure the US should even remain a United Nations member. "The American people need to decide if it's worth it," she said. There was a lot of abuse and waste in the organization, she said, and it was often "politically unfair" to the US and its allies. But she said the UN could be useful as a "vehicle" for imposing sanctions on a country like North Korea over its nuclear program, or an arms embargo on South Sudan. "There are rays of light," she said. "But the verdict is still out."[24]

Haley's December 2018 exit interviews included liberal-internationalist *The Atlantic* and right-leaning *Weekly Standard*, the flagship (soon to be grounded) of American neoconservative thought. Both offered wide-ranging reflections on her ambassadorship. *The Atlantic* was especially interested in Ambassador Haley's parting thoughts for multilateralism. "The one thing I learned at the UN is that countries resent America," she said, tacitly acknowledging the problem before pivoting to preferred themes. "It's a tough place. But they want us to lead. And we have to always lead on our values and our freedoms and what we believe is right. I think those freedoms are every person's God-given right. It doesn't cost us anything to fight for democracy, to fight for human rights, and to fight for the dignity of people. . . . We have to understand the leverage we have: that when we call out a country or we call out a wrong, everyone takes notice."[25] Writer Uri Friedman asked if Mitt Romney had been prescient in 2012 to warn that Russia was "America's No. 1 geopolitical foe." Haley said that Russia and China "both equally are concerns and both equally need a lot of attention" as geopolitical foes of the US.

The *Weekly Standard*'s farewell profile seemed more interested in the inner workings of the Trump administration and what they might mean for the Republican Party and for conservatives opposed to Trump. "Haley insists that her goals at the U.N. and the president's were the same," writer Michael Warren said. "But what's notable from our interview is how rarely she mentions Trump. As she tells it, she is the active agent—bringing ideas and proposals *to* the president." Haley told Warren the threat to withhold aid from countries that voted against the US was her idea: "A little over a year ago, I went to the president, I gave him a binder and I said, 'I want you to look at this.' And it listed every country, the number of times they voted with us or against us, and how much money in aid we give to them. And he was shocked, furious, but determined to do something about it."

The *Weekly Standard* interview also asked Haley about "her popularity with women at a time when the GOP's standing with that group of voters couldn't be much worse." The ambassador said,

> Young girls and women come up and say something, and it's humbling but I get it . . . because women balance so much and they try so hard to be great at everything, and it's not so much as they look up to me, but I think they see one of them doing it, too. . . .
>
> We're doing the best we can and we know that there is someone out there looking at us as we do it, and we don't want to disappoint. I don't think women have more challenges. . . . I've never thought that. I think our challenges can be different, but I don't think we have more challenges.
>
> The frustrations are literally what every other woman goes through. Balancing your marriage and your kids and your finances and your work and wanting to really make people proud. Making sure your parents are okay. Loving the job you do and wanting to be great at it.[26]

Was Haley a feminist, Michael Warren wondered? If so, he concluded, "she's unquestionably a conservative one."

In South Carolina, Andy Shain summed up Haley's legacy in a "Palmetto Politics" piece for Charleston's *Post and Courier*. "Since 2010," he said, "the Bamberg native has been an active international political figure as South Carolina's governor and the United States' ambassador to the United Nations, building a cult following for her leadership, accomplishments, and relatable personality." Now that Haley was disappearing from "mandatory public view," he said, she might find time to "sleep in and binge watch TV," as she had suggested in a recent interview, but her "every interview, every statement, every photo op, every decision from now on will be calculated on running for the White House." Shain recalled repeatedly how during her rise in South Carolina, Haley had denied ambition for higher office.

Shain credited Haley with "escaping cleanly" from the Trump administration; the column's headline predicted, "The cult of Nikki Haley will grow after she leaves the UN."[27] When she renamed and archived @Amb NikkiHaley, the Twitter account in which—despite government watchdog warnings—she had mixed personal and official business, it had nearly 1.7 million followers.[28]

Back in New York, Laura Kirkpatrick waited until January, after Ambassador Haley's departure, to offer *PassBlue*'s assessment of "her legacy at the UN." Haley, she said, left the job "as much an enigma as the day she arrived." Kirkpatrick quoted an anonymous former cabinet-level Trump administration official who said Haley "got up to speed on almost every issue immediately" and was "an incredibly hard worker." There were times at the National Security Council, the former administration official said, when "she was a stronger voice than anybody" and had her facts right.[29]

She also noted Ambassador Haley's "outspoken" responses to human rights violations. But she was selective in her criticisms, focusing on states such as Venezuela, Iran, and the Democratic Republic of the Congo, but not the Philippines or Egypt. She "did not stand up for women's rights while at the UN in a noticeable way—a glaring lack of commitment to a cause dear to millions of women in the US and abroad, especially amid the MeToo movement."

Haley, Laura Kirkpatrick said, was also partisan: she reportedly "removed Democrats' names from a list of former personnel of the US mission to the UN, to not invite them to events and parties." The reporter tried to get a comment on this measure from the press office at the US mission. It said it couldn't give a statement: the US government was partially shut down, over President Trump's demands on congressional Democrats for $5 billion to build his southern border wall.

★ ★ ★

After leaving the UN, Haley said she would be staying in New York for a period, while her son Nalin finished high school. She and her husband Michael sold their Lexington, South Carolina, home, the *Post and Courier* reported. In late January, not quite a month after her departure, CNBC reported that Haley had signed with the Washington Speakers Bureau and was "quoting $200,000 and the use of a private jet for domestic speaking engagements," according to seven anonymous sources. "Haley's lucrative fee," CNBC said, "propels her into a league populated by U.S. presidents, former Federal Reserve Chairman Ben Bernanke, former first lady Michelle Obama and former Secretary of State Hillary Clinton."[30]

Haley rejoined the South Carolina educational charity she founded in 2011, the Original Six Foundation, as chair.[31] She toured South Carolina schools, including one in Bamberg. She also joined the board at Boeing, the American multinational aerospace company. Haley was governor when Boeing announced a $1 billion expansion in North Charleston that included economic incentives worth $120 million from the state. She also opposed efforts to unionize workers at the North Charleston plant, saying unions weren't needed in South Carolina. As Haley joined Boeing's board, the company was facing public-relations fiascos, first with the fatal crashes of two passenger 737 Max planes in separate overseas incidents, after which the aircraft type was grounded over concerns about its flight control systems, and separately, over whistleblower accounts of shoddy assembly work on the 787 Dreamliner in North Charleston.[32] "Every company has its ups and downs," Haley told the *Post and Courier* from an elementary school in Bamberg. "I think that Boeing needs to take this seriously and be as transparent as they possibly can."[33]

In Grand Rapids, Michigan, in May 2019, Haley told an economic club that socialism threatened the United States, echoing a favorite Trump theme. "Capitalism is the greatest force for ending poverty and lifting up human beings in history," Haley said. "America's dangerous flirtation with socialism is in colleges, in the media and in Congress. We have an obligation to remind everyone that if you care about global poverty, you should support capitalism."[34] In June, Haley visited Iowa to stump for Senator

Joni Ernst's reelection. At Ernst's annual Roast and Ride at the Central Iowa Expo grounds in Boone, Haley said she felt sorry for Iowans, what with a parade of twenty-three Democrats coming to the state to campaign for the 2020 presidential election.

"It's a really odd collection of liberals, radicals, and socialists and I know a lot about liberals, radicals, and socialists," Haley told the Iowa crowd. "In case you forgot, I used to work at the United Nations."[35]

★ ★ ★

In the fall of 2019, Haley managed to sometimes break into a news season dominated by the Democratic-led impeachment inquiry into President Trump's alleged withholding of military assistance from Ukraine in its ongoing conflict with Russia as a means of pressuring its newly elected president, Volodymyr Zelensky, to pursue investigations into Joe Biden, the former vice president campaigning for the 2020 presidential election, and his son Hunter.

In October, Nikki and Michael Haley bought a $2.4 million, 5,774-square-foot home on resort-oriented Kiawah Island, the *Post and Courier* reported, "sparking rumors that her return to South Carolina signals a return to politics and a potential bid for the presidency in 2024."[36] According to the property's Zillow listing, the paper reported, it features a pool and "Mediterranean architectural elements with an outdoor kitchen, a garden and several terraces that look out onto the river." The Kiawah River lies south and west of Charleston, where, as Marjory Wentworth's 2014 poem for Haley's second inaugural said, all the rivers become "One River," and history is "One Boat."

That same month, Haley was honored at an annual dinner of the American Enterprise Institute, the conservative think tank in Washington, DC. AEI gave the former ambassador its Irving Kristol Award, named for the late neoconservative thinker and awarded for "notable intellectual or practical contributions to improved public policy and social welfare." Haley's remarks at AEI suggested a path for reconciliation among conservatives, if not for the country.

"President Trump is a disruptor," she said. "That makes some people very happy, and it makes some people very mad. But if we are a country that lives by the rule of law, we must accept that we have one president at a time, and that president attained his office by the choice of the American people."[37] To support Trump, for now, was to support the Constitution for all time. This line of reasoning had the considerable additional attraction of pointing out that so long as the rule of law prevailed—and why wouldn't it?—there would be another election for president in just over a year, and another in 2024.

Haley's second memoir since 2012, *With All Due Respect: Defending America with Grit and Grace*, was published in November 2019. The book picked up with the former governor's abbreviated second term, and focused mainly on her UN ambassadorship. In one widely reported passage, Haley slammed Rex Tillerson and Trump's second chief of staff, former US Marines general John Kelly, for attempting to recruit her to "save the country" by helping them undermine the president. This "bombshell" led the book's coverage by CNN, Fox News, *The Guardian*, *The Independent*, the *Times of Israel*, the *New York Times*, NPR, the *Washington Post*, and many others. The president, Haley said Kelly and Tillerson said, didn't know what he was doing. Tillerson, she said, even went so far as to say gravely that "he resisted the president's decisions"—she didn't say if he said which ones—"because, if he didn't, people would *die*."[38]

President Trump tweeted on November 10, "Make sure you order your copy today, or stop by one of her book tour stops to get a copy and say hello. Good luck Nikki!"

The next day, CBS News' *Sunday Morning* featured Haley for a sit-down interview, which turned quickly to her former cabinet colleagues. "They should have been saying that to the president, not asking me to join them on their sidebar plan. It should have been, go tell the president what your differences are, and quit if you don't like what he's doing. But to undermine a president is really a very dangerous thing. And it goes against the Constitution, and it goes against what the American people want, and it was offensive."[39]

When interviewer Norah O'Donnell asked Haley whether President Trump would be impeached and ultimately removed from office, Haley was incredulous. "No. On what?" she said. "You're gonna impeach a president for asking for a favor that didn't happen and—and giving money, and it wasn't withheld. I don't know what you would impeach him on."[40] Haley said impeachment was "like the death penalty for a public official," and said the American people should render their verdict on Trump in the upcoming election.

Writing for *The Atlantic*, David Frum, a former speechwriter for President George W. Bush and a frequent critic of President Donald Trump, said Haley's book and her promotion of it represented an "audacious bet" and "a gamble that the future of the Republican Party looks a lot like Trump."[41] At the *New Yorker*, economic journalist and staff writer John Cassidy offered a more cynical take on the same theme. "Haley, who is often mentioned as a possible Presidential candidate for 2024, is a prime example of a Republican who is supporting Trump for opportunistic reasons," he wrote. "For Haley, helping Trump is helping herself."[42]

At the *Washington Post*, conservative columnist Henry Olsen said, "Haley's short stint as U.N. ambassador made her a national Republican heroine." He remarked, "Haley artfully used her position to make people notice her." The book release, he said, showed "the Haley marketing machine in action." Haley was signaling to Republicans that she "is capable of steering an independent course without stabbing Trump in the back, a quality that would help her build the next version of the party without alienating Trump's die-hard base." But Olsen said "the Republican world is changing fast" and "Haley's recent forays" didn't really clarify where she stood on key intra-party debates "about the role of government power in domestic affairs and the limitations of government power in foreign affairs." He pointed to Marco Rubio as someone who was positioning to "reform capitalism so that business more effectively serves U.S. workers and the national interest"; he noted Senator Josh Hawley's (R-Missouri) similar themes.

Olsen said, "Haley's choice to play it safe makes sense for now," since her position as a former administration official made her "more constrained in differing from Trump."[43] Still, Haley eventually would "have to chart her own path," and "if that path is simply a recitation of the pre-Trump GOP consensus, she'll likely find her star fading while her more adventurous competitors rise." As noted in this book's opening chapter, *New York Times* columnist David Brooks, another in-house conservative at an establishment newspaper, has made much the same argument: the GOP's future may be Rubio redux, or Hawley, not Haley.

But will it? Trump's 2016 campaign was bereft of policy ideas to "reform capitalism"—Get Mexico to pay for the wall! Get China to pay for tariffs!—but long on nostalgia and big on attitude. Isn't it at least as plausible that Nikki Haley's callbacks to pre-Trumpian conservatism, combined with her Trump administration credentials and her solid blocking game for the president, could keep her on the field? Maybe the nostalgic fantasy is to expect that the GOP's hope in the near term would rest on a renaissance of supposed policy intellectuals—Young(ish) Men, mostly white, with Big Ideas.

Nikki Haley's vision may seem more vague, but she may be seeing something that others don't, or don't want to see. Rewatching Rubio's GOP State of the Union response from 2013, then Haley's from 2016, which of these pre-Trump "rising stars" has held up better under pressure and over time?

★ ★ ★

In December 2019, Haley was a guest on conservative-libertarian commentator Glenn Beck's video podcast for BlazeTV. Beck promoted her appearance heavily across his social media platforms. Beck, who gained his widest audience a decade earlier (sometimes spinning elaborate conspiracy theories about President Obama and billionaire philanthropist George Soros) had opposed Trump's 2016 candidacy, but now strongly supported his reelection. Throughout the hour-long interview, Glenn Beck seemed enraptured with Nikki Haley.

With a fatherly mien far removed from his formerly wild-eyed persona, Beck cold-started the episode in his unadorned studio, speaking into a hanging microphone and looking into the camera. "Everybody is shaped by their family, their upbringings, their life experiences," he said. "Some of us go through more hardships than others," he continued, adjusting his reading glasses. "But true leaders are the ones who can take that adversity in stride and use it as propellent"—he drew his hands in, as if summoning—"something that pushes them to a higher stratosphere. And if they do it right, they do it with humility." He recounted how his next guest had "witnessed firsthand the racist attitudes of others, directed toward her and her Indian immigrant parents." He told the Bamberg "beauty pageant" story. He mentioned South Carolina's experiences with tragedy and "the slaughter on the streets" and the taking down of the Confederate flag.[44]

"She's one of the only females in a male dominated arena, she's never quit fighting for her integrity, her principles, and for the American people," Beck continued, in a rendition likely to see many reprises and variations. He introduced Nikki Haley as former South Carolina governor and former US ambassador, and said, "perhaps someday she will be known as the first female president." The introduction was recorded separately from the sit-down interview, so after the cut (and Beck's quick pitch for an electric toothbrush), Haley was suddenly on set, across a roundtable from Beck, and no need to demur following his grand prediction for her future.

The full interview has since drawn over seventy-five thousand views on YouTube—not exactly network numbers, but in the media ecosphere of President Trump's base, it was event TV. Shorter snippets were widely shared on social media, particularly a clip picked up by NBC News and other mainstream outlets, in which Haley talked about how the Mother Emanuel mass shooting in 2015 led to South Carolina's decision to take down the Confederate flag. Compared to her contemporaneous statements as governor about the Emmanuel Nine murders and (eventually) the Confederate flag, Haley's rendition of this history for Beck's audience was more elliptical.

"Here is this guy that comes out with this manifesto, holding the Confederate flag. And [he] had just hijacked everything that people thought of—we don't have hateful people in South Carolina. It's a small minority; it's always going to be there. People saw it as service, and sacrifice, and heritage." The "it" seemed to refer to the Confederate flag; the former governor didn't say who "people" were, or acknowledge that Black and white South Carolinians had expressed sharply polarized views on flying the flag before the murders. "But once he did that, there was no way to overcome it," she said. She still didn't say Dylann Roof's name. This time, she didn't name his "hateful" motives as those of a white supremacist.

Critics in the media saw Haley's comments as a regression, as if she were walking back her 2015 position, when she called unequivocally for the flag's removal.[45] Haley's comments about many South Carolinians seeing the flag as "heritage" weren't really any different from things she had said before. But they came close on the heels of her defense of President Trump while on her book tour circuit, and it seemed like something had shifted, at least in the mainstream media's orientation to her. Was Haley's audition for their favor now over?

While Haley still made niche news from the sidelines, 2019's big bequest to 2020 was the COVID-19 global pandemic, caused by a novel coronavirus originating in Wuhan, China. President Trump had never enjoyed majority approval in national polls, but he reached a peak 49 percent approval in January 2020,[46] when US stock market averages were at record highs and unemployment at fifty-year lows, even as many working Americans experienced low wages and lacked health care, and even as the virus was silently spreading from Asia and Europe to the United States.

The Trump administration announced restrictions on flights from China in January, but otherwise stumbled in its early response to the pandemic, with the president blaming Beijing and the World Health Organization for failing to prevent the spread and downplaying the danger even as community transmission already had begun in hot spots on the West and East Coasts of the United States. Trump's approval rebounded momentarily in May amid daily presidential briefings on the pandemic response, but his messaging became increasingly erratic. State governors diverged on extending stay-at-home orders or "reopening" the economy, as US unemployment now hit levels not seen since the Great Depression. By early summer, the US led the world in COVID-19 cases. State and local health officials sought to persuade Americans to wear cloth face coverings and maintain "social distancing" so as to flatten the rising curve that charted new infections, and to avoid overwhelming hospitals.

President Trump's approval numbers fell as Democratic challenger Joe Biden took solid leads in national polling and in key swing states won by Trump in 2016. Biden had struggled through the Democratic primaries to fend off progressive challengers Sen. Elizabeth Warren and, especially, Sen. Bernie Sanders. But Biden's campaign turned around, in South Carolina, on the last day of a leap-year February, when Black Democratic voters came out in favor of the former vice president despite questions about his record and whether a seventy-seven-year-old white man was the right candidate for the party.

On February 26, South Carolina's seventy-nine-year-old, fourteen-term US congressman Jim Clyburn gave Biden an endorsement that analysts called "game-changing" and "an inflection point" for the campaign.[47] Rep. Clyburn was the Black American who had read Marjory Wentworth's "One River, One Boat" into the Congressional Record after the poem was cut from Governor Nikki Haley's second inauguration in January 2015, and who along with another Black American, Sen. Tim Scott, had stood with the governor when she had called for taking down the Confederate flag six months later.

The same day, Joe Biden spoke to a Georgetown, South Carolina, crowd. He said he was "a little emotional" at Clyburn's endorsement and was thinking about the congressman's late wife, Emily, whom he had come to know over the years. *Post and Courier* reporter Jamie Lovegrove tweeted coverage from Biden's rally, "Biden has started criticizing @Nikki Haley more directly in South Carolina recently for declining to expand Medicaid here. In Georgetown, he appears to start saying she 'didn't have the brains' before stopping himself and changing it to 'foresight' because he wants to 'be polite.'"

Seven minutes later, @NikkiHaley responded: "Hold up Joe. I will put my brain up against yours anytime. Bring it."[48]

In early August 2020, twelve weeks before the November general election, Biden named a former primary challenger, Kamala Harris, as his running mate. The US senator and former state attorney general from California was the first Black woman—and the first Indian American, South Asian American, and Asian American—on an American presidential ticket. Kamala Devi Harris, the daughter of an Indian physician-researcher-activist mother and Jamaican economist father, described herself simply as "a proud American." Her 2019 memoir *The Truths We Hold* proudly explored her mother's progressive family roots in India, where her grandfather was a civil servant.[49]

Vanita Gupta, head of the Justice Department's Civil Rights Division under President Obama, told the *New York Times* that having Kamala Harris on the presidential ticket was "a stand-alone milestone, irrespective of who the opponent is." She added, "But it is particularly poignant given what this country has endured for the last several years, with this administration that at every turn has sought to divide us and use racism for political gain."[50]

Ten years after backing Nikki Haley's first gubernatorial campaign, Sarah Palin, the last woman to land on a presidential ticket, posted a snark-free message of congratulations for Harris on her Instagram account. "Congrats to the democrat VP pick," the former Alaska governor wrote. "Climb upon Geraldine Ferraro's and my shoulders, and from the most amazing view in your life consider lessons we learned." Palin offered several pieces of advice to Harris, saying, "out of the chute trust no one new," "fight mightily to keep your own team with you," "don't get muzzled," and "don't forget the women who came before you."[51]

In their first joint appearance after the announcement, on August 12, 2020, Joseph Robinette Biden Jr. and Kamala Devi Harris wore cloth face coverings, stood together before assembled media and no assembled crowd in Wilmington, Delaware—where Biden won his first Senate campaign in 1972, the year Nimrata Nikki Randhawa was born—and promised to lead the United States of America out of crisis.

As a high-profile woman in American politics, Nikki Haley could have offered friendly advice to Kamala Harris, much like what Sarah Palin wrote. But she opted for a different kind of statement. Retweeting a *Newsweek* headline, @NikkiHaley wrote on August 13, "Biden's pick for his VP running mate, Democratic California Senator Kamala Harris, was ranked as being more liberal than Democratic Vermont Senator Bernie Sanders, the congressperson often considered the furthest left within the Democratic caucus."

★ ★ ★

With no federal or state responsibilities in the pandemic response, citizen Nikki Haley could tailor her frequent words and occasional actions to enhance her conservative credentials. In late February 2020, even before the pandemic had become the dominant issue, Haley weighed in with an op-ed for the *Wall Street Journal*, amid the moderate-vs.-progressive tussles of the Democratic primaries and efforts by even some Republicans to offer bold ideas for reforming the US economic system. The headline of Haley's piece, "This Is No Time to Go Wobbly on Capitalism," most likely was written by editors (per the standard practice), and not by Haley herself. But it was an explicit callback to one of Margaret Thatcher's most famous sayings, and the column's theme was similarly Thatcheresque:

> There's an important debate happening in America right now, a competition among three distinct views of the world. The first view is held by those who think capitalism is the best and fairest economic system the world has ever seen. The second is held by those who think socialism is the answer to a host of problems from climate change to inequality. Then there are those who are pushing a watered-down or hyphenated capitalism, which is the slow path to socialism.
>
> Mark me down as a capitalist. I grew up in South Carolina as the daughter of Indian immigrants. My mom started a small business selling clothes and gifts. She worked hard and showed my brothers, my sister and me what it meant to live the American dream. The U.S. is a country where people can find jobs that match their talents and passions. America has lifted up more people and unleashed more prosperity than any other country in human history.[52]

As COVID-19 outbreaks roiled the markets, shuttered businesses, and put millions of Americans out of work, congressional Republicans voted for a bipartisan $2 trillion stimulus package in March that included direct payments to taxpayers, expanded unemployment benefits, and a $500 billion fund to assist struggling companies. But Haley that same month resigned from her seat on the Boeing Company's board, less than a year after joining, to protest its bid for government assistance. In a letter to Boeing's management released by the company, the former Tea Party governor who had opposed unionization efforts at its North Charleston factory wrote, "I cannot support a move to lean on the federal government for a stimulus or bailout that prioritizes our company over others and relies on taxpayers to guarantee our financial position. I have long held strong convictions that this is not the role of government."[53]

In April, when President Trump sought to lay with US governors the primary responsibility for responding to the pandemic just days after claiming he had "total control" over decision-making as president, Haley was on the spot with another op-ed, this one for the *New York Times*. Haley said "overheated" critics of the president's response should "look no further than the governors" whose complaints about the Trump administration's feckless response were "in some cases, attempting to distract from their own failures to plan and execute."

Tellingly, an editor's note below her byline simply said, "Ms. Haley is a former governor of South Carolina." The former *ambassador* was nowhere to be found in this op-ed on a major global crisis; the former *governor* trumpeted, "During my six years as governor of South Carolina, I dealt with a thousand-year flood, damaging hurricanes, a racially driven church shooting, a white police officer who killed an innocent black victim, and a school shooting."[54] It didn't seem to have occurred to the former governor that while all of these had been significant challenges for South Carolina, none were remotely like the twin public health and economic crises brought on by the pandemic that impacted *all* states and indeed most countries simultaneously, however unevenly.

On Fox News's morning program *Fox & Friends*, Haley was asked about Trump's daily presidential briefings on the coronavirus pandemic, which sometimes stretched to two hours, with the president's meandering monologues. She applauded Trump's willingness to "over-communicate" to "show up every day and let people know he is on it," but said, "I also think he needs to let his experts speak. Let them talk about it."[55] At the time, Dr. Anthony Fauci, an accomplished immunologist physician-researcher and the director of the National Institute of Allergy and Infectious Diseases since 1984, was a frequent presence at the president's daily briefings. Fauci's poll numbers were much better than Trump's.

On July 23, 2020, amid accelerated research efforts and billions in federal spending to support the administration's public-private initiative, Operation Warp Speed, to back the development, manufacturing, and distribution of COVID-19 vaccines and treatments, Nikki Haley tweeted, "Any coronavirus cure will be thanks to capitalism" with a heart emoji and US flag.

And she was just like ordinary Americans! In August, @NikkiHaley wanted everyone to know she was shopping online, too, and frustrated with home delivery delays. She tweeted to complain that the Popcorn Factory had twice "messed up birthday orders missed delivery dates with no explanation. First time I gave you benefit of the doubt. Second one tells me not to buy from you again. #DisappointedNephew."[56]

Even at billionaire-friendly *Forbes*, staff writer Lisette Voytko had to note, "Reaction was swift and intense, as business leaders, politicians, journalists and activists criticized Haley for displaying entitlement and pointed out that the United States Postal Service, one of the company's main delivery partners, is slower to deliver mail these days due to cost-cutting measures under the Trump administration."[57] It wasn't clear whether Haley had opted for USPS or FedEx delivery, but NBC News correspondent Stephanie Ruhle wanted to know if Haley would be "tweeting at the Postmaster General"—who since June 2020 had been Louis DeJoy, a wealthy businessman and Republican donor from North Carolina, who the president's treasury secretary Steven Mnuchin reportedly helped put forward to lead the financially struggling USPS.[58]

Sometimes her grit seemed to get the better of her grace. But as rhetorical misfires go, @NikkiHaley's #popcorngate seemed hardly career-ending.

She may be just getting started. Curiously, while Haley served as UN ambassador for only days past the halfway mark of the turbulent Trump presidency, the events of 2019 and 2020—including the president's impeachment and especially the COVID-19 pandemic—seemed to bend time in a way that made it harder to register this plain fact: as Trump's time sputtered to a close, she'd been gone from the administration for as long as she had served in it. (It didn't hurt Haley's profile that her successor, Kelly Craft, was not nearly as visible in the UN role.)

Since stepping out of her part in the administration that had once seemed so unlikely, Nikki Haley's every public move has seemed to hint that she could be positioning herself to run for the presidency of the United States. The American people may wish to bring their own popcorn.

Afterword

The events of January 6, 2021, did not just bring Donald Trump's presidency to an ignominious finale. To be sure, Trump's treacherous endgame unleashed without irony "American carnage" at the same US Capitol steps where the forty-fifth president had delivered his inaugural address on January 20, 2016—the very day Governor Nikki Haley turned forty-five. Now, private citizen Haley's forty-ninth birthday would mark the inauguration of Joseph R. Biden and the swearing in of Kamala Harris as vice president. But with Trump refusing to attend Biden's inauguration or even to acknowledge the legitimacy of the election, it would be for January 6 and its aftermath to stand as the billionaire outsider's final-for-now moment at the center of the national psyche. It would also elicit Haley's public break from Trump, in a way that neither Charlottesville nor any of the scandals of the Trump presidency had done previously. This was "Nikki Haley's Time for Choosing," as *Politico* titled an enlightening profile by Tim Alberta.[1] And it just might mark the end of the unlikely association between Haley and Trump.

On January 6, Haley watched live images of the storming of the Capitol by a pro-Trump mob seeking to disrupt Congress's counting of the states' certified Electoral College votes, and tweeted, "Every American has the right to peacefully protest. What's happening now at the U.S. Capitol building is wrong and un-American. We are better than that." Earlier that same day, Haley had tweeted to acknowledge Democratic victories the night before in the runoff races for Georgia's two US Senate seats, which had just produced a 50–50 Senate with Vice President–elect Harris poised to break ties in favor of the Democrats (on votes not bound by the chamber's arcane filibuster). Haley said, "The results of these two Senate races are a major wake up call for the Republican Party and our country. There's no whining in politics. Time to get to work."

The next day, Haley spoke at a private dinner at the Republican National Committee meeting in Florida. Taking to Twitter once again to preview her remarks, she said, "It will be a conversation about where we are, some hard truths, and where I believe we go from here." As reported by *Politico*, according to "a person familiar with her remarks" at the closed-door event, Haley, referring to the president's speech at the so-called Stop the Steal rally in Washington just before the Capitol attack, said Trump "was badly wrong with his words yesterday." She added, "And it wasn't just his words. His actions since Election Day will be judged harshly by history," seeming to refer to Trump's conspiratorial rhetoric about the election.[2] (As it happened, at around 9:30 that night in a Washington hospital, US Capitol Police Officer Brian Sicknick died from injuries sustained in the attack. Two other officers died by suicide in the days that followed. On January 6 itself, a California woman who had attempted to enter the Capitol through a broken window, a US Air Force veteran, was also killed by police fire, and at least one other death resulted from medical emergency.)

But Haley did not stick publicly to her private RNC message, in which she also reportedly told GOP colleagues, "We must stop turning the American people against each other" and "If we are the party of personal responsibility, we need to take personal responsibility." Instead, in an appearance on Laura Ingraham's Fox News program *The Ingraham Angle* on January 25, she focused her criticism on congressional Democrats for pressing ahead with the second impeachment of the president, this time for his role in inciting the Capitol attack. While offering a lukewarm rebuke of Trump's conduct as "not great," she now criticized Democrats for *their* divisiveness: "They beat him up before he got into office and they're beating him up after he leaves office. I mean, at some point, give the man a break. I mean, move on if you are truly about moving on."

In an interview with Haley just days after the January 6 insurrection, Alberta's *Politico* profile captured her seeming difficulty in processing what had transpired, and uncertainty over how to position herself amid the crisis it presented for the GOP and for American democracy. Haley told Alberta that Trump "went down a path he shouldn't have, and we shouldn't have followed him. . . . We can't let that ever happen again." Looking ahead for her party, she said, "I don't think he's going to be in the picture. I don't think he can. He's fallen so far." (She also said she thought Trump truly believed the election had been subject to widespread vote fraud.)

Haley's criticism of Trump led the wider media reporting on Alberta's essay, which was actually a deep dive into Haley's political biography (including new reporting on her tenure in South Carolina). But since she had at least partly retreated from her previous position by the time the piece was published, the effect was to create confusion about what the presumptive 2024 candidate really believed—and what she stood for. It was all a long way from "With all due respect, I don't get confused."

As the GOP split into a pro-Trump majority and a small minority of congressional and state Republicans willing to speak out against the former president, Haley sought to stay in the game. She wrote an op-ed for the *Wall Street Journal* explaining that people (like her) who both praised Trump's record and criticized his conduct were not "having it both ways" but rather simply "using their brains."[3]

The next day, citing what it described as "a source familiar," *Politico* reported that Haley had reached out to Trump, their first communication since before the January 6 insurrection. The former ambassador sought an audience with the former president at his Mar-a-Lago resort in Florida. Trump turned her down.[4]

★ ★ ★

I did not seek an interview with Nikki Haley for this book. In my judgment, there was already ample material in the public record to work with: Haley was basically an "open book," having written a memoir and topical op-eds for various major media outlets, delivered speeches to various general and interest-group audiences, and sat for multiple major interviews with TV and print journalists. I determined early on that even if I had been able to get access to Governor Haley (which seemed unlikely, based on the experiences of South Carolina reporters),[5] I didn't think it would be worth the time to ask a busy governor to cover subjects she'd already addressed, with fair consistency, on many occasions. I also thought I could use my limited time visiting South Carolina to learn things I couldn't necessarily learn from Governor Haley directly, but which still had bearing on the cultural and political contexts around her governorship. When she went to New York to represent the United States at the United Nations, she was even more omnipresent through public statements and media coverage (and presumably, would have been less accessible).

I did meet Nikki Haley briefly, in a different setting, on September 27, 2019. She was the Fall Convocation speaker at Elon University, where I teach political science and international relations. I'd been hearing for months beginning in late 2018 and early 2019, even while Ambassador Haley was still at the United Nations, that she might come speak to our campus—something about a connection, maybe with a donor or trustee, that might make it happen. Well, why not? She spoke at nearby Duke

University toward the end of her tenure at the UN. When Elon's president, Connie Book, confirmed the campus chatter in a committee meeting, I approached her afterward and mentioned that I was working on this book. "Oh, that's good to know," President Book said. "You can give the introduction."

Before I introduced Ambassador Nikki Haley to over four thousand people at the university's Schar Center arena, we gathered in a waiting room, and President Book introduced me to the former South Carolina governor whose career I'd started following when our kids—and the former governor's kids—were all in elementary school. This was, as a favorite uncle of mine would have said, "pretty neat." We spoke briefly. Haley was outgoing, but self-contained. We took a picture together, and then it was time to go on stage. She joked that she'd have to follow me, so she wouldn't get lost along the way. I quipped back: I'd only been in the new arena once before, and never backstage.

My introductory remarks did what such things do: I had something like 120 seconds to distill some of the highlights of Haley's governorship and ambassadorship, to touch on the acclaim as well as some of the criticisms. I talked about Charleston and the Confederate flag. I mentioned human rights groups calling Ambassador Haley out over the Human Rights Council withdrawal. I expected when I brought up her response to Larry Kudlow's comment about her "momentary confusion" over Russia policy—"With all due respect, I don't get confused"—that it might get applause from the audience. I was wary: this wasn't a pep rally. But I knew I had to bring it up as context for the title of her coming memoir, *With All Due Respect: Defending America With Grit and Grace*. And when the audience did applaud, I was grateful for a sip of water. I accidentally left the glass when I gave the lectern to Ambassador Haley. Rookie mistake. She discreetly moved it, as she opened a neatly arranged binder containing her speaking notes.

I'd heard most of what she had to say before, so I tried to focus equally on the response in the room—and it was exuberant. After I introduced Ambassador Haley, I was able to step down from the podium and take a seat in the front row, where I could be quickly forgotten. I listened, and watched people listening, as she told stories about her family and growing up in Bamberg. She talked about Charleston. She talked much more about foreign policy, which surprised me a little. She said, slowing down for emphasis, "Russia is not our friend." She gestured at the lectern and recalled what I ("the professor") had said about criticisms she took from

Photo by Kim Walker.
Courtesy of Elon University.

human rights groups—which, given the time constraint, was only to mention that there *had* been criticisms, but even this required rebuttal. She said Americans generally and students specifically should not confuse the Human Rights Council for a pro–human rights body, "just because it's in the name." She criticized other college campuses for trying to silence conservative speech by students and speakers. There were bursts of applause throughout. Most faculty were more restrained, as I tried to appear to be: it was a day at the office.

Haley arrived not long before the Convocation, and left not long after. Though organizers had requested it, she initially had declined a request to meet with student groups before the event, citing the travel time from South Carolina and her plan to return home the same day. But about ninety minutes before we were due backstage, I got a call from one of our senior administrative staff: Haley would have a few minutes after all, he said, and could I round up a few political science students? (The College Republicans had been alerted already.) It was a quiet Friday afternoon on campus, but I contacted a few students I knew would come quickly. They came.

Afterward, one of them—a young white man from Raleigh, North Carolina, who had sat at a table in Amritsar, Punjab, six months earlier and listened to me talk about this book project—emailed me to say, "I wanted to thank you for the opportunity for meeting Nikki Haley today! It was really exciting and she was really nice. It was honestly a dream come true and I couldn't wait until Tuesday to thank you."

Well. What more can you say about that?

Notes

1. Jason A. Kirk, "Indian-Americans and the U.S.-India Nuclear Agreement: Consolidation of an Ethnic Lobby?," *Foreign Policy Analysis* 4, no. 3 (May 2008): 275–300.
2. James C. Cobb, *Away Down South: A History of Southern Identity* (New York: Oxford University Press, 2007).
3. This book will adhere to the capitalization of Black, but not brown and white (except in quoted material, where the various styles of original sources will be preserved).

    In mid-2020, amid the new national Black Lives Matter protests and civil unrest that followed the police killing of George Floyd in Minneapolis, the Associated Press and several other major news organizations announced that they would begin capitalizing *Black* (but not *white*) as a racial designation. The AP did not change its formal Stylebook recommendation regarding *brown*, which is to "avoid the broad and imprecise term brown in racial, ethnic or cultural references," though of course some Americans—including Nikki Haley—specifically self-identify as brown (or Brown). In not endorsing the capitalization of white, an internal staff memo at the AP further informally suggested that "capitalizing the term white, as is done by white supremacists, risks subtly conveying legitimacy to such beliefs." The National Association of Black Journalists, however, "recommends that whenever a color is used to appropriately describe race then it should be capitalized, including White and Brown."

    Editorial standards in this area will likely continue to evolve differently for different types of publishers. The University of Arkansas Press uses *The Chicago Manual of Style* as its default style guide. In June 2020, *The Chicago Manual* updated its section 8.38 and explained, "Specifically, we now prefer to write *Black* with a capital *B* when it refers to racial and ethnic identity. At the same time, we acknowledge that, as a matter of editorial consistency, *White* and similar terms *may* [emphasis added] also be capitalized when used in this sense." Chicago Manual, "Black and White: A Matter of Capitalization," *CMOS Shop Talk* (blog), June 22, 2020, http://cmosshoptalk.com/2020/06/22/black-and-white-a-matter-of-capitalization/.
4. William Faulkner, *Requiem for a Nun* (New York: Random House, 1951), act 1, scene 3.
5. Here, "political time" is intended to carry both general and US presidency-centered meanings. Australian political scientist and India specialist Donald F. Miller defined political time as "the timing of our affairs; the union of an event

with its time and place; the particular context of our actions, each one seemingly unique. To cope with chance; to grab an opportunity or be thrown by the unexpected"; see Donald F. Miller, "The Problem of Timing and Chance," *Time & Society* 2, no. 2 (May 1993): 139–57. Stephen Skowronek, the scholar of American political development, has used the phrase to refer to a historical pattern of the US presidency that has repeated itself over two hundred years; see Stephen Skowronek, *Presidential Leadership in Political Time: Reprise and Reappraisal?*, 2nd ed. (Lawrence: University Press of Kansas, 2011). Applying his taxonomy to the 2016 US presidential election, Skowronek has called Trump's election a "disjunctive" event; see Richard Kreitner, "What Time Is It? Here's What the 2016 Election Tells Us About Obama, Trump, and What Comes Next," *The Nation*, November 22, 2016.

6. Nikki Haley, *With All Due Respect: Defending America With Grit and Grace* (New York: St. Martin's Press, 2019), 56.

7. Sean Wilentz, *The Age of Reagan: A History, 1974–2008* (New York: HarperCollins, 2008).

8. For a classic account of the possibilities and perils of writing contemporary history, see Arthur Schlesinger Jr., "On the Writing of Contemporary History," *The Atlantic*, March 1967.

ACKNOWLEDGMENTS

1. Jerry Garcia and Robert Hunter, "Uncle John's Band," *Workingman's Dead* (Grateful Dead album), Warner Bros. Records, 1970.

2. Kurt Vonnegut, *Slaughterhouse-Five, or The Children's Crusade: A Duty-Dance With Death* (New York: Dell Publishing, 1969).

3. Bruce Springsteen, "I'll See You in My Dreams," *Letter to You*, Columbia Records, 2020.

4. Graham Nash, "Teach Your Children," *Déjà Vu* (Crosby, Stills, Nash & Young album), Atlantic Records, 1970.

CHAPTER 1: THIS LAND IS YOUR LAND

1. In the first of her two memoirs, Haley briefly discusses her relationship to the Tea Party movement, without precisely identifying herself with it. On April 15 (tax day), 2010, SC rep. Haley spoke as a gubernatorial candidate at a Tea Party gathering on the State House steps and said, "I've never seen people so spirited about their government and elected officials so scared. It's a beautiful thing!" In the book, she says it was beautiful to see "all these South Carolinians who didn't care about party and didn't care about race or gender," but just wanted to be heard in Columbia and in Washington, DC. She writes that she "welcomed and cherished the support of the Tea Party movement." Nikki Haley, *Can't Is Not an Option: My American Story* (New York: Sentinel, 2012), 131–32.

2. See preface, note 3, for a discussion of different editorial standards and rationales for capitalizing (or not) the terms Black, brown, and white when referring to racial and ethnic designations. As noted, quoted material here retains the style of the original source (in this case, Nikki Haley's memoir *Can't Is Not an Option*).

3. For a detailed history, see Michael K. Prince, *Rally 'Round the Flag, Boys! South Carolina and the Confederate Flag* (Columbia: University of South Carolina Press, 2004).

4. Yvonne Wegner, "NAACP Attacks Haley Over Flag," *Post and Courier* (Charleston), July 27, 2011.

5. Mary Quinn O'Connor, "South Carolina Governor Rejects NAACP Push to Remove Confederate Flag," Fox News, July 29, 2011, www.foxnews.com.

6. There *is* a lesser-known history of solidarity between American Blacks and Indian nationalists, from the late nineteenth century to the 1960s; see Nico Slate, *Colored Cosmopolitanism: The Shared Struggle for Freedom in the United States and India* (Cambridge, MA: Harvard University Press, 2012), and Nico Slate, *Lord Cornwallis Is Dead: The Struggle for Democracy in the United States and India* (Cambridge, MA: Harvard University Press, 2019).

7. In announcing Senator Scott's appointment, Governor Haley said, "It is important to me, as a minority female, that Congressman Scott earned this seat. He earned this seat for the person that he is. He earned this seat with the results he has shown." Aaron Blake and Chris Cillizza, "Nikki Haley Appoints Rep. Tim Scott to Senate," *Washington Post*, December 17, 2012.

8. For a particularly critical review of Haley's early governorship that sees considerable hypocrisy in her calls for ethics and transparency reforms, see Corey Hutchins, "Nikki Haley's Pay-to-Play Politics," *The Nation*, July 4, 2011, https://www.thenation.com/article/archive/nikki-haleys-pay-play-politics/. See also Gina Smith, "Ethics Probe of S.C. Gov. Haley Shines Light on Dark Side of State's Politics," *The State* (Columbia, SC), June 18, 2012; and Tom Jensen, "Haley Vulnerable in South Carolina," Public Policy Polling, December 11, 2012, www.publicpolicypolling.com.

9. Phillip Rucker, "Nikki Haley Talks about Why She Endorsed Mitt Romney," *Washington Post*, December 18, 2011.

10. Rachel Weiner, "Reince Priebus Gives GOP Prescription for Future," *Washington Post*, March 18, 2013.

11. Mark S. Brodin, "From Dog-Whistle to Megaphone: The Trump Regime's Cynical Assault on Affirmative Action," *National Lawyers Guild Review* 74, no. 2 (2017): 65–71. For background, see Ian Haney López, *Dog Whistle Politics: How Coded Racial Appeals Have Reinvented Racism and Wrecked the Middle Class* (New York: Oxford University Press, 2014).

12. Ashish Kumar Sen, "Sikh American Woman Is Republican Whip," *The Tribune* (Chandigarh, India), January 18, 2006, www.tribuneindia.com.

13. Haley, *Can't Is Not an Option*.

14. Nikki R. Haley, *With All Due Respect: Defending America with Grit and Grace* (New York: St. Martin's Press, 2019).

15. Cindy Simon Rosenthal, *When Women Lead: Integrative Leadership in State Legislatures* (New York: Oxford University Press, 1998), 161.

16. Center for American Women and Politics, Rutgers, The State University of New Jersey, cited in Lori Cox Han, *Women and US Politics: The Spectrum of Political Leadership*, 2nd ed. (Boulder: Lynne Rienner, 2010), 108, table 5.3.

17. Quoted from Haley's remarks at Elon University Fall Convocation, Elon, NC, September 27, 2019, as noted by the author (in attendance) and as reported by Dawn Baumgartner Vaughan, "Former Trump Official Haley on Working

for the President: 'We Never Had a Conflict,'" *News and Observer* (Raleigh), September 27, 2019. Haley uses nearly identical language in Haley, *With All Due Respect*.

18. Quoted in Annie Gowan and Tyler Bridges, "From Piyush to Bobby: How Does Jindal Feel about His Family's Past?," *Washington Post*, June 23, 2015. For a more sympathetic perspective on Jindal's position, see Saurabh Jha, "Give Bobby Jindal a Break—He's as Indian as the Rest of Us," *Quartz*, August 7, 2015, https://qz.com/474583/give-bobby-jindal-a-break-hes-as-indian-as -the-rest-of-us/.

19. Yvonne Wegner, "Gov. Haley Releases Fundraising Totals, Including Many Out-of-State Donations," *Post and Courier*, October 11, 2011.

20. David Brooks, "Where Do Republicans Go from Here?," *New York Times*, August 7, 2020, https://www.nytimes.com/2020/08/07/opinion/sunday /republican-party-trump-2020.html.

21. Brooks, "Where Do Republicans Go?"

22. Brooks, "Where Do Republicans Go?" The online column was corrected late in the day, with an editor's note: "An earlier version of this article misspelled the given name of a former UN ambassador. She is Nikki Haley, not Nicki." The Sunday, August 9, 2020 print version of Brooks's column rendered the correct spelling.

23. Brooks, "Where Do Republicans Go?"

24. Reflective Democracy Campaign, cited in Alexa Lardieri, "Despite Diverse Demographics, Most Politicians Are Still White Men," *U.S. News and World Report*, October 24, 2017, https://www.usnews.com/news/politics/articles /2017-10-24/despite-diverse-demographics-most-politicians-are-still -white-men.

25. López, *Dog Whistle Politics,* 151, citing the *New York Times*/CBS, "Poll: National Survey of Tea Party Supporters," April 5–12, 2010, 41, as reported in "Polling the Tea Party," *New York Times*, April 14, 2010, https://www.nytimes. com/interactive/projects/documents/new-york-timescbs-news-poll-national -survey-of-tea-party-supporters.

26. López, *Dog Whistle Politics,* 253n39.

27. "Trump Gets Better Grades on North Korea, Quinnipiac University National Poll Finds; But Voters Say Trump Is Making World Less Safe," Quinnipiac University Poll, April 25, 2018, https://poll.qu.edu/images/polling/us/us042 52018_uhms25.pdf.

28. Caitlyn Byrd, "Nikki Haley One of the Most Admired Women in the World, Poll Finds," *Post and Courier*, December 28, 2017.

29. Peter J. Boyer, "The Color of Politics: A Mayor of the Post-Racial Generation," *New Yorker*, February 4, 2008.

30. Michael Tesler and David O. Sears, *Obama's Race: The 2008 Election and the Dream of a Post-Racial America* (Chicago: University of Chicago Press, 2010).

31. Desmond S. King and Rogers M. Smith, *Still a House Divided: Race and Politics in Obama's America* (Princeton, NJ: Princeton University Press, 2011), 9 (emphasis in original).

32. Paul Taylor and D'Vera Cohn, "A Milestone En Route to Becoming a Majority Minority Nation," Pew Research Center, Washington, DC, November 7, 2012.

33. Matthew Frye Jacobson, *Whiteness of a Different Color: European Immigrants*

and the Alchemy or Race (Cambridge, MA: Harvard University Press, 1999); Eric L. Goldstein, *The Price of Whiteness: Jews, Race, and American Identity* (Princeton, NJ: Princeton University Press, 2008); Noel Ignatiev, *How the Irish Became White* (New York: Routledge, 2008).

34. George Yancey, *Who Is White? Latinos, Asians, and the New Black/Nonblack Divide* (Boulder, CO: Lynne Rienner, 2003), 3, 4.

35. Author's telephone interview with Sanjay Puri, Chairman, US-India Political Action Committee (USINPAC), August 2012.

36. The Original Six Foundation mission is to serve "as a resource to build bridges now for a better quality of life tomorrow" in "South Carolina's neediest communities." Original Six Foundation, "About Us," www.originalsixfoundation .org, accessed June 23, 2019.

37. Author's conversation with an Indian American former resident on a visit to the state, Mount Pleasant, South Carolina, January 26, 2018.

38. Haley, *Can't Is Not an Option*, 46.

39. Haley, *Can't Is Not an Option*, 28.

40. Haley, *Can't Is Not an Option*, 47.

41. Haley, *Can't Is Not an Option*, 10.

42. Haley, *Can't Is Not an Option*, 17.

43. Haley, *Can't Is Not an Option*, 16.

44. Haley, *Can't Is Not an Option*, 17–18.

45. "Election Results: South Carolina," *New York Times*, November 2, 2010.

46. Emily Bohatch, "In a State That Votes Republican, These SC Counties Hit the Polls for Democrats," *The State*, June 5, 2018, https://www.thestate.com/news /politics-government/election/article212557829.html. Not surprisingly, *The State* found that when averaging contested US Senate, US House, presidential, and gubernatorial races in South Carolina from 2008 to 2016, Bamberg County voted 64.5 percent Democratic to 33.8 percent Republican, while Lexington County voted 68.1 percent Republican to 27.6 percent Democratic.

47. Haley, *Can't Is Not an Option*, 37.

48. Author's visits to Mt. Horeb United Methodist Church, Lexington, South Carolina, and Gurdwara Guru Nanaksar, Chapin, South Carolina, October 13, 2013.

49. Sikh Religious Society of South Carolina, www.carolinasikhs.org/photos.html, accessed January 29, 2019.

50. A classic account is in Joan Jensen, *Passage From India: Asian Indian Immigrants in North America* (New Haven, CT: Yale University Press, 1988).

51. Mark A. Noll, *God and Race in American Politics: A Short History* (Princeton, NJ: Princeton University Press, 2008).

52. For a critical perspective on the 1965 reform as a product of "liberal nationalism," see Mae M. Ngai, "The Unlovely Residue of Outworn Prejudices: The Hart-Celler Act and the Politics of Immigration Reform, 1945–1965," in Michael Kazin and Joseph A. McCartin, eds., *Americanism: New Perspectives on the History of an Ideal*, 108–127 (Chapel Hill: University of North Carolina Press, 2006).

53. Sanjoy Chakravorty, Devesh Kapur, and Nirvikar Singh, *The Other One Percent: Indians in America* (New York: Oxford University Press, 2017), x.

54. Vijay Prashad, *The Karma of Brown Folk* (Minneapolis: University of

Minnesota Press, 2000); Sharmila Rudrappa, *Ethnic Routes to Becoming American: Indian Immigrants and the Cultures of Citizenship* (New Brunswick, NJ: Rutgers University Press, 2004); Khyati Y. Joshi, *New Roots in America's Sacred Ground: Religion, Race, and Ethnicity in Indian America* (New Brunswick, NJ: Rutgers University Press, 2006); Sunil Bhatia, *American Karma: Race, Culture, and Identity in the Indian Diaspora* (New York: New York University Press, 2007).

55. Vivek Bald, *Bengali Harlem and the Lost Histories of South Asian America* (Cambridge, MA: Harvard University Press, 2013).

56. Manan Desai, "The 'Tan Stranger' From Ceylon," *Tides* (digital magazine), South Asian American Digital Archive, July 8, 2014, https://www.saada.org /tides/article/tan-stranger-from-ceylon.

57. For a range of more recent perspectives, see Khyati Y. Joshi and Jigna Desai, eds., *Asian Americans in Dixie: Race and Migration in the South* (Urbana: University of Illinois Press, 2013).

58. Ajantha Subramanian, "North Carolina's Indians: Erasing Race to Make the Citizen," in James L. Peacock, Harry L. Wilson, and Carrie M. Matthews, eds., *The American South in a Global World* (Chapel Hill: University of North Carolina Press, 2005), 193.

59. Chakravorty, Kapur, and Singh, *Other One Percent.*

60. Sangay K. Mishra, *Desis Divided: The Political Lives of South Asian Americans* (Minneapolis: University of Minnesota Press, 2016).

61. Prema Kurien, "Race, Religion, and the Political Incorporation of Indian Americans," *Journal of Religious and Political Practice* 2, no. 3 (2016): 273.

62. Vijay Prashad, *Uncle Swami: South Asians in America Today* (Noida, Uttar Pradesh: HarperCollins India, 2012), ix.

63. See especially Deepa Iyer, *We Too Sing America: South Asian, Arab, Muslim, and Sikh Immigrants Shape Our Multiracial Future* (New York: New Press, 2015).

64. Janelle S. Wong, Karthick Ramakrishnan, Taeku Lee, and Jane Junn, *Asian American Political Participation: Emerging Constituents and Their Political Identities* (New York: Russell Sage Foundation, 2012), 203, table 6.5.

65. Pew Research Center, "Indian Americans," *The Rise of Asian Americans* (report), Washington, DC: Pew Research Center, 2012, 44–46. Updated edition: April 4, 2013.

66. Lisa Miller, "We Are All Hindus Now," *Newsweek*, August 15, 2009.

67. Pew Research Center, "Trends in Party Identification of Religious Groups," Religion and Public Life Project, Washington, DC, February 2, 2012, https:// www.pewforum.org/2012/02/02/trends-in-party-identification-of-religious -groups/.

68. Democracy Corps, "Inside the GOP: Report on Focus Groups with Evangelical, Tea Party, and Moderate Republicans," Washington, DC, October 3, 2013.

69. Lisa Anderson, "Evangelicals in S.C. Not Just Voting on Faith," *Chicago Tribune*, January 13, 2008.

70. Jason A. Kirk and Jason Husser, "What Makes a Successful Indian American Political Candidate?," *South Asian Diaspora* 9, no. 2 (2017): 207–23.

71. Shyam Krishnan Sriram and stonegarden grindlife, "The Politics of Deracialization: South Asian American Candidates, Nicknames, and Campaign Strategies." *South Asian Diaspora* 9, no. 1 (2017): 17–31.

72. David Brody, "Nikki Haley Reflects More Christian Tone," *Brody File* (blog), Christian Broadcasting Network News, June 3, 2010, https://www1.cbn.com /thebrodyfile/archive/2010/06/03/nikki-haley-reflects-more-christian-tone.

73. Brody, "Nikki Haley Reflects More Christian Tone."

74. Brody, "Nikki Haley Reflects More Christian Tone."

75. Brody, "Nikki Haley Reflects More Christian Tone," emphasis in original.

76. Jim Geraghty, "Hey, Look Who's Calling Nikki Haley a 'Christian, Indian-American Woman' Today," *Campaign Spot* (blog), *National Review Online*, June 23, 2010, https://www.nationalreview.com/the-campaign-spot/hey-look -whos-calling-nikki-haley-christian-indian-american-woman-today-jim/.

77. Yvonne Wegner, "Gov. Haley Listed Her Race as White on Her Voter Registration Card," *Post and Courier*, July 28, 2011.

78. Siddhartha Mahanta, "Indian Nikki Haley Says She Is White," *Political Mojo* (blog), *Mother Jones*, July 29, 2011, https://www.motherjones.com /politics/2011/07/indian-nikki-haley-says-she-is-white/.

79. Prashad, *Uncle Swami*, 95–96.

80. Ian Goldin, Geoffrey Cameron, and Meera Balarajan, *Exceptional People: How Migration Shaped Our World and Will Define Our Future* (Princeton, NJ: Princeton University Press, 2011).

81. Dylan's lyrics adorn the 1999 song's driving rhythm with apocalyptic imagery. The singer, "who used to care" (before things changed) ambles a landscape populated by spectral presences like a woman with "white skin" and "assassin's eyes"; he stands on the gallows with his "head in a noose," any minute "expecting all hell to break loose." It is possible to hear "Things Have Changed" as a nihilistic inversion of the songwriter's own 1964 anthem, "The Times They Are A-Changin.'"

   In 2012, Dylan told an interviewer, "This country is just too fucked up about color. It's a distraction. People at each other's throats just because they are a different color. It's the height of insanity and it would hold any nation back—or any neighborhood back.... It's doubtful that America's ever going to get rid of that stigmatization." Mikal Gilmore, "Bob Dylan Unleashed," *Rolling Stone*, September 27, 2012.

82. Angie Maxwell, *The Indicted South: Public Criticism, Southern Inferiority, and the Politics of Whiteness* (Chapel Hill: University of North Carolina Press, 2014).

83. Maxwell, *Indicted South*, 248.

84. James L. Peacock, *Grounded Globalism: How the U.S. South Embraces the World* (Athens: University of Georgia Press, 2007).

85. Raymond A. Mohl, "Globalization, Latinization, and the *Nuevo* New South," in *Globalization and the American South*, ed. James C. Cobb and William Stueck (Athens: University of Georgia Press, 2005), 66–99. See also the other contributions in this volume, and contemporaneously in James L. Peacock, Harry L. Watson, and Carrie R. Matthews, eds., *The American South in a Global World* (Chapel Hill: University of North Carolina Press, 2005).

86. Shaila Dewan and Robbie Brown, "All Her Life, Nikki Haley Was the Different One," *New York Times*, June 13, 2010.

87. Haley, *Can't Is Not an Option*, chapter 6.

88. "SC Sen. Jake Knotts Calls Barack Obama and Nikki Haley 'Ragheads,'" *BuzzFeed*, May 15, 2012, video at www.youtube.com/watch?v=Zq5xMT3z560, accessed July 18, 2013. Also reported in John O'Connor, "Knotts' Slur Stirs the Haley Storm," *The State*, June 3, 2010.

89. Mark Halperin and John Heilemann, *Double Down: Game Change 2012* (New York: Penguin, 2013), 100.

90. Halperin and Heilemann, *Double Down*, 408–9.

91. "Haley Wins South Carolina GOP Runoff for Governor," NPR, June 22, 2010, https://www.npr.org/templates/story/story.php?storyId=128018612.

92. Arian Campo-Flores, "The Face of the New South," *Newsweek*, July 12, 2010.

93. Kyle Wingfield, "Southern Conservatives Show Signs of Color-Blindness," *Atlanta Journal-Constitution*, June 23, 2010.

94. Campo-Flores, "Face of the New South."

95. "Nikki Haley, GOP Gubernatorial Nominee, Bears Cultural Distinction," *Tell Me More*, NPR, June 23, 2010, https://www.npr.org/templates/story/story.php?storyId=128047094.

96. Bilal Ahmed, "Performative Whiteness," *South Asia Journal* 9, September 2013, http://southasiajournal.net/performative-whiteness/.

97. Aseem Shukla, "Haley, Jindal and America's New Religious Litmus Test," *On Faith* (blog), *Washington Post*, June 23, 2010.

98. David Gibson, "Nikki Haley's Win: A Victory for Assimilation, Not Acceptance," *Politics Daily*, June 25, 2010.

99. Reihan Salam, "How Ethnic Can Our Politicians Be?," *Daily Beast*, June 11, 2010.

100. Prashant Agrawal, "An Indian in the White House?" *India Real Time* (blog), *Wall Street Journal*, June 23, 2010.

101. Tunku Varadarajan, "Nikki Haley and the New Racial Face of the South," *Daily Beast*, June 9, 2010.

102. Varadarajan, "Nikki Haley and the New Racial Face of the South."

103. Peter Beinhart, "The Jesus Litmus Test," *Daily Beast*, July 15, 2010.

104. Henry Barbour, Sally Bradshaw, Ari Fleischer, Zori Fonalledas, and Glenn McCall, *Growth and Opportunity Project*, Republican National Committee, March 2013, 7.

105. Alan Rosenthal, *The Best Job in Politics: Exploring How Governors Succeed as Policy Leaders* (Thousand Oaks, CA: Sage Publishing, 2012).

106. Luther F. Carter and Richard D. Young, "The Governor: Powers, Practices, Roles and the South Carolina Experience," South Carolina Governance Project, Center for Governmental Services, Institute for Public Service and Policy Research, University of South Carolina, no date, accessed August 18, 2014, http://www.ipspr.sc.edu/grs/SCCEP/Articles/governor.htm.

107. Keith G. Bentele and Erin E. O'Brien, "Jim Crow 2.0? Why States Consider and Adopt Restrictive Voter Access Policies," *Perspectives on Politics* 11, no. 4 (December 2013): 1088–116.

108. "Transcript: Remarks by Gov. Nikki Haley on South Carolina's Voter ID Law," January 17, 2012.

109. Del Quentin Wilbur, "Court Approves South Carolina Voter ID Law but Delays It Until at Least 2013," *Washington Post*, October 10, 2012.

110. Nikki Haley "Nikki on the Issues: Immigration," May 20, 2010, https://www.youtube.com/watch?v=KTqNMH_elto&feature=youtu.be, accessed August 19, 2014.

111. Andrew Shain, "SC Drops Effort at Enforcing Immigration Law," *The State*, March 3, 2014.

112. Quoted in Richard Kim, "'We Can't Afford It': The Big Lie About Medicaid Expansion," *The Nation*, July 20, 2012, https://www.thenation.com/article/archive/we-cant-afford-it-big-lie-about-medicaid-expansion/. The URL for Haley's original op-ed in the *Post and Courier* is nonfunctioning.

113. Kim, "'We Can't Afford It,'" July 20, 2012.

CHAPTER 2: CHARLESTON: "WE ARE AT WAR WITH OURSELVES"

1. Quoted in "Gov. Haley Responds to Wis. Shooting at Sikh Temple," WLTX (Columbia, SC), August 5, 2012, www.wltx.com/article/news/gov-haley-responds-to-wis-shooting-at-sikh-temple/101-376769560.

2. Jeremy Turnage, "Haley and Family Respond to Sikh Temple Shooting," WISTV, August 6, 2012, https://www.wistv.com/story/19207368/haley-and-family-respond-to-sikh-temple-shooting/.

3. Marjory Wentworth, "The Weight It Takes," September 11, 2011, www.marjorywentworth.net/newmarj/the-weight-it-takes/. Used by permission. The poet credits the final line of James Dickey's "The Strength of Fields" (1992) for inspiring the first line of the stanza: *My life belongs to the world. I will do what I can.*

4. Marjory Wentworth, "One River, One Boat," no date, www.marjorywentworth.net/newmarj/one-river-one-boat/. Used by permission.

5. Andy Brack, "An Interview with Marjory Wentworth," *Statehouse Report*, January 9, 2015, https://www.statehousereport.com/2015/01/09/wentworth-interview/.

6. Jeremy Borden, "Marjory Wentworth, Poet Laureate, Cut Out of Haley Inauguration," *Post and Courier* (Charleston), January 9, 2015. https://www.postandcourier.com/politics/no-time-for-poem-at-haley-inaugural-poet-laureate-writes-of-states-painful-history-with/article_692ac81a-f763-5caa-9786-6b9de0b96ec6.html.

7. Jamie Self and Andrew Shain, "SC's Official Poet Silenced at Haley Inaugural," *The State* (Columbia, SC), January 9, 2015.

8. Borden, "Marjory Wentworth, Poet Laureate, Cut Out of Haley Inauguration."

9. Melissa Harris-Perry, "A Letter to Gov. Nikki Haley: Time to Take Down the Confederate Flag in South Carolina," MSNBC, October 18, 2014, https://www.msnbc.com/melissa-harris-perry/letter-gov-nikki-haley-time-take-down-the-confederate-flag-south-carolina-msna438521.

10. Critics have pointed out numerous loopholes in the law, and the state has devoted few resources to its effective administration, putting the burden mostly on local police departments. See Daniel J. Gross, "Some Police Shootings in South Carolina Aren't Captured on Body Camera," *Greenville News*, June 17, 2020, https://www.greenvilleonline.com/in-depth/news/local

/south-carolina/2019/09/29/body-camera-use-sc-police-shootings-is
-inconsistent-heres-why/3210213002/.

11. In 2017, Slager was sentenced to twenty years in prison for second-degree murder.

12. Emily Shapiro, "Judge Declares Mistrial in Michael Slager Murder Trial," ABC News, December 5, 2016, https://abcnews.go.com/US/judge-declares-mistrial
-michael-slager-murder-trial/story?id=43980554.

13. Ray Sanchez and Ed Payne, "Charleston Church Shooting: Who Is Dylann Roof?" CNN, December 16, 2016, https://www.cnn.com/2015/06/19/us
/charleston-church-shooting-suspect/index.html.

14. Frances Robles, "Dylann Roof Photos and a Manifesto Are Posted on Website," New York Times, June 20, 2015, https://www.nytimes.com/2015/06/21/us
/dylann-storm-roof-photos-website-charleston-church-shooting.html.

15. "'I Hate the Sight of the American Flag': Dylann Roof's Racist Rant Read in Court," CNN Wire, Fox 8 News, https://myfox8.com/news/i-hate-the-sight
-of-the-american-flag-dylann-roofs-racist-rant-read-in-court/.

16. Nikki R. Haley, *With All Due Respect: Defending America With Grit and Grace* (New York: St. Martin's Press, 2019), 14.

17. Though Governor Haley and her father, Ajit Randhawa, both issued statements of sympathy after the Wisconsin temple shootings, surprisingly few reporters after the Charleston shootings recalled the killing of six coreligionists of the Randhawas under similar circumstances nearly three years earlier. An exception was a Charleston reporter who drew the parallel, but who did not indicate whether she discussed it with the governor; see Jennifer Berry Hawes, "Grieving Gov. Nikki Haley Forever Changed by Church Massacre," *Post and Courier*, July 18, 2015, https://www.postandcourier.com/archives
/on-my-watch-grieving-governor-forever-changed-by-church-massacre
-on-my-watch-grieving-governor/article_e8494588-52a8-5a47-b6fc-799
1b99f48c4.html.

18. Julia Craven, "South Carolina Governor Releases Strangely Obtuse Statement on Black Church Shooting," *Huffington Post*, June 18, 2015, https://www.huff
post.com/entry/nikki-haley-charleston-shooting_n_7612398.

19. Nick Gass, "Nikki Haley: Charleston Shooter Deserves Death Penalty," *Politico*, June 19, 2015, https://www.politico.com/story/2015/06/dylann-roof-deserves
-death-pentalty-nikki-haley-119200.

20. Hawes, "Grieving Governor Haley Forever Changed by Church Massacre." After spending time with his Emanuel AME family, Haley would later tell Hawes, "I knew Sen. Pinckney. I'm now more thankful that I know Rev. Pinckney."

21. Hawes, "Grieving Governor Haley Forever Changed by Church Massacre."

22. Jennifer Berry Hawes, *Grace Will Lead Us Home: The Charleston Church Massacre and the Hard, Inspiring Journey to Forgiveness* (New York: St. Martin's Press, 2019), 97.

23. Justin Wm. Moyer, "Why South Carolina's Confederate Flag Isn't at Half-Staff After Church Shooting," *Washington Post*, June 19, 2015, https://www
.washingtonpost.com/news/morning-mix/wp/2015/06/19/why-south
-carolinas-confederate-flag-isnt-at-half-mast-after-church-shooting/.

24. Ta-Nehisi Coates, "Take Down the Confederate Flag—Now," *The Atlantic*, June 18, 2015, https://www.theatlantic.com/politics/archive/2015/06/take-down-the-confederate-flag-now/396290/.
25. Hawes, *Grace Will Lead Us Home*, 97.
26. Paige Lavender, "Nikki Haley, Mark Sanford Weigh in on Confederate Flag Debate," *Huffington Post*, June 19, 2015, https://www.huffpost.com/entry/confederate-flag-south-carolina_n_7620490.
27. Colleen McCain Nelson, "Tragedy Thrusts Haley Into National Spotlight," *Wall Street Journal*, June 20–21, 2015, A4.
28. Scott Calvert and Cameron McWhirter, "Charleston Killings Rekindle Flag Furor," *Wall Street Journal*, June 20–21, 2015, A4.
29. "Sanford: Confederate Flag Issue a Pandora's Box," *Morning Joe*, MSNBC, June 19, 2015, https://www.msnbc.com/morning-joe/watch/sanford--confederate-flag-issue-a-pandoras-box-468066371560.
30. Alan Blinder and Manny Fernandez, "Outrage vs. Tradition, Wrapped in a High-Flying Flag of Dixie," *New York Times*, June 19, 2015.
31. "Sen. Graham: 'Time to Revisit' Confederate Flag Decision," *New Day*, CNN, June 22, 2015.
32. Nelson, "Tragedy Thrusts Haley Into National Spotlight."
33. Haley, *With All Due Respect*, 30.
34. For other details and essential nuances of this historic tableau, see Hawes, *Grace Will Lead Us Home*, 99–102.
35. Josh Dawsey and Cameron McWhirter, "Governor: Time to Furl Flag," *Wall Street Journal*, June 23, 2015, A1, A6.
36. In North Carolina, the governor's announcement backfired: it led to a surge of new orders for the specialty Sons of Confederate Veterans plate, with the NC Department of Motor Vehicles temporarily running out of stock. State lawmakers argued over who had the authority to discontinue the plate. Five years after McCrory's announcement and under the Democratic governor who defeated him in 2016, Roy Cooper, the SCV plate remained available from the NC DMV.
37. Eugene Scott, "Nikki Haley: Confederate Flag 'Should Have Never Been There,'" CNN, July 10, 2015, https://www.cnn.com/2015/07/10/politics/nikki-haley-confederate-flag-removal/index.html.
38. Ben Schreckinger, "Nikki Haley's Star Rises as Rebel Flag Comes Down," *Politico*, July 10, 2015, https://www.politico.com/story/2015/07/nikki-haleys-star-rises-as-confederate-flag-comes-down-119940.
39. Dawsey and McWhirter, "Governor: Time to Furl Flag."
40. Joan Walsh, "No, I Won't Praise Nikki Haley: It Shouldn't Have Taken a Massacre to Do the Right Thing on the Confederate Flag," *Salon*, June 23, 2015, https://www.salon.com/2015/06/23/no_i_won%E2%80%99t_praise_nikki_haley_it_shouldnt_have_taken_a_massacre_to_do_the_right_thing_on_the_confederate_flag/.
41. "Ann Coulter Attacks Gov. Nikki Haley as 'An Immigrant' Who 'Does Not Understand America's History,'" YouTube video, June 24, 2015, https://www.youtube.com/watch?v=JtNQ6joCGSk.
42. Rush Limbaugh, "See, I Told You So: Democrats Are Using the Confederate

Flag to Destroy the GOP Southern Stronghold (And the American Flag is Next)" (transcript), *Rush Limbaugh Show*, June 25, 2015, www.rushlimbaugh .com.

43. Rush Limbaugh, "I'm Not Arguing to Keep It, But This is Not Really About the Confederate Flag in South Carolina" (transcript), *Rush Limbaugh Show*, June 23, 2015.

44. Schreckinger, "Haley's Star Rises."

45. "Remarks by the President in Eulogy for the Honorable Reverend Clementa Pinckney," June 26, 2015, College of Charleston, Charleston, South Carolina, https://obamawhitehouse.archives.gov/the-press-office/2015/06/26/remarks -president-eulogy-honorable-reverend-clementa-pinckney.

46. Amber Phillips, "6 Key Moments from the South Carolina Senate's Strikingly Blunt Confederate Flag Debate," *The Fix* (blog), *Washington Post*, July 6, 2015, https://www.washingtonpost.com/news/the-fix/wp/2015/07/06/4-key -moments-from-the-south-carolina-senates-strikingly-blunt-confederate -flag-debate/.

47. Phillips, "6 Key Moments."

48. Campbell Robertson, Monica Davey, and Jule Bosman, "Calls to Drop Confederate Emblems Spread Nationwide," *New York Times*, June 23, 2015, https://www.nytimes.com/2015/06/24/us/south-carolina-nikki-haley -confederate-flag.html.

49. Schreckinger, "Haley's Star Rises."

50. Schreckinger, "Haley's Star Rises."

51. "Rep. Mike Pitts Said He Took Hearing Aids Out When Gov. Haley Spoke," *Greenville Online*, July 8, 2015, https://www.greenvilleonline.com/videos /news/politics/2015/07/08/29885427/.

52. Schreckinger, "Haley's Star Rises."

53. Michael E. Miller, "Jenny Horne: How a Descendent of the President of the Confederacy Helped Vanquish His Flag," *Washington Post*, July 9, 2015, https:// www.washingtonpost.com/news/morning-mix/wp/2015/07/09/south -carolina-rep-jenny-horne-on-her-historic-and-surprisingly-personal -speech-it-needed-to-be-done/.

54. Miller, "Jenny Horne."

55. Nikki Haley, Facebook post, www.facebook.com/NikkiHaley/posts/101530 52425093226.

56. Valerie Bauerlein, "After Battle, Disputed Flag to Get New Home," July 10, 2015, *Wall Street Journal*, A3.

57. The other two former governors who stood behind Haley were Democrats Jim Hodges and Richard Riley.

58. Schreckinger, "Haley's Star Rises."

59. Valerie Bauerlein, "Rebel Flag's Lowering Ends an Era in South Carolina," *Wall Street Journal*, July 11–12, 2015, A2.

60. Stephanie McCrummen and Elahe Izadi, "Confederate Flag Comes Down on South Carolina's Statehouse Grounds," *Washington Post*, July 10, 2015, https:// www.washingtonpost.com/news/post-nation/wp/2015/07/10/watch-live-as -the-confederate-flag-comes-down-in-south-carolina/.

61. Scott, "Haley: Confederate Flag 'Should Have Never Been There.'"

62. The poll found a sharp racial divide among respondents, with 72 percent of Blacks and 25 percent of whites saying the flag was a symbol of racism. In the South, the gulf was even wider. Among whites with a college degree, 51 percent said it's a symbol of pride, 41 percent said of racism. Among those whites without a college degree, 73 said it's a sign of southern pride, 18 percent racism. CNN/ORC International Poll, conducted June 26–28, 2015, margin of error plus or minus 3 percentage points. http://i2.cdn.turner.com/cnn/2015/images/07/01/confederate.flag.pdf.

63. "Gov. Nikki Haley on the Removal of the Confederate Flag" (video), CNN, July 10, 2015. https://www.cnn.com/videos/politics/2015/07/10/nikki-haley-talks-removal-of-confederate-flag.cnn

64. Transcript, *Meet the Press*, July 12, 2015, https://www.nbcnews.com/meet-the-press/meet-press-transcript-july-12-2015-n390781; Myra Ruiz, "Governor Nikki Haley on Meet the Press," WYFF NBC 4 (Greenville, SC), July 12, 2015, https://www.wyff4.com/article/gov-nikki-haley-appears-on-meet-the-press/7015935.

65. Jennifer Berry Hawes, "'On My Watch' Grieving governor forever changed by church massacre," *Post and Courier*, July 17, 2015, updated Nov 2, 2016, https://www.postandcourier.com/archives/on-my-watch-grieving-governor-forever-changed-by-church-massacre-on-my-watch-grieving-governor/article_e8494588-52a8-5a47-b6fc-7991b99f48c4.html.

66. Doug Heye, "On Confederate Flag Issue, Nikki Haley Shows Republicans a Way Forward," *Washington Wire* (blog), *Wall Street Journal*, July 10, 2016, https://www.wsj.com/articles/BL-WB-56541.

67. James C. Cobb, "Why Nikki Haley Finally Called for the Removal of the Confederate Flag," *Time*, July 6, 2015. www.time.com

68. Hawes, *Grace Will Lead Us Home*, 103.

69. Hawes, *Grace Will Lead Us Home*, 103.

70. Ali Vitali, Kasie Hunt, and Frank Thorp V, "Trump Referred to Haiti and African Nations as 'Shithole' Countries," January 11, 2018, NBC News, https://www.nbcnews.com/politics/white-house/trump-referred-haiti-african-countries-shithole-nations-n836946.

71. Lindsey Graham, "Nikki Haley," *Time*, April 21, 2016.

CHAPTER 3: UN-LIKELY AMBASSADOR

1. Transcript: Gov. Haley's Response to the State of the Union, *The State* (Columbia, SC), Jan. 12, 2016, https://www.thestate.com/news/politics-government/politics-columns-blogs/the-buzz/article54410190.html.

2. "Deport Nikki Haley" (op-ed), *Wall Street Journal*, January 13, 2016, https://www.wsj.com/articles/deport-nikki-haley-1452729872.

3. Anand Giridharadas, "How Nikki Haley Was Redeemed by Donald Trump," Notebook, *New York Times Magazine*, January 13, 2016, https://www.nytimes.com/2016/01/13/magazine/how-donald-trump-redeemed-nikki-haley.html.

4. Giridharadas, "How Nikki Haley Was Redeemed by Donald Trump."

5. Janell Ross, "As Republicans Salivate over a Possible Rubio-Haley Ticket, a Word of Caution," *Washington Post*, February 18, 2016, https://www

.washingtonpost.com/news/the-fix/wp/2016/02/18/as-republicans-salivate
-over-a-possible-rubio-haley-ticket-a-word-of-caution/.

6. Cynthia Roldan, "Nikki Haley and Marco Rubio: The GOP's Future?," *Post and Courier* (Charleston), February 17, 2016, https://www.postandcourier.com /politics/nikki-haley-and-marco-rubio-the-gop-s-future/article_22499860 -1694-5b41-951f-317b44595add.html.

7. Tim Smith, "Haley Undecided on Endorsement but It Won't Be Trump," *Greenville News*, February 16, 2016, https://www.greenvilleonline.com/story /news/politics/elections/2016/02/16/haley-undecided-endorsement-but-wont -trump/80450230/. On Haley's position on accepting Syrian refugees into South Carolina, see Tim Smith, "Syrian Refugees Arrive in the Midlands, More Coming to SC," *The State*, December 15, 2015, https://www.thestate.com/news /local/article50152865.html. On Haley's position on the Obama administra-tion's proposed closure of the Guantánamo detention center and transfer of prisoners to the United States, see Vera Bergengruen, "Nikki Haley Says She'll Help Obama Find the Money to Keep Guantanamo Open," McClatchy, April 28, 2016, https://www.mcclatchydc.com/news/politics-government /congress/article74421512.html.

8. Deirdre Shesgreen, "S.C. Gov. Haley Urges Defeat of Clinton without Mentioning Trump," *USA Today*, July 20, 2016, https://www.usatoday.com /story/news/politics/onpolitics/2016/07/20/sc-gov-haley-urges-defeat -clinton-without-mentioning-trump/87342054/.

9. Tom Kludt, "Nikki Haley 'not a fan' of Trump—but still going to vote for him," CNN, October 27, 2016, https://www.cnn.com/2016/10/27/politics/nikki -haley-donald-trump/index.html.

10. Timothy Snyder, *The Road to Unfreedom: Russia, Europe, America* (New York: Tim Duggan Books, 2018), 261.

11. Snyder, *Road to Unfreedom*, 260.

12. "Putin's Revenge (Part 2)," *Frontline*, PBS/WGBH Boston, November 1, 2017.

13. Elise Labott, "Donald Trump Told Nikki Haley She Could Speak Her Mind. She's Doing Just That," *State*, CNN (September 2017), https://www.cnn.com /interactive/2017/politics/state/nikki-haley-donald-trump-united-nations/. "Withdrew from consideration" was how Haley's staff asked the author to phrase it when introducing Haley before her remarks at Elon University's Fall Convocation in September 2019.

14. Maggie Haberman, Michael S. Schmidt, and Julie Hirschfeld Davis, "Jeff Sessions Appears Headed to a Trump Cabinet Position," *New York Times*, November 17, 2016, https://www.nytimes.com/2016/11/17/us/politics /donald-trump-transition.html.

15. Jim Acosta and Daniella Diaz, "Source: Haley Under Consideration for State Dept., Trump Meeting Thursday," CNN, November 16, 2016, https://www.cnn .com/2016/11/16/politics/donald-trump-nikki-haley-transition.

16. Michael Levenson, "Did Mitt Romney Get Played by the King of Reality TV?," *Boston Globe*, December 13, 2016, https://www.bostonglobe.com/metro/2016 /12/13/romney-passed-over-for-secretary-state-ending-bizzare-courtship -with-trump/TtogpbgjArtdQZG0ico7dJ/story.html.

17. Rad Berky, "Haley 'Encouraged' after Meeting with Trump," WCNC

(Charlotte), November 17, 2016, https://www.wcnc.com/article/news/politics /national-politics/haley-encouraged-after-meeting-with-trump/275-352913501.

18. Maggie Haberman, "Nikki Haley Chosen as U.N. Ambassador," *New York Times*, November 23, 2016, https://www.nytimes.com/2016/11/23/us/politics /nikki-haley-donald-trump-un-ambassador.html.

19. Philip Rucker and Carol Leonnig, *A Very Stable Genius: Donald J. Trump's Testing of America* (New York: Penguin Press, 2020), 17.

20. Abigail Tracy, "Nikki Haley Led the Way on Syria—but Will She Set Off a War with State?," *Hive* (blog), *Vanity Fair*, April 15, 2017, https://www.vanityfair .com/news/2017/04/nikki-haley-trump-foreign-policy. In the state's 2018 gubernatorial election, McMaster beat Democratic nominee James Smith 54–46 percent.

21. Labott, "Donald Trump Told Nikki Haley She Could Speak Her Mind."

22. David Bosco, "Why is the United Nations Ambassador in the Cabinet?," *The Multilateralist* (blog), *Foreign Policy*, July 17, 2013, https://foreignpolicy .com/2013/07/17/why-is-the-united-nations-ambassador-in-the-cabinet/.

23. Richard Fausset and Somini Sengupta, "Nikki Haley's Path: From Daughter of Immigrants to Trump's Pick for U.N.," *New York Times*, November 23, 2016, https://www.nytimes.com/2016/11/23/us/nikki-haley-donald-trump-un -ambassador.html.

24. Amber Phillips, "Last Month, Nikki Haley Was 'Not a Fan' of Donald Trump. Now She Has Agreed to Join His Administration," *Washington Post*, November 23, 2016, https://www.washingtonpost.com/news/the-fix /wp/2016/11/23/last-month-nikki-haley-was-not-a-fan-of-donald-trump -now-shes-agreed-to-join-his-administration/.

25. Jerry Markon, Robert Costa, and Emma Brown, "Trump Nominates Two Prominent GOP Women: DeVos as Education Secretary, Haley as U.N. Ambassador," *Washington Post*, November 23, 2016, https://www.washington post.com/politics/trump-nominates-nikki-haley-to-be-un-ambassador/2016 /11/23/401f4a7a-b183-11e6-be1c-8cec35b1ad25_story.html.

26. Lindsey Graham on Twitter, November 23, 2016, https://twitter.com/lindsey grahamsc/status/801429937509040128?lang=en.

27. Bristow Marchant, "What SC Officials Are Saying About Nikki Haley's UN Nomination," *The State*, November 23, 2016, https://www.myrtlebeachonline .com/news/state/south-carolina/article116714123.html.

28. Amy Lieberman, "Development Experts React to Nikki Haley's Appointment as US Ambassador to UN," *Devex*, November 23, 2016, https://www.devex .com/news/development-experts-react-to-nikki-haley-s-appointment-as-us -ambassador-to-un-89218.

29. Steve Coll, *Private Empire: ExxonMobil and American Power* (New York: Penguin Books, 2012).

30. All quotations in this section were transcribed by the author from the unedited video, "U.N. Ambassador to the United Nations confirmation hearing," C-SPAN, January 18, 2017, https://www.c-span.org/video/?421753-1/un-ambassador -nominee-governor-nikki-haley-testifies-confirmation-hearing.

31. Coons would tell a CNN reporter later in the year that he had come to respect Haley's diplomacy.

32. Larry Buchanan, Andrew W. Lehren, Jugal K. Patel, and Adam Pearce, "How Much People in the Trump Administration are Worth," *New York Times*, April 3, 2017, https://www.nytimes.com/interactive/2017/04/01/us/politics /how-much-people-in-the-trump-administration-are-worth-financial -disclosure.html.

33. In 2018, the *New York Times* capped a story about a pricey mechanized curtain installation in Haley's penthouse with the headline, "Nikki Haley's View of New York is Priceless. Her Curtains? $52,701." The story quickly drew a backlash for linking the purchase to the ambassador, which in fact had been made during the Obama administration. This led the *Times* to publish a rare recasting of the story with an editor's note, which said that the original version had created "an unfair impression about who was responsible for the purchase in question," and added, "The article should not have focused on Ms. Haley, nor should a picture of her have been used." Gardiner Harris, "State Department Spent $52,701 on Curtains for Residence of U.N. Envoy," *New York Times*, September 13, 2018, https://www.nytimes.com/2018/09/13/us/politics /state-department-curtains.html.

CHAPTER 4: TAKING NAMES

1. Richard Roth, "US Ambassador Nikki Haley at UN: 'We're Taking Names,'" CNN, January 27, 2017, https://www.cnn.com/2017/01/27/politics/haley-un -first-day.

2. "A Conversation with Nikki Haley," Council on Foreign Relations, New York, March 29, 2017, https://www.cfr.org/event/conversation-nikki-haley.

3. "A Conversation with Nikki Haley."

4. Matt Apuzzo, Maggie Haberman, and Matthew Rosenberg, "Trump Told Russians That Firing 'Nut Job' Comey Eased Pressure from Investigation," *New York Times*, May 19, 2017, https://www.nytimes.com/2017/05/19/us /politics/trump-russia-comey.html.

5. Matthew Rosenberg and Eric Schmitt, "Trump Revealed Highly Classified Intelligence to Russia, in Break with Ally, Officials Say," *New York Times*, May 15, 2017, https://www.nytimes.com/2017/05/15/us/politics/trump -russia-classified-information-isis.html.

6. Abigail Tracy, "Nikki Haley Led the Way on Syria—But Will She Set Off a War With State?" *The Hive* (blog), *Vanity Fair*, April 15, 2017, https://www.vanity fair.com/news/2017/04/nikki-haley-trump-foreign-policy.

7. Eliana Johnson, "Haley Eclipses Tillerson on Trump's Foreign Policy Ladder," *Politico*, April 3, 2017, https://www.politico.com/story/2017/04/nikki-haley-rex -tillerson-foreign-236806.

8. "Transcript: Afghan Officials Say 36 ISIS Fighters Killed by MOAB; National Security Adviser to Head to Afghanistan Soon; Trump Administration to Keep White House Visitor Logs Private; Nikki Haley Emerges as Strong Voice on Trump Foreign Policy," CNN, April 14, 2017, http://edition.cnn.com /TRANSCRIPTS/1704/14/wolf.02.html.

9. Pamela Falk, "All Eyes Should Be on Nikki Haley," *The Hill*,

August 10, 2017, https://thehill.com/blogs/pundits-blog/
foreign-policy/346035-All-eyes-should-be-on-Nikki-Haley.

10. Nahal Toosi, "Two Top Aides to Nikki Haley Quit," *Politico*, August 10, 2017, https://www.politico.com/story/2017/08/10/nikki-haley-2-top-aides-quit
-241479.

11. Dexter Filkins, "Rex Tillerson at the Breaking Point," *New Yorker*, October 16, 2017, https://www.newyorker.com/magazine/2017/10/16/rex-tillerson-at-the
-breaking-point.

12. Dulcie Leimbach, "Where's Samantha Power? Her Rare Appearances Rankle the Press Corps at the UN," *PassBlue*, May 8, 2015, https://www.passblue
.com/2015/05/08/wheres-samantha-power-her-rare-appearances-rankle
-the-press-corps-at-the-un/.

13. Kacie Candela, "The US Ambassador's Love Affair with TV News Shows," *PassBlue*, August 25, 2017, https://www.passblue.com/2017/08/25/the-us
-ambassadors-love-affair-with-tv-news-shows/.

14. Irwin Arieff, "Nikki Haley's Balancing Act," *PassBlue*, July 25, 2017, https://
www.passblue.com/2017/07/25/the-us-ambassadors-balancing-act/.

15. Elise Labott, "Donald Trump Told Nikki Haley She Could Speak Her Mind. She's Doing Just That," *State,* CNN, September 2017, https://www.cnn.com
/interactive/2017/politics/state/nikki-haley-donald-trump-united-nations/.

16. Labott, "Donald Trump Told Nikki Haley She Could Speak Her Mind."

17. Arieff, "Nikki Haley's Balancing Act."

18. Nahal Toosi, "Nikki Haley's Twitter Account Raises Protocol Concerns," *Politico*, May 20, 2018, https://www.politico.com/story/2018/05/20/nikki
-haley-personal-twitter-account-597279.

19. Toosi, "Nikki Haley's Twitter Account Raises Protocol Concerns."

20. See Helena Andrews-Dyer, "Rocker Joan Jett and Gov. Nikki Haley Hang Out in New York," *Washington Post*, May 20, 2014, https://www.washingtonpost
.com/news/reliable-source/wp/2014/05/20/rocker-joan-jett-and-gov-nikki
-haley-hang-out-in-new-york/; and Caitlyn Byrd, "Nikki Haley's Love of Joan Jett Is About to Hit the Big Screen," *Post and Courier* (Charleston), September 18, 2018, https://www.postandcourier.com/politics/nikki-haleys
-love-of-joan-jett-is-about-to-hit-the-big-screen/article_e22f21d6-bb55
-11e8-b1dc-3f2ef6f3f882.html.

21. Rob Dozier, "Nikki Haley's Instagram Is an Odd Window into the Life of a Woman Who Wants You to Know She Has It All," *Slate*, June 29, 2018, https://
slate.com/technology/2018/06/nikki-haleys-instagram-is-a-bizarre-window
-into-one-woman-who-manages-to-have-it-all.html.

22. "Digital Diplomacy: Is Nikki Haley's Twitter Account Violating Protocol?," *Sputnik News*, May 20, 2018, https://sputniknews.com/us/2018052010646
27626-nikki-haley-twitter-protocol-breach/.

23. Somini Sengupta and Rick Gladstone, "Nikki Haley Says U.S. May 'Take Our Own Action' on Syrian Chemical Attack," *New York Times*, April 5, 2017, https://www.nytimes.com/2017/04/05/world/middleeast/syria-chemical
-attack-un.html.

24. Theodore Shleifer, "Haley Says Trump Doesn't Limit Her Foreign Policy

Bullhorn," CNN, April 13, 2017, https://www.cnn.com/2017/04/13/politics /nikki-haley-profile-jamie-gangel.

25. "Transcript and Video: Trump Speaks About Strikes in Syria," *New York Times*, April 6, 2017, https://www.nytimes.com/2017/04/06/world/middleeast /transcript-video-trump-airstrikes-syria.html.

26. Everett Rosenfeld, "The US warned the Russians ahead of Syrian missile strikes," CNBC, April 7, 2017, https://www.cnbc.com/2017/04/06/the-us -warned-the-russians-ahead-of-syria-missile-strikes-official.html.

27. Nikki Haley, "Nikki Haley: An Unprecedented Step on Human Rights," CNN, April 19, 2017, https://www.cnn.com/2017/04/19/opinions/human-rights -cycle-violence-nikki-haley.

28. "Trump Jokes (?) About Firing Nikki Haley: 'She Could Easily Be Replaced,'" *Washington Post*, April 24, 2017, https://www.washingtonpost.com/news/the -fix/wp/2017/04/24/trump-jokes-about-firing-nikki-haley-she-could-easily -be-replaced/.

29. David Nakamura and Anne Gearan, "Obama Warned Trump on North Korea. But Trump's 'Fire and Fury' Strategy Wasn't What Obama Aides Expected," *Washington Post*, August 9, 2017, https://www.washingtonpost.com/politics /obama-warned-trump-on-north-korea-but-trumps-fire-and-fury-strategy -wasnt-what-obama-aides-expected/2017/08/09/f3f02e0e-7d19-11e7-9d08 -b79f191668ed_story.html.

30. Zachary Cohen, "Trump Claims (Without Evidence) Obama Nearly Launched War with North Korea," CNN, WRAL, https://www.wral.com/trump-claims -without-evidence-obama-nearly-launched-war-with-north-korea/17876057 /?version=amp.

31. "Trump Says North Korea 'Behaving Very Badly,' China Has Done Little to Help," Reuters, March 17, 2017, https://www.reuters.com/article/us-north korea-trump/trump-says-north-korea-behaving-very-badly-china-has -done-little-to-help-idUSKBN16O1OX.

32. Michelle Nichols, "United Nations Bans Key North Korean Exports Over Missile Tests," Reuters, August 5, 2017, https://www.reuters.com/article/uk -northkorea-missiles-un-idUKKBN1AL0NS.

33. Ambassador Nikki Haley, "Remarks at an Emergency UN Security Council Briefing on North Korea," US Mission to the United Nations, September 4, 2017, https://usun.usmission.gov/remarks-at-an-emergency-un-security -council-briefing-on-north-korea/.

34. Quoted in D. Parvaz, "North Korea Isn't 'Begging for War'—It's Fighting for Survival," *ThinkProgress*, September 6, 2017, https://archive.thinkprogress .org/north-korea-begging-for-war-23ece17ac1e2/.

35. Maxwell Tani, "Nikki Haley Defends Trump's Nickname for Kim Jong Un: 'Every Other International Community is Now Referring to Him as Rocket Man,'" Yahoo! Life, September 20, 2017, https://www.yahoo.com/lifestyle /nikki-haley-defends-trumps-nickname-151239409.html.

36. David Albright, Sarah Burkhard, Allison Lach, and Andrea Stricker, "Countries Involved in Violating UNSC Resolutions on North Korea," Institute for Science and International Security, December 5, 2017, https://isis-online.org/isis

-reports/detail/countries-involved-in-violating-unsc-resolutions-on-north
-korea/10.

37. Aaron Blake, "Trump's Big Win at the United Nations," *Washington Post*,
August 7, 2017, https://www.washingtonpost.com/news/the-fix/wp/2017/08
/07/trumps-big-win-at-the-united-nations/.

38. Ben Evansky, "How Nikki Haley Brought Trump's Maximum Pressure
Campaign Down on North Korea at UN Security Council," Fox News, June 11,
2018, https://www.foxnews.com/politics/how-nikki-haley-brought-trumps
-maximum-pressure-campaign-down-on-north-korea-at-un-security-council.

39. Evansky, "How Nikki Haley Brought Trump's Maximum Pressure Campaign
Down."

40. See Allison Colburn, "Haley Wrongly Says Congress Had No Input on Iran
Nuclear Deal," Politifact, Poynter Institute, October 19, 2017, https://www
.politifact.com/factchecks/2017/oct/19/nikki-haley/haley-wrongly-says
-congress-had-no-input-iran-nucl/.

41. Nikki Haley, *With All Due Respect: Defending America With Grit and Grace*
(New York: St. Martin's Press, 2019), 157.

42. "UN Ambassador Nikki Haley: Considerations on US Policy Towards Iran,"
American Enterprise Institute, Washington, DC, September 5, 2017, https://
www.youtube.com/watch?v=gwa7lHhFKRM.

43. On the "chosen trauma" concept, see Vamik D. Volkan, "Large Group
Identity, International Relations and Psychoanalysis," *International Forum
of Psychoanalysis* 18, No. 4 (2009): 206–13.

44. Colum Lynch and Dan de Luce, "With Saudi Blockade Threatening Famine in
Yemen, U.S. Points Finger at Iran," *Foreign Policy*, November 22, 2017, https://
foreignpolicy.com/2017/11/22/with-saudi-blockade-threatening-famine-in
-yemen-u-s-points-finger-at-iran/.

45. Lynch and de Luce, "With Saudi Blockade Threatening Famine in Yemen."

46. John Ismay and Helene Cooper, "U.S. Accuses Iran of U.N. Violation, but
Evidence Falls Short," *New York Times*, December 14, 2017, https://www
.nytimes.com/2017/12/14/world/middleeast/nikki-haley-iran-weapons
-yemen.html.

47. Ismay and Cooper, "U.S. Accuses Iran of U.N. Violation."

48. Ismay and Cooper, "U.S. Accuses Iran of U.N. Violation."

49. Colum Lynch and Robbie Gramer, "Haley's 'Smoking Gun' on Iran Met with
Skepticism at U.N.," *Foreign Policy*, December 4, 2017, https://foreignpolicy
.com/2017/12/14/nikki-haley-yemen-houthi-rebels-iran-missiles-press
-conference-pentagon-skepticism-united-nations-trump-nuclear-deal
-diplomacy/.

50. Benny Avni, "How Nikki Haley is Pushing Europe to Get Tough on Iran," *New
York Post*, January 30, 2018, https://nypost.com/2018/01/30/how-nikki-haley
-is-pushing-europe-to-get-tough-on-iran/.

51. Nikki Haley, "The U.N.'s Uncomfortable Truths About Iran," op-ed, *New York
Times*, February 17, 2018, https://www.nytimes.com/2018/02/17/opinion
/nikki-haley-united-nations-iran.html.

52. Nicole Gaouette, "Despite Haley Threat, UN Votes to Condemn Trump

Jerusalem Decision," CNN, December 22, 2017, https://www.cnn.com/2017
/12/21/politics/haley-un-jerusalem/index.html.

53. Colum Lynch, "Corrupt Guatemalans' GOP Lifeline," *Foreign Policy*,
February 5, 2019, https://foreignpolicy.com/2019/02/05/trump-republican
-lawmakers-weaken-u-n-anti-corruption-commission-guatemala-jimmy
-morales-white-house-putin/.

54. Lynch, "Corrupt Guatemalans' GOP Lifeline."

55. David M. Halbfinger, Isabel Kershner and Declan Walsh, "Israel Kills Dozens
at Gaza Border as U.S. Embassy Opens in Jerusalem," *New York Times*, May 14,
2018, https://www.nytimes.com/2018/05/14/world/middleeast/gaza-protests
-palestinians-us-embassy.html.

56. Adriene Masha Varkiani, "Nikki Haley Walks Out of U.N. Security Council
Meeting as Palestinian Envoy Begins to Speak," *ThinkProgress*, May 15, 2018,
https://archive.thinkprogress.org/nikki-haley-walks-out-of-the-un-3459a4
ac3c2e/. See also "Nikki Haley Defends Israel after Gaza Violence, Walks Out
of Meeting," CBS News, May 16, 2018, https://www.cbsnews.com/news/nikki
-haley-defends-israel-walks-out-of-un-meeting/.

57. Rick Gladstone, "U.S. Vetoes U.N. Resolution on Gaza, Fails to Win Second
Vote on its Own Measure," *New York Times*, June 1, 2018, https://www.nytimes
.com/2018/06/01/world/middleeast/gaza-israel-palestinians-.html.

58. David A. Fahrenthold, "Trump Recorded Having Extremely Lewd
Conversation About Women in 2005," *Washington Post*, October 8, 2016,
https://www.washingtonpost.com/politics/trump-recorded-having-extremely
-lewd-conversation-about-women-in-2005/2016/10/07/3b9ce776-8cb4-11e6
-bf8a-3d26847eeed4_story.html.

59. Emma Dumain, "Nikki Haley May Have Had the Defining Moment of Her
Career—Again," *Post and Courier*, April 9, 2017, https://www.postandcourier
.com/news/nikki-haley-may-have-had-the-defining-moment-of-her/article
_4d561b00-1bba-11e7-92ac-d3baeb87821d.html.

60. "Cornel West & Rev. Traci Blackmon: Clergy in Charlottesville Were Trapped
by Torch-Wielding Nazis," *Democracy Now!*, August 14, 2017, https://www
.democracynow.org/2017/8/14/cornel_west_rev_toni_blackmon_clergy.

61. "Full Text: Trump's Comments on White Supremacists, 'Alt-left' in
Charlottesville," *Politico*, August 15, 2017, https://www.politico.com/story
/2017/08/15/full-text-trump-comments-white-supremacists-alt-left
-transcript-241662.

62. Gregory Favre, "For Pointers on Handling Charlottesville, Trump Could Have
Asked Nikki Haley," *Sacramento Bee*, August 18, 2017, https://www.sacbee
.com/opinion/op-ed/article168048917.html.

63. Sophie Tatum, "Nikki Haley to Staff on Charlottesville: 'We Must Denounce
Them at Every Turn,'" CNN, September 8, 2017, https://www.cnn.com/2017
/09/08/politics/un-ambassador-nikki-haley-charlottesville-email-state.

64. "Transcript: Nikki Haley on 'Face the Nation,' Dec. 10, 2017," CBS News,
https://www.cbsnews.com/news/transcript-nikki-haley-on-face-the-nation
-dec-10-2017/.

65. Catherine Powell, "#MeToo Goes Global and Crosses Multiple Boundaries,"
blog post, Council on Foreign Relations, December 14, 2017, https://www.cfr
.org/blog/metoo-goes-global-and-crosses-multiple-boundaries.

66. Abigail Tracy, "'Barely Disguised Political Ambitions': Are Nikki Haley's Chess Moves Putting Her in Danger?," *Hive* (blog) *Vanity Fair*, December 12, 2017, https://www.vanityfair.com/news/2017/12/nikki-haley-donald-trump-accusers.

67. Jonathan Lemire and Richard Lardner, "Trump Says Female Senator 'Would Do Anything' for Money," Associated Press, December 12, 2017, https://apnews.com/article/e3b50b28fa73426799e6ac63839057fb.

68. Andrea Mitchell, tweeted statement, @mitchellreports, Twitter, December 11, 2017.

69. Eliana Johnson, "An Affair with Trump? Nikki Haley on 'Disgusting' Rumors and Her Rise to a Top Foreign Policy Role," *Women Rule* (podcast), *Politico*, January 26, 2018, https://www.politico.com/story/2018/01/26/nikki-haley-trump-foreign-policy-370851.

70. Archive: Ambassador Nikki Haley, Twitter, January 28, 2018, https://twitter.com/ambnikkihaley/status/957813664207245313?lang=en.

71. Bari Weiss, "The Slut-Shaming of Nikki Haley," op-ed, *New York Times*, January 29, 2018, https://www.nytimes.com/2018/01/29/opinion/nikki-haley-slutshaming-clinton-grammys.html.

72. "Trump Answers Questions on Rex Tillerson and Mike Pompeo: Full Transcript," *New York Times*, March 13, 2018, https://www.nytimes.com/2018/03/13/us/politics/trump-pompeo-tillerson.html.

73. Jeremy Diamond, Kevin Liptak, Kaitlan Collins, and Elise Labott, "Haley's Response to WH Blame over Sanctions: 'I Don't Get Confused,'" CNN, April 18, 2018, https://www.cnn.com/2018/04/17/politics/nikki-haley-russia-sanctions/index.html.

74. Aaron Blake, "Nikki Haley's Extraordinary Rebuke of the White House," *Washington Post*, April 17, 2018, https://www.washingtonpost.com/news/the-fix/wp/2018/04/17/nikki-haleys-extraordinary-public-rebuke-of-the-white-house/.

75. Grant Gambling, "Nikki Haley: 'With All Due Respect, I Don't Get Confused,'" *RedState*, April 17, 2018, https://redstate.com/grantgambling/2018/04/17/nikki-haley-due-respect-dont-get-confused-n88197.

76. Blake, "Nikki Haley's Extraordinary Rebuke of the White House."

77. Peter Baker, Julie Hirschfeld Davis, and Maggie Haberman, "Sanctions Flap Erupts into Open Conflict Between Haley and White House," *New York Times*, April 17, 2018, https://www.nytimes.com/2018/04/17/world/europe/trump-nikki-haley-russia-sanctions.html.

CHAPTER 5: HEDGING BETS

1. "Donald Trump's Humiliation in Helsinki," *The Economist*, July 21, 2018, https://www.economist.com/leaders/2018/07/21/donald-trumps-humiliation-in-helsinki.

2. Abigail Tracy, "'Not a Good Look': Inside Nikki Haley's Retreat to Trump Island," *Hive* (blog), *Vanity Fair*, January 25, 2018, https://www.vanityfair.com/news/2018/01/nikki-haley-donald-trump-united-nations.

3. Gabriel Debenedetti, "Dems Prep for Pence, Kasich, Haley to Run in 2020," *Politico*, August 22, 2017, https://www.politico.com/story/2017/08/22/democrats-2020-trump-primary-241866.

4. Peter Baker, Julie Hirschfeld Davis, and Maggie Haberman, "Sanctions Flap Erupts into Open Conflict Between Haley and White House," *New York Times*, April 17, 2018, https://www.nytimes.com/2018/04/17/world/europe/trump-nikki-haley-russia-sanctions.html.

5. Maggie Haberman, "Pence Hires Haley Aide as National Security Advisor, Creating Unusual Dual Role," *New York Times*, April 13, 2018, https://www.nytimes.com/2018/04/13/us/politics/pence-jon-lerner-nikki-haley.html.

6. Jonathan Swan, "Scoop: Trump Tried to Block Pence National Security Appointment," *Axios*, April 15, 2018, https://www.axios.com/trump-pence-block-national-security-lerner-haley-1256a68a-718e-42e2-a4d5-e52b7d86b402.html.

7. Reuters, "Haley: Relationship with Trump Is 'Perfect,'" *Voice of America*, April 18, 2018, https://www.voanews.com/usa/us-politics/haley-relationship-trump-perfect.

8. Alex Ward, "Exclusive: Trump Promised Kim Jong Un He'd Sign a Statement to End the Korean War," *Vox*, August 29, 2018, https://www.vox.com/2018/8/29/17795452/trump-north-korea-war-summit-singapore-promise.

9. Stephan M. Haggard, "Those North Korean Sanctions Might Be Working. Here's Why," *Monkey Cage* (blog), *Washington Post*, April 6, 2018, https://www.washingtonpost.com/news/monkey-cage/wp/2018/04/06/those-north-korea-sanctions-might-be-working-heres-why/.

10. Jamie Tarabay, "Pompeo's North Korea Meeting Went 'As Badly as It Could Have Gone,'" CNN, July 11, 2018, https://www.cnn.com/2018/07/11/politics/pompeo-north-korea-intl/index.html.

11. Joel Gehrke, "Nikki Haley Unveils 89 Examples of North Korea Smuggling Oil, Calls for Supply Cutoff," *Washington Examiner*, July 12, 2018, https://www.washingtonexaminer.com/policy/defense-national-security/nikki-haley-unveils-89-examples-of-north-korea-smuggling-oil-calls-for-supply-cutoff.

12. "Remarks With Permanent Representative to the United Nations Nikki Haley," U.S. Embassy & Consulates in China, July 20, 2018, https://china.usembassy-china.org.cn/remarks-with-permanent-representative-to-the-united-nations-nikki-haley/.

13. Ian Talley and Anatoly Kurmanaev, "Thousands of North Korean Workers Enter Russia Despite U.N. Ban," *Wall Street Journal*, August 2, 2018, https://www.wsj.com/articles/russia-is-issuing-north-korean-work-permits-despite-u-n-ban-1533216752.

14. Don Lee, "China Is Quietly Relaxing Its Sanctions against North Korea, Complicating Matters for Trump," *Los Angeles Times*, August 3, 2018, https://www.latimes.com/business/la-fg-china-north-korea-sanctions-2018-story.html.

15. Josh Rogin, "Why Trump canceled Pompeo's trip to North Korea," *Washington Post*, August 27, 2018, https://www.washingtonpost.com/news/josh-rogin/wp/2018/08/27/why-trump-cancelled-pompeos-trip-to-north-korea/.

16. "Presentation of the Jeane J. Kirkpatrick Award to U.N. Ambassador Nikki Haley," Foundation for Defense of Democracies, August 28, 2018, https://s3.us-east-2.amazonaws.com/defenddemocracy/uploads/documents/FDD-Summit-Ambassador-Haley.pdf.

17. Julian E. Barnes and Eric Schmitt, "Trump Promotes Diplomatic Gains, but

North Korea Continues Building Missiles," *New York Times*, July 31, 2018, https://www.nytimes.com/2018/07/31/us/politics/north-korea-missiles.html.

18. "Presentation of the Jeane J. Kirkpatrick Award to U.N. Ambassador Nikki Haley."

19. Secretary Mike Pompeo, Secretary of State, United States, and Ambassador Nikki Haley, U.S. Permanent Representative to the United Nations, "Remarks on the UN Human Rights Council," U.S. Permanent Mission to the United Nations, Washington, D.C., June 19, 2018, https://usun.usmission.gov /remarks-on-the-un-human-rights-council/.

20. Carol Morello, "U.S. Withdraws from U.N. Human Rights Council over Perceived Bias against Israel," *The Washington Post*, June 19, 2018, https://www .washingtonpost.com/world/national-security/us-expected-to-back-away -from-un-human-rights-council/2018/06/19/a49c2d0c-733c-11e8-b4b7 -308400242c2e_story.html.

21. Morello, "U.S. Withdraws from U.N. Human Rights Council."

22. Nick Cumming-Bruce, "U.N. Rights Chief Tells U.S. to Stop Taking Migrant Children From Parents," *New York Times*, June 18, 2018, https://www.nytimes .com/2018/06/18/world/europe/trump-migrant-children-un.html.

23. Press Release, Spokesman for UN Secretary General António Guterres, "Secretary-General Says Refugees, Migrants Should Be Treated With Dignity," June 18, 2018, https://www.un.org/press/en/2018/sgsm19094.doc.htm.

24. "US Migrant Children Policy Reversal, Still 'Fails' Thousands of Detained Youngsters: UN Rights Experts," *UN News*, June 22, 2018, https://news.un.org /en/story/2018/06/1012832.

25. Gardiner Harris, "Haley Blames Watchdog Groups for U.S. Withdrawal from U.N. Rights Council," *New York Times*, June 20, 2018, https://www.nytimes .com/2018/06/20/us/politics/haley-un-human-rights-council.html.

26. Letter from Amnesty International to Ambassador Haley, June 22, 2018, https://www.amnesty.org/download/Documents/AMR5186502018 ENGLISH.PDF.

27. Brian Houser, "Letter: The U.S. Has Abandoned the Crusade for Human Rights," *Chicago Tribune*, July 11, 2018, https://www.chicagotribune.com /opinion/letters/ct-letters-un-human-rights-council-nikki-haley-20180629 -story.html.

28. "Statement on Visit to the USA, by Professor Philip Alston, United Nations Special Rapporteur on Extreme Poverty and Human Rights," Office of the High Commissioner for Human Rights, United Nations, December 15, 2017, https://www.ohchr.org/EN/NewsEvents/Pages/DisplayNews.aspx?NewsID =22533.

29. "Report of the Special Rapporteur on Extreme Poverty and Human Rights on His Mission to the United States of America," United Nations, distributed by the Secretariat to the General Assembly, May 4, 2018, Human Rights Council thirty-eighth session, June 18–July 6, 2018, Agenda item 3. Online at http:// undocs.org/A/HRC/38/33/ADD.1.

30. Jeff Stein, "Nikki Haley: It Is Patently Ridiculous for the United Nations to Examine Poverty in America," *Washington Post*, June 21, 2018, https://www .washingtonpost.com/news/wonk/wp/2018/06/21/nikki-haley-it-is-patently -ridiculous-for-the-united-nations-to-examine-poverty-in-america/.

31. Nikki Haley, "The United Nations' Patently Ridiculous Report on American Poverty," *National Review*, July 9, 2018, https://www.nationalreview.com/2018/07/united-nations-report-on-american-poverty-distorts-and-misrepresents/.

32. Barbara Crossette, "Donald Trump and Nikki Haley Take Aim at the Human Rights Council," *The Nation*, January 8, 2018, https://www.thenation.com/article/archive/donald-trump-and-nikki-haley-take-aim-at-the-un-human-rights-council/.

33. Jeff Stein, "The U.N. Says 18.5 million Americans Are in 'Extreme Poverty.' Trump's Team Says Just 250,000 Are," *Washington Post*, June 25, 2018, https://www.washingtonpost.com/news/wonk/wp/2018/06/25/trump-team-rebukes-u-n-saying-it-overestimates-extreme-poverty-in-america-by-18-million-people/.

34. Jeff Stein and Tracy Jan, "The Trump Administration has a new argument for dismantling the social safety net: It worked.," *Washington Post*, July 14, 2018, https://www.washingtonpost.com/business/economy/white-house-declares-war-on-poverty-largely-over-amid-push-to-revamp-social-programs/2018/07/13/8f9536ea-86b2-11e8-8f6c-46cb43e3f306_story.html.

35. Evie Fordham, "Nikki Haley Shames Washington Post into Issuing Correction after Spreading False Reporting about Her," *Daily Caller*, July 15, 2018, https://dailycaller.com/2018/07/15/nikki-haley-washington-post-correction/.

36. Fordham, "Nikki Haley Shames Washington Post into Issuing Correction."

37. Vicente Fox Quesada, Twitter, June 19, 2018, https://twitter.com/vicentefoxque/status/1009214660309078016?lang=en.

38. June 19, 2018.

39. Stephen Schlesinger, "Nikki Haley's Dimming Star," CNN.com, June 26, 2018, https://www.cnn.com/2018/06/25/opinions/nikki-haley-dimming-star-schlesinger.

40. Clifford D. May, "Nikki Haley, a Woman for Our Times," *Washington Times*, June 26, 2018, https://www.washingtontimes.com/news/2018/jun/26/nikki-haley-a-woman-for-our-times/.

41. Jeane J. Kirkpatrick, "Standing Alone," in *Legitimacy and Force*, Vol. 1, *Political and Moral Dimensions* (New Brunswick, NJ: Transaction Books), p. 195 and 193–4; emphasis in original.

42. Jeff Manning, "Immigration Crackdown Brings 123 Migrants to Sheridan, Outrage from Oregon Democrats," *The Oregonian*/OregonLive, June 16, 2018.

43. Sonia Smith, "Asylum Politics," *Texas Monthly*, August 2014.

44. See Mark Dow, *American Gulag: Inside U.S. Immigration Prisons* (Berkeley: University of California Press, 2004), 105–9.

45. Ajay Lele, "Will India Be Able to Balance Ties with US without Damaging Relations with Iran and Russia?" *DailyO*, July 4, 2018, https://www.dailyo.in/politics/2-plus-2-dialogue-india-us-nikki-haley-sushma-swaraj-nirmala-sitharaman/story/1/25273.html.

46. Joanna Slater, "Mike Pompeo Was Supposed to Meet with His Indian Counterpart. He Went to North Korea Instead." *Washington Post*, July 6, 2018, https://www.washingtonpost.com/news/worldviews/wp/2018/07/06/mike-pompeo-was-supposed-to-meet-with-his-indian-counterpart-he-went-to-north-korea-instead/.

47. "India, Top Iranian Oil Importer, Says Will Not Heed U.S. Sanctions," Radio Free Europe/Radio Liberty, May 29, 2018, https://www.rferl.org/a/india-top -iranian-oil-importer-says-will-not-honor-us-sanctions-swaraj/29256213.html.

48. Michelle Nichols, "U.S. Envoy Tells Modi Important to Cut Imports of Iranian Oil," Reuters, June 27, 2018, https://www.reuters.com/article/us-usa-iran-india /u-s-envoy-haley-tells-modi-important-to-cut-imports-of-iranian-oil-idUSK BN1JN24K.

49. Indrani Bagchi, "Nikki Haley Talks Tough on Iran Import Curbs," *Times of India*, June 29, 2018, https://timesofindia.indiatimes.com/business/india -business/us-firm-india-may-cut-energy-imports-from-iran/articleshow /64782981.cms.

50. Reuters, "India Preparing for Cut in Oil Imports From Iran," *Deccan Chronicle*, June 29, 2018, https://www.deccanchronicle.com/business/in-other-news /290618/india-preparing-for-cut-in-oil-imports-from-iran.html.

51. Mat McDermott, "In Pulling Photo of Nikki Haley in Front of Hindu Swastika, Reuters Failed as Journalists," Samudra (blog), July 2, 2018, https://www .patheos.com/blogs/samudra/2018/07/pulling-photo-nikki-haley-hindu -swastika-reuters-failed-journalists/.

52. "Reuters Shows Its Ignorance by Removing Picture of Nikki Haley with 'Swastika' at Hindu Temple," *Daily News and Analysis*, June 30, 2018, https:// www.dnaindia.com/india/report-reuters-shows-its-ignorance-by-removing -picture-of-nikki-haley-with-swastika-at-hindu-temple-2631306.

53. "DSGMC Takes Up with Nikki Haley Issue of 52 Indians Held in US," *The Tribune* (Chandigarh), June 28, 2018, https://www.tribuneindia.com/news /archive/nation/dsgmc-takes-up-with-nikki-haley-issue-of-52-indians-held -in-us-611920.

54. Sunita Sohrabji, "Sikh Nationals Seeking Asylum Allowed to Leave Sheridan, Oregon, Prison on Bond; ACLU Drops Lawsuit," *India West*, December 20, 2018, https://www.indiawest.com/news/global_indian/sikh-nationals-seeking -asylum-allowed-to-leave-sheridan-oregon-prison-on-bond-aclu-drops -lawsuit/article_5ac8b1f4-03d9-11e9-ba46-833ad74cb2c4.html?.

55. "Advancing India-US Relations—Special Address by Amb. Nikki R. Haley," Observer Research Foundation, New Delhi, June 28, 2018, https://www.orf online.org/research/advancing-india-us-relations-special-address-nikki-haley/.

56. "Advancing India-US Relations—Special Address by Amb. Nikki R. Haley."

57. "U.S. Ambassador to the U.N., Nikki Haley, Address to UH," YouTube, May 22, 2018, https://www.youtube.com/watch?v=Lgoy56KsPfU.

58. Ambassador Nikki Haley, Remarks at the Christians United for Israel Annual Summit (as delivered), July 23, 2018, Washington, DC. United States Mission to the United Nations. Online at https://usun.state.gov/remarks/8528.

59. Adam K. Raymond, "Nikki Haley Tells Conservative Teens to Stop Trying to 'Own the Libs,'" *Intelligencer* (blog), *New York*, July 24, 2018, https://nymag .com/intelligencer/2018/07/nikki-haley-to-conservative-teens-stop-owning -the-libs.html.

60. Penny Starr, "Nikki Haley Scolds Students: You Shouldn't 'Own the Libs,'" *Breitbart*, July 24, 2018, https://www.breitbart.com/national-security/2018/07 /24/haleys-mixed-message-high-schoolers-dont-own-libs-stand-up-mob/.

61. Aaron Blake, "Nikki Haley Warns Against 'Owning the Libs.' That's Basically Trump's Entire Political Strategy," *Washington Post*, July 24, 2018, https://www.washingtonpost.com/news/the-fix/wp/2018/07/24/nikki-haley-warns-against-owning-the-libs-thats-basically-trumps-entire-political-strategy/.

62. Anonymous senior official in the Trump administration, "I Am Part of the Resistance inside the Trump Administration," *New York Times*, September 5, 2018, https://www.nytimes.com/2018/09/05/opinion/trump-white-house-anonymous-resistance.html.

63. Chris Cillizza, "13 People Who Might Be the Author of the New York Times Op-Ed," *The Point with Chris Cillizza* (blog), CNN, September 6, 2018, https://www.cnn.com/2018/09/05/politics/donald-trump-mystery-op-ed/index.html.

64. Nikki Haley, "When I Challenge the President, I Do It Directly. My Anonymous Colleague Should Have, Too," *Washington Post*, September 7, 2018, https://www.washingtonpost.com/opinions/when-i-challenge-the-president-i-do-it-directly-my-anonymous-colleague-should-have-too/2018/09/07/d453eaf6-b2ae-11e8-9a6a-565d92a3585d_story.html.

65. Ed Kilgore, "Nikki Haley Shows How to Exploit a Crisis With Op-Ed on Anonymous White House Writer," *Intelligencer* (blog), *New York*, September 8, 2018, https://nymag.com/intelligencer/2018/09/nikki-haley-shows-again-how-to-exploit-a-crisis.html.

66. Joseph P. Duggan, "Nikki Haley's 'Song of Myself,'" *American Spectator*, September 12, 2018, https://spectator.org/nikki-haleys-song-of-myself/.

67. David Nakamura, "'People Actually Laughed at a President': At U.N. Speech, Trump Suffers the Fate He Always Feared," *Washington Post*, September 25, 2018, https://www.washingtonpost.com/politics/people-actually-laughed-at-a-president-at-un-speech-trump-suffers-the-fate-he-always-feared/2018/09/25/990b1d52-c0eb-11e8-90c9-23f963eea204_story.html.

CHAPTER 6: CITIZEN HALEY

1. Maggie Haberman, Mark Landler, and Edward Wong, "Nikki Haley to Resign as Trump's Ambassador to U.N.," *New York Times*, October 9, 2018, https://www.nytimes.com/2018/10/09/us/politics/nikki-haley-united-nations.html.

2. Jacob Pramuk and Bryan Schwartz, "Nikki Haley Will Resign as Trump's UN Ambassador at the End of the Year," CNBC, October 9, 2018, https://www.cnbc.com/2018/10/09/nikki-haley-resigns-as-trumps-un-ambassador.html.

3. Haberman, Landler, and Wong, "Nikki Haley to Resign as Trump's Ambassador to U.N."

4. Andy Shain, "Nikki Haley Reportedly Seeking $200,000 for Speeches, More Than a Year's Pay at Her Old Jobs," *Post and Courier* (Charleston), January 30, 2019, https://www.postandcourier.com/politics/nikki-haley-reportedly-seeking-200-000-for-speeches-more-than-years-pay-at-her-old/article_ca21241c-24ab-11e9-af15-ffb30a6769f4.html.

5. Jeffry Bartash, "Nikki Haley's 2-Year Stint as Trump's U.N. Ambassador Not Unusual for a Job That's Often Been a Revolving Door," MarketWatch, October 9, 2018, https://www.marketwatch.com/story/nikki-haleys-2-year-stint-as-trumps-un-ambassador-not-usual-for-a-job-thats-often-been-a-revolving-door-2018-10-09.

6. Andy Shain, "Watchdog Group Wants Investigation of Nikki Haley Flights to SC," *Post and Courier*, October 8, 2018, https://www.postandcourier.com /politics/watchdog-wants-investigation-of-nikki-haleys-private-jet-flights -to-sc/article_d32bcbb0-cb2e-11e8-8c2a-076e4f7ad7a1.html.

7. Jennifer Rubin, "Why Nikki Haley's Resignation Is No Surprise," *Washington Post*, October 9, 2018, https://www.washingtonpost.com/news/opinions/wp /2018/10/09/why-nikki-haleys-resignation-is-no-surprise/.

8. Stephen Collinson, "Nikki Haley May Have Timed Her Exit Perfectly," CNN, October 10, 2018, https://www.cnn.com/2018/10/10/politics/nikki-haley -donald-trump-election-2020-2024/index.html.

9. Peter Feaver, "Nikki Haley Will Be Back," *Foreign Policy*, October 9, 2018, https://foreignpolicy.com/2018/10/09/nikki-haley-will-be-back-un-trump/.

10. Zack Beauchamp, "How Nikki Haley Played the White House Game—And Won," *Vox*, October 9, 2018, https://www.vox.com/policy-and-politics/2018 /10/9/17955654/nikki-haley-resign-news.

11. Alex Ward, "The Paradox of Nikki Haley," *Vox*, October 9, 2018, https://www .vox.com/2018/10/9/17955618/nikki-haley-resigns-un-ambassador-trump.

12. Daniel W. Drezner, "Assessing Nikki Haley," *Washington Post*, October 10, 2018, https://www.washingtonpost.com/outlook/2018/10/10/assessing-nikki-haley/.

13. John Nichols, "Nikki Haley Was Never the Adult in the Room," *The Nation*, October 9, 2018, https://www.thenation.com/article/archive/nikki-haley-was -never-the-adult-in-the-room/.

14. Zak Cheney-Rice, "Nikki Haley Represents the GOP's Doomed Flirtation with Racial Inclusiveness," *Intelligencer* (blog), *New York*, October 10, 2018, https:// nymag.com/intelligencer/2018/10/nikki-haley-was-co-opted-by-the-trump -administration.html.

15. John Wagner, "At Charity Dinner, Nikki Haley Takes Jabs at Trump and Other Political Elites," *Washington Post*, October 19, 2018, https://www.washington post.com/politics/at-charity-dinner-nikki-haley-takes-playful-jabs-at-trump- and-other-political-elites/2018/10/19/f91dcd7e-d389-11e8-b2d2-f397227 b43f0_story.html.

16. Jack Holmes, "Trump's Defenders Keep Turning to False-Equivalence Propaganda to Defend Him," *Esquire*, October 30, 2018, https://www.esquire .com/news-politics/a24430904/nikki-haley-trump-pittsburgh-shooting -charleston/.

17. John Fund, "How About Nikki Haley for Speaker?," *National Review*, October 28, 2018, https://www.nationalreview.com/2018/10/nikki-haley -house-speaker-could-unite-parties/.

18. Matt Lewis, "Trump Should Dump Pence and Run with Nikki Haley," *Daily Beast*, November 13, 2018, https://www.thedailybeast.com/trump-should -dump-pence-and-run-with-nikki-haley.

19. Krishnadev Calamur, "After Nikki Haley, Will Anyone Stand Up to Russia?," *The Atlantic,* November 26, 2018, https://www.theatlantic.com/international /archive/2018/11/nikki-haley-russia-ukraine/576670/.

20. Michael Schwirtz, "In Blow to Haley, U.N. Rejects Measure Condemning Hamas," *New York Times*, December 6, 2018, https://www.nytimes.com/2018 /12/06/world/middleeast/israel-hamas-haley-united-nations.html.

21. Benjamin Wittes, "Five Things I Learned From the Mueller Report," *The*

Atlantic, April 29, 2019, https://www.theatlantic.com/ideas/archive/2019/04/ben-wittes-five-conclusions-mueller-report/588259/.

22. Shane Harris, "Testimony by Intelligence Chiefs on Global Threats Highlights Differences with President," *Washington Post*, January 29, 2019, https://www.washingtonpost.com/world/national-security/intelligence-officials-will-name-biggest-threats-facing-us-during-senate-hearing/2019/01/28/f08dc5cc-2340-11e9-ad53-824486280311_story.html.

23. Katie Reilly, "Nikki Haley Boasted That the U.S. is More Respected Under Trump. Polls Say Otherwise," *Time*, October 9, 2018, https://time.com/5419603/nikki-haley-donald-trump-united-states-global-respect/. See Julie Ray, "World's Approval of U.S. Leadership Drops to New Low," Gallup, January 18, 2018, https://news.gallup.com/poll/225761/world-approval-leadership-drops-new-low.aspx; and Richard Wike, Bruce Stokes, Jacob Poushter, Laura Silver, Janell Fetterolf and Kat Devlin, "Trump's International Ratings Remain Low, Especially Among Key Allies," Pew Research Center, October 1, 2018, https://www.pewresearch.org/global/2018/10/01/trumps-international-ratings-remain-low-especially-among-key-allies/.

24. Eli Lake, "Nikki Haley Isn't So Sure About the UN," *Bloomberg*, December 21, 2018, https://www.bloomberg.com/opinion/articles/2018-12-21/nikki-haley-asks-should-the-u-s-stay-in-the-un.

25. Uri Friedman, "Read Nikki Haley's Full Interview with *The Atlantic*" (transcript), December 7, 2018, https://www.theatlantic.com/international/archive/2018/12/nikki-haley-interview-transcript/577555/.

26. Michael Warren, "Nikki Haley Is Fierce," *Weekly Standard*, December 13, 2018, linked from https://www.weeklystandard.com/ to the *Washington Examiner* after *Weekly Standard*'s closure, at https://www.washingtonexaminer.com/weekly-standard/outgoing-u-n-ambassador-nikki-haley-sounds-like-shes-running-for-something.

27. Andy Shain, "Palmetto Politics: The Cult of Nikki Haley Will Grow After She Leaves the UN," *Post and Courier*, December 8, 2018, https://www.postandcourier.com/politics/palmetto-politics-the-cult-of-nikki-haley-will-grow-after/article_ed5fb0f4-fa37-11e8-97ff-ebea6b1c0c44.html.

28. Brian Hicks, "All Atwitter About Nikki Haley's Setback? Don't Worry, She'll Be Fine," *Post and Courier*, January 6, 2019, https://www.postandcourier.com/columnists/hicks-column-all-atwitter-about-nikki-haleys-setback-dont-worry-shell-be-fine/article_9e17db02-103a-11e9-9ea3-23a7256f02b5.html.

29. Laura E. Kirkpatrick, "Now That She's Gone: Nikki Haley's Legacy at the UN," *Nikki Haley Watch* (blog), *PassBlue*, January 9, 2019, https://www.passblue.com/2019/01/09/now-that-shes-gone-nikki-haleys-legacy-at-the-un/.

30. Kayla Tausche, "Haley Is Charging a Whopping $200,000 per Speaking Gig," CNBC, January 30, 2019, https://www.cnbc.com/2019/01/30/ex-un-ambassador-nikki-haley-charging-200000-per-speaking-gig.html.

31. Bristow Marchant, "Nikki Haley rejoins her SC charity's board after leaving the UN," *The State* (Columbia), February 13, 2019, https://www.thestate.com/news/politics-government/article226151210.html.

32. Natalie Kitroeff and David Gelles, "Claims of Shoddy Production Draw Scrutiny to a Second Boeing Jet," *New York Times*, April 20, 2019, https://

www.nytimes.com/2019/04/20/business/boeing-dreamliner-production
-problems.html.

33. Andy Shain, "Boeing Board Nominee Nikki Haley Says Company Must Be
'Accountable' about Jet Woes," *Post and Courier*, April 24, 2019, https://www
.postandcourier.com/business/boeing-board-nominee-nikki-haley-says
-company-must-be-accountable-about-jet-woes/article_e0233512-66d6
-11e9-bb0d-53e1fb81b0a7.html.

34. Eliana Johnson, "Nikki Haley Begins Experiment in Political Life after Trump,"
Politico, May 30, 2019, https://www.politico.com/story/2019/05/30/nikki-haley
-2020-elections-1348432.

35. Shane Vander Hart, "Haley in Iowa Touts Efforts to Change United Nations'
Culture," *Caffeinated Thoughts*, June 17, 2019, https://caffeinatedthoughts
.com/2019/06/nikki-haley-iowa-united-nations/.

36. Fleming Smith, "Nikki Haley buys $2.4 million home in SC, stokes 2024 presi-
dential speculation," *Post and Courier*, October 13, 2019, https://www.postand
courier.com/business/real_estate/nikki-haley-buys-2-4-million-home-in-sc
-stokes-2024-presidential-speculation/article_7c7ed13e-ede4-11e9-a451
-3be0ac4150b9.html.

37. "Nikki Haley—AEI Annual Dinner 2019," American Enterprise Institute,
Washington, D.C., October 30, 2019, available at YouTube, https://www
.youtube.com/watch?v=lpAiFsWgY38.

38. Haley, *With All Due Respect: Defending America With Grit and Grace* (New
York: St. Martin's Press, 2019), 150, emphasis in original.

39. "Nikki Haley: I Was Asked by Cabinet Members to Take Sides against the
President," CBS News, WNCT (Greenville, NC), November 10, 2019, https://
www.wnct.com/news/nikki-haley-i-was-asked-by-cabinet-members-to-take
-sides-against-the-president/.

40. Cited in John Cassidy, "Nikki Haley Embodies What's Wrong with the
Republican Party," *New Yorker*, November 11, 2019, https://www.newyorker
.com/news/our-columnists/nikki-haley-embodies-whats-wrong-with-the
-republican-party.

41. David Frum, "Nikki Haley's Audacious Bet," *The Atlantic*, November 10, 2019,
https://www.theatlantic.com/ideas/archive/2019/11/nikki-haleys-book
-audacious-bet/601726/.

42. Cassidy, "Nikki Haley Embodies What's Wrong with the Republican Party."

43. Henry Olsen, "Nikki Haley Wants to Lead the Post-Trump GOP. She'll Have to
Get a Lot More Specific," *Washington Post*, November 22, 2019, https://www
.washingtonpost.com/opinions/2019/11/11/nikki-haley-wants-lead-post
-trump-gop-shell-have-get-lot-more-specific/.

44. Glenn Beck, "UN Ambassador and Beyond: Always Taking Names / Nikki
Haley / Ep 62 / The Glenn Beck Podcast," YouTube, December 6, 2019, https://
www.youtube.com/watch?v=mP_3yrzNoKo.

45. See for example, among many pithier responses, political scientists Logan
Strother, Thomas Ogorzalek, and Spencer Piston in "What Nikki Haley gets
wrong about the Confederate flag," for the *Washington Post*'s Monkey Cage,
December 7, 2019, https://www.washingtonpost.com/politics/2019/12/07
/what-nikki-haley-gets-wrong-about-confederate-flag/; and historian

Adam H. Domby's very similarly titled "Nikki Haley Gets the History of the Confederate Flag Very Wrong," *Washington Post*, December 8, 2019, https://www.washingtonpost.com/opinions/2019/12/08/nikki-haley-gets-history-confederate-flag-very-wrong/.

46. Gallup periodic multiday polls, "Presidential Approval Ratings—Donald Trump," January 2017-January 2021, https://news.gallup.com/poll/203198/presidential-approval-ratings-donald-trump.aspx.

47. Donna M. Owens, "Jim Clyburn Changed Everything for Joe Biden's Campaign. He's Been a Political Force for a Long Time," *Washington Post*, April 1, 2020, https://www.washingtonpost.com/lifestyle/style/jim-clyburn-changed-everything-for-joe-bidens-campaign-hes-been-a-political-force-for-a-long-time/2020/03/30/7d054e98-6d33-11ea-aa80-c2470c6b2034_story.html.

48. John Bowden, "Nikki Haley Responds to Biden: 'I Will Put My Brain Up against Yours Anytime,'" *The Hill*, February 27, 2020, https://thehill.com/homenews/campaign/485022-nikki-haley-responds-to-biden-i-will-put-my-brain-up-against-yours-anytime.

49. See Nia-Malika Henderson, "Race in the Race: What Kamala Harris' identity brings to 2020," CNN, January 28, 2019, https://www.cnn.com/2019/01/28/politics/kamala-harris-identity-2020-trump; and Shashank Bengali and Melanie Mason, "The Progressive Indian Grandfather Who Inspired Kamala Harris," *Los Angeles Times*, October 25, 2019, https://www.latimes.com/politics/story/2019-10-25/how-kamala-harris-indian-family-shaped-her-political-career.

50. Matt Stevens and Rebecca R. Ruiz, "'Feeling Seen for the First Time,' Indian-Americans Cheer Kamala Harris's Selection," *New York Times*, August 13, 2020, https://www.nytimes.com/2020/08/13/us/politics/kamala-harris-south-asians-indian.html.

51. Kate Sullivan, "Sarah Palin offers advice and congratulations to Kamala Harris," CNN, August 12, 2020, https://www.cnn.com/2020/08/11/politics/sarah-palin-advice-congratulations-kamala-harris/index.html.

52. Nikki Haley, "This Is No Time to Go Wobbly on Capitalism," op-ed, *Wall Street Journal*, February 26, 2020, https://www.wsj.com/articles/this-is-no-time-to-go-wobbly-on-capitalism-11582739248.

53. "Former U.N. Ambassador Nikki Haley Leaves Boeing Board, Opposing Federal Aid," Reuters, March 19, 2020, https://www.reuters.com/article/us-boeing-board-nikki-haley/former-u-n-ambassador-nikki-haley-leaves-boeing-board-opposing-federal-aid-idUSKBN2163Y0.

54. Nikki R. Haley, "Nikki Haley: Focus on Your Governor, Not Trump," op-ed, *New York Times*, April 8, 2020, https://www.nytimes.com/2020/04/08/opinion/nikki-haley-governor-coronavirus-trump.html.

55. Quint Forgey, "'He Needs to Let His Experts Speak': Haley Offers Trump Messaging Advice amid Pandemic," *Politico*, April 10, 2020, https://www.politico.com/news/2020/04/10/nikki-haley-offers-trump-advice-amid-pandemic-178744.

56. Nikki Haley on Twitter, August 10, 2020, https://twitter.com/nikkihaley/status/1292810162344988672?lang=en.

57. Lisette Voytko, "Nikki Haley's Gripe Over Late Popcorn Factory Delivery Draws Backlash Amid USPS Woes," *Forbes*, August 10, 2020, https://www.forbes.com/sites/lisettevoytko/2020/08/10/nikki-haleys-gripe-over-late-popcorn-factory-delivery-draws-backlash-amid-usps-woes/?sh=e99f00517bc8.
58. Louis DeJoy was CEO of New Breed Logistics (based in High Point, NC) from 1983 to 2014. He serves on the Board of Trustees at Elon University, where this book's author is professor of political science. DeJoy is married to Aldona Wos, a Polish-American physician and former US ambassador to Estonia under President George W. Bush, who was nominated by President Trump in February 2020 to serve as US ambassador to Canada.

At Elon University's Convocation with Nikki Haley on September 27, 2019, the former Estonian ambassador moderated a question-and-answer period with the former UN ambassador, following Haley's prepared remarks. Seated with Haley on a stage to the side of the podium, Wos asked her own questions and read a small selection of questions pre-submitted by Elon University students. (As noted in the afterword, this book's author introduced Ambassador Haley before her prepared remarks, and also introduced Ambassador Wos before her contribution.)

On Louis DeJoy's selection as postmaster general (the president does not appoint the position, but appeared in this case to have influenced the process, via Mnuchin's involvement with the USPS Board of Governors), see for example Kenneth P. Vogel, Jessica Silver-Greenberg, Alan Rappeport, and Hailey Fuchs, "Mnuchin Paved Way for Postal Service Shake-up," *New York Times*, August 22, 2020, https://www.nytimes.com/2020/08/22/business/economy/dejoy-postmaster-general-trump-mnuchin.html.

AFTERWORD

1. Tim Alberta, "Nikki Haley's Time for Choosing," *Politico*, February 12, 2021, https://www.politico.com/interactives/2021/magazine-nikki-haleys-choice/.
2. Alex Isenstadt, "Haley Criticizes Trump over Capitol Riot, Election Claims in RNC Speech," *Politico*, January 7, 2021, https://www.politico.com/news/2021/01/07/nikki-haley-criticizes-trump-456320.
3. Nikki R. Haley, "The Media Tries to Divide Republicans," op-ed, *Wall Street Journal*, February 17, 2021.
4. Tara Palmeri, Eli Okun, and Garrett Ross, "Playbook PM: Trump Snubs Haley," *Politico*, February 18, 2021, https://www.politico.com/newsletters/playbook-pm/2021/02/18/trump-snubs-haley-491802.
5. Six months into Haley's first term as governor, *The Nation*'s Corey Hutchins reported that "since taking office she's refused every sit-down interview request with *The State*, one of South Carolina's largest newspapers," and "Print and TV reporters throughout the state have complained about her administration's press relations"; see "Nikki Haley's Pay-to-Play Politics," July 4, 2011, https://www.thenation.com/article/archive/nikki-haleys-pay-play-politics/.

Selected Bibliography

Ahmed, Bilal. "Performative Whiteness." *South Asia Journal* 9. September 9, 2013. http://southasiajournal.net/2013/09/performative-whiteness/.

Bald, Vivek. *Bengali Harlem and the Lost Histories of South Asian America.* Cambridge, MA: Harvard University Press, 2013.

Bentele, Keith G., and Erin E. O'Brien. "Jim Crow 2.0? Why States Consider and Adopt Restrictive Voter Access Policies." *Perspectives on Politics* 11, no. 4 (December 2013): 1088–116.

Bhatia, Sunil. *American Karma: Race, Culture, and Identity in the Indian Diaspora.* New York: New York University Press, 2007.

Bosco, David. "Why Is the United Nations Ambassador in the Cabinet?" *The Multilateralist* (blog), *Foreign Policy*, July 17, 2013. https://foreignpolicy .com/2013/07/17/why-is-the-united-nations-ambassador-in-the-cabinet/.

Brodin, Mark S. "From Dog-Whistle to Megaphone: The Trump Regime's Cynical Assault on Affirmative Action." *National Lawyers Guild Review* 74, no. 2 (2017): 65–71.

Bullock, Charles S., III, and Mark J. Rozell, eds. *The New Politics of the Old South: An Introduction to Southern Politics.* 5th ed. Lanham, MD: Rowman & Littlefield, 2013.

Bullock, Charles S., III, and Mark J. Rozell, eds. *The Oxford Handbook of Southern Politics.* New York: Oxford University Press, 2012.

Carter, Luther F., and Richard D. Young. "The Governor: Powers, Practices, Roles and the South Carolina Experience." The South Carolina Governance Project, Center for Governmental Services, Institute for Public Service and Policy Research, University of South Carolina, accessed April 2021. http://www.ipspr .sc.edu/grs/SCCEP/Articles/governor.htm.

Cash, W. J. *The Mind of the South.* New York: Vintage Books, 1941.

Chakravorty, Sanjoy, Devesh Kapur, and Nirvikar Singh. *The Other One Percent: Indians in America.* New York: Oxford University Press, 2017.

Cobb, James C. *Away Down South: A History of Southern Identity.* New York: Oxford University Press, 2007.

Desai, Manan. "The 'Tan Stranger' From Ceylon." *Tides* (digital magazine), South Asian American Digital Archive, July 8, 2014. https://www.saada.org/tides /article/tan-stranger-from-ceylon.

Goldin, Ian, Geoffrey Cameron, and Meera Balarajan. *Exceptional People: How Migration Shaped Our World and Will Define Our Future.* Princeton, NJ: Princeton University Press, 2011.

Goldstein, Eric L. *The Price of Whiteness: Jews, Race, and American Identity.* Princeton: Princeton University Press, 2008.

Haley, Nikki. *Can't Is Not an Option: My American Story.* New York: Sentinel, 2012.

Haley, Nikki R. *With All Due Respect: Defending America with Grit and Grace*. New York: St. Martin's Press, 2019.

Han, Lori Cox. *Women and US Politics: The Spectrum of Political Leadership*. 2nd ed. Boulder: Lynne Rienner, 2010.

Hawes, Jennifer Berry. *Grace Will Lead Us Home: The Charleston Church Massacre and the Hard, Inspiring Journey to Forgiveness*. New York: St. Martin's Press, 2019.

Ignatiev, Noel. *How the Irish Became White*. New York: Routledge, 2008.

Iyer, Deepa. *We Too Sing America: South Asian, Arab, Muslim, and Sikh Immigrants Shape Our Multiracial Future*. New York: New Press, 2015.

Jacobson, Matthew Frye. *Whiteness of a Different Color: European Immigrants and the Alchemy of Race*. Cambridge, MA: Harvard University Press, 1999.

Jensen, Joan. *Passage from India: Asian Indian Immigrants in North America*. New Haven, CT: Yale University Press, 1988.

Joshi, Khyati Y. *New Roots in America's Sacred Ground: Religion, Race, and Ethnicity in Indian America*. New Brunswick, NJ: Rutgers University Press, 2006.

Joshi, Khyati Y., and Jigna Desai, eds. *Asian Americans in Dixie: Race and Migration in the South*. Urbana: University of Illinois Press, 2013.

King, Desmond S., and Rogers M. Smith. *Still a House Divided: Race and Politics in Obama's America*. Princeton, NJ: Princeton University Press, 2011.

Kirk, Jason A. "Indian-Americans and the U.S.-India Nuclear Agreement: Consolidation of an Ethnic Lobby?" *Foreign Policy Analysis* 4, no. 3 (May 2008): 275–300.

Kirk, Jason A. "'What Would Gandhi Do?': Nikki Haley and South Carolina in American Politics, Black, White, and Brown." In *The American Governor: Power, Constraint, and Leadership in the States*, edited by David Redlawsk, 155–76. New York: Palgrave Macmillan, 2015.

Kirk, Jason A., and Jason Husser. "What Makes a Successful Indian American Political Candidate?" *South Asian Diaspora* 9, no. 2 (2017): 207–23.

Kurien, Prema. "Race, Religion, and the Political Incorporation of Indian Americans." *Journal of Religious and Political Practice* 2, no. 3 (2016): 273–95.

López, Ian Haney. *Dog Whistle Politics: How Coded Racial Appeals Have Reinvented Racism and Wrecked the Middle Class*. New York: Oxford University Press, 2014.

Maxwell, Angie. *The Indicted South: Public Criticism, Southern Inferiority, and the Politics of Whiteness*. Chapel Hill: University of North Carolina Press, 2014.

Miller, Donald F. "The Problem of Timing and Chance." *Time & Society* 2, no. 2 (May 1993): 139–57.

Mishra, Sangay K. *Desis Divided: The Political Lives of South Asian Americans*. Minneapolis: University of Minnesota Press, 2016.

Mohl, Raymond A. "Globalization, Latinization, and the *Nuevo* New South." In *Globalization and the American South*, edited by James C. Cobb and William Stueck, 66–99. Athens: University of Georgia Press, 2005.

Ngai, Mae M. "The Unlovely Residue of Outworn Prejudices: The Hart-Celler Act and the Politics of Immigration Reform, 1945–1965." In *Americanism: New Perspectives on the History of an Ideal*, edited by Michael Kazin and Joseph A. McCartin, 108–27. Chapel Hill: University of North Carolina Press, 2006.

Noll, Mark A. *God and Race in American Politics: A Short History*. Princeton, NJ: Princeton University Press, 2008.

Peacock, James L. *Grounded Globalism: How the U.S. South Embraces the World*. Athens: University of Georgia Press, 2007.

Peacock, James L., Harry L. Watson, and Carrie R. Matthews, eds. *The American South in a Global World*. Chapel Hill: University of North Carolina Press, 2005.

Pew Research Center. "Indian Americans." *The Rise of Asian Americans* (report), 44–46. Updated edition: April 4, 2013. Washington, DC: Pew Research Center, 2012.

Pew Research Center. "Trends in Party Identification of Religious Groups." Religion and Public Life Project, February 2, 2012. Washington, DC: Pew Research Center. https://www.pewforum.org/2012/02/02/trends-in-party-identification-of-religious-groups/.

Prashad, Vijay. *The Karma of Brown Folk*. Minneapolis: University of Minnesota Press, 2000.

Prashad, Vijay. *Uncle Swami: South Asians in America Today*. Noida, Uttar Pradesh: HarperCollins India, 2012.

Prince, Michael K. *Rally 'Round the Flag, Boys!: South Carolina and the Confederate Flag*. Columbia: University of South Carolina Press, 2004.

Rosenthal, Alan. *The Best Job in Politics: Exploring How Governors Succeed as Policy Leaders*. Thousand Oaks, CA: Sage Publishing, 2012.

Rosenthal, Cindy Simon. *When Women Lead: Integrative Leadership in State Legislatures*. New York: Oxford University Press, 1998.

Rudrappa, Sharmila. *Ethnic Routes to Becoming American: Indian Immigrants and the Cultures of Citizenship*. New Brunswick, NJ: Rutgers University Press, 2004.

Schlesinger, Arthur, Jr. "On the Writing of Contemporary History." *The Atlantic*, March 1967. https://www.theatlantic.com/magazine/archive/1967/03/on-the-writing-of-contemporary-history/305731/.

Skowronek, Stephen. *Presidential Leadership in Political Time: Reprise and Reappraisal?* 2nd ed. Lawrence: University Press of Kansas, 2011.

Slate, Nico. *Colored Cosmopolitanism: The Shared Struggle for Freedom in the United States and India*. Cambridge, MA: Harvard University Press, 2012.

Slate, Nico. *Lord Cornwallis Is Dead: The Struggle for Democracy in the United States and India*. Cambridge, MA: Harvard University Press, 2019.

Snyder, Timothy. *The Road to Unfreedom: Russia, Europe, America*. New York: Tim Duggan Books, 2018.

Sriram, Shyam Krishnan, and stonegarden grindlife. "The Politics of Deracialization: South Asian American Candidates, Nicknames, and Campaign Strategies." *South Asian Diaspora* 9, no. 1 (2017): 17–31.

Subramanian, Ajantha. "North Carolina's Indians: Erasing Race to Make the Citizen." In Peacock et al., *American South in a Global World*, 192–204.

Taylor, Paul, and D'Vera Cohn. "A Milestone En Route to Becoming a Majority Minority Nation." November 7, 2012. Washington, DC: Pew Research Center.

Tesler, Michael, and David O. Sears. *Obama's Race: The 2008 Election and the Dream of a Post-Racial America*. Chicago: University of Chicago Press, 2010.

Volkan, Vamik D. "Large Group Identity, International Relations, and Psychoanalysis." *International Forum of Psychoanalysis* 18, no. 4 (2009): 206–13.

Wilentz, Sean. *The Age of Reagan: A History, 1974–2008.* New York: HarperCollins, 2008.

Wong, Janelle S., Karthick Ramakrishnan, Taeku Lee, and Jane Junn. *Asian American Political Participation: Emerging Constituents and Their Political Identities.* New York: Russell Sage Foundation, 2012.

Yancey, George. *Who Is White? Latinos, Asians, and the New Black/Nonblack Divide.* Boulder, CO: Lynne Rienner, 2003.

Index